**UNIVERSITY OF WALES SWANSEA**
**PRIFYSGOL CYMRU ABERTAWE**
**LIBRARY/LLYFRGELL**

Classmark    PB 2115 Ait

Location    Swm Larary

1005551473

KU-691-282

LANGU

The Cha

Welsh Language in the Twentieth Century

# LANGUAGE, ECONOMY AND SOCIETY

THE CHANGING FORTUNES OF THE
WELSH LANGUAGE IN THE TWENTIETH CENTURY

John Aitchison

and

Harold Carter

CARDIFF
UNIVERSITY OF WALES PRESS
2000

© John Aitchison and Harold Carter, 2000

All rights reserved. No part of this book may be reproduced, stored in a retrieval system, or transmitted, in any form or by any means, electronic, mechanical, photocopying, recording or otherwise, without clearance from the University of Wales Press, 6 Gwennyth Street, Cardiff CF24 4YD. www.wales.ac.uk/press

**British Library Cataloguing-in-Publication Data**

A catalogue record for this book is available from the British Library


ISBN  0-7083-1552-6

Cover design by Olwen Fowler, The Beacon Studio
Typeset at the University of Wales Press
Printed at The Alden Press, Oxford

# Contents

# CONTENTS

# Preface

This book is an updated and substantially extended version of an earlier text entitled *A Geography of the Welsh Language, 1961-1991*, published by the University of Wales Press in 1994. In new chapters it considers more detailed statistical information concerning migration, social class and household structures and reflects on recent institutional developments that have impacted greatly upon the status of the Welsh language during the 1990s. It also re-evaluates prospects for the language as we enter the new millennium.

As was noted in the Preface to the previous edition, this study continues a long-standing academic commitment on the part of geographers at the University of Wales, Aberystwyth to the analysis of language patterns and associated cultural processes. Indeed, the very first geographical analysis of the Welsh language followed immediately upon the establishment of the Gregynog Chair and the Honours School of Geography in 1917. This was a paper by Trevor Lewis which appeared in the *Annales de Géographie* of 1926, entitled: 'Sur la distribution du parler gallois dans Le Pays de Galles d'après le recensement de 1921'. Thereafter, each succeeding decennial census has been mapped and analysed by Aberystwyth geographers – Trevor Williams, J. Gareth Thomas, Emrys Jones and E. G. Bowen.

Interestingly, the one Gregynog Professor of Geography who made no specific contribution to such language studies was C. Daryll Forde. However, he did publish a book which became very widely used in the teaching of human geography – *Habitat, Economy and Society*. It is in sympathy with the concept of that volume, and of the particular tradition which it represents, that we have called the present book *Language, Economy and Society: The Changing Fortunes of the Welsh Language in the Twentieth Century*. Here, through analyses of spatial distributions, we seek to delineate those aspects of the Welsh economy and those characteristics of the nature of Welsh society which have determined the present condition of the language.

It is evident that the condition of the Welsh language today can be viewed from two sharply differing perspectives. On the one hand it could be claimed that the fight for the language has been won, and on the other that an assured future is far from having been secured. The first of these viewpoints has been identified by Dylan Phillips, 'Mewn teitl bras ar dudalen flaen y *Western Mail* ym mis Chwefror eleni [1998] cyhoeddwyd yn ddewr "Language war is over". Mae Prys Edwards yn mynnu bod protestwyr iaith bellach yn greaduriaid prin iawn – yn wir, eu bod wedi diflannu mwy neu lai wedi'r Gymraeg ennill ei phlwyf yn y byd.' [In banner headlines the front page of the *Western Mail* in February of this year [1998] proclaimed "Language war is over". Prys Edwards declared that the language protesters were now an endangered species – indeed they had largely disappeared since Welsh had won its place in the world] (Phillips, 1998, 13). As we seek to demonstrate, there is certainly much evidence to support Prys Edwards's assertion. Thus, an attitude survey commissioned by the Welsh Language Board suggests that the vast majority of Welsh people support all the measures that have been promoted to ensure the future of the language, and that those disaffected constitute no more than a small, if vociferous, minority. A key basis of a new security is the Welsh Language Act of 1993. Reflecting on such matters, the present authors have observed: 'The case for the view that the fight for the language has been won can be stated quite succinctly. Attitudes which were once antagonistic to the language and its propagation have been reversed, for support is now almost universal; all the domains of language use, which were lost from the Act of Union onwards, have been reclaimed; and finally, all this is evidenced in the data of the 1991 census which suggest that a turnaround of historic proportions is nigh' (D. Dunkerley and A. Thompson, 1999, 98).

The opposed view that the language is still in a parlous condition can, paradoxically, also be supported through evidence drawn from census data and parallel surveys. One of the clear bases of a language's vitality is the number of people who speak it, especially the number who regard it as their mother tongue, rather than as a second language. Censuses do not yield insights into such matters, but a Welsh Office survey of 1992 revealed that only 56 per cent of Welsh-speakers regarded Welsh as their mother tongue. More disconcertingly, the proportion dropped to only 27 per cent amongst those between three and fifteen years old. Again, data from primary schools show that in 1996/7 only 6.4 per cent of the pupils came from homes where Welsh was regarded as the household language. These, and other more recent disaggregated statistics, are examined in this book. Suffice it to say that all the past problems of the language, such as the continuing impact of in-migration, are still extant. Indeed, the contemporary crisis in agriculture along with the increasing price differential in property between rural Wales and parts of England, could well exacerbate the weakening of the language in its heartland through rural depopulation on the one hand and in-migration on the other. Certainly the notion often trailed, that somehow due to the Welsh Language Act and creation of the National Assembly for Wales (*Y Cynulliad*) the language issue has been wholly resolved and depoliticized seems untenable. Activists still regard the Act as little more than tokenism writ large, and that the Welsh-language schemes it demands are merely cosmetic. Moreover, the language will always be a competitor for resources, and the allocation of scarce resources amongst competing interests is the very heart of politics.

The Welsh language is clearly at a critical juncture in its long history. There are certainly forces at work which suggest that it will be carried forward by a process of normalization, and that it will come to hold a reinvigorated position of considerable significance at the heart of a truly bilingual Wales. At the same time, however, it might also be argued that for the language no more than yet another false dawn has broken, and that despite advancing numbers of speakers the depth and quality of its integration into the everyday life of Wales will be tenuous and markedly transformed in nature. Although this book is essentially a formal study in cultural geography, it is hoped that its various findings and arguments will contribute substantively to ongoing debates concerning the future of the language in Wales – both the challenges and the opportunities.


John Aitchison and Harold Carter
University of Wales, Aberystwyth
January, 2000

# CHAPTER 1

## Language and Ethnicity

The importance of your learning – and conforming to – the rules spelled out, entry by entry, in *The Official Politically Correct Dictionary and Handbook* cannot be overemphasized. For, as linguists Edward Sapir and Benjamin Wharf suspected as early as the 1940s – and postmodernist theory has confirmed – language is not merely the mirror of society, it is the major force in 'constructing' what we perceive as 'reality'. (Beard and Cerf, 1992, xiii).

### Linguistic Relativism

It might seem odd, even perverse, to begin an analysis of the changing geography of the Welsh language with a quotation from *The Official Politically Correct Dictionary and Handbook* (Beard and Cerf, 1992). Its relevance to the present study is that it serves to emphasize the importance that is attached to language, even to the extent of using it to manipulate culture and ideology. Significantly, Beard and Cerf preface their tract with a reference to George Orwell's 1984 – 'It was intended that when Newspeak had been adopted once and for all and Oldspeak forgotten, a heretical thought . . . should be literally unthinkable, at least so far as thought is dependent on words.'

The attempt to impose a politically correct vocabulary, the Sapir–Wharf hypothesis, and George Orwell's Newspeak are all expressions of the same belief – that the languages people speak profoundly shape the way in which they think and act. As Mandelbaum has observed:

> Human beings do not live in the objective world alone, nor alone in the world of social activity as ordinarily understood, but are very much at the mercy of the particular language which has become the medium of expression for the society. It is quite an illusion to imagine that one adjusts to reality essentially without the use of language and language is merely an incidental means of solving problems of communication and reflection. (Mandelbaum, 1949, 162)

Needless to say, such a relativistic stance, which can also be seen as 'a reaction against the nominalist position originating in Platonic and Aristotlian [*sic*] philosophy and popular throughout the nineteenth century, that knowledge of reality is not affected by language'

(Steinfatt, 1989), is not universally accepted. It would seem, for instance, to be at odds with Chomsky's proposal of 'an innate schema of grammar in humans as a necessary postulate to account for language acquisition in children' (Steinfatt, 1989, 39). Be this as it may, linguistic relativism, developed in the 1940s and current since, is in keeping with post-modernism. Postmodernism is obsessed with deconstruction, iconography and semiotics. These are concerned respectively with the significance of language, visual images, and signs and symbols – all modes of perception and expression of the environment in which people live and have their being. Likewise, all are deeply ritualized and conditioned by language. To quote from an interpretation of the cultural anthropology of Mary Douglas,

> Ritual carries or transmits collective information, like language. But it is also true that language acts like a ritual, and its structures – its codes – are part of society's arsenal of ritual utilized in the periodic affirmation of social order. To speak is to perform a ritual, and partake, intentionally or not, in the affirmation and reproduction of basic social relations and commonly held values. (Wuthnow, 1984, 104)

Socio-linguists have articulated similar views. Thus, Tabouret-Keller writes, 'the language spoken by somebody and his or her identity as a speaker of this language are inseparable. This is surely a piece of knowledge as old as human speech itself. Language acts are acts of identity' (Tabouret-Keller, 1997, 315). Likewise, Fishman has argued:

> that there should be some link between language and ethnicity is obvious, since the major symbolic system of the human species must be associated with the perceived dimensions of human aggregation. If people group themselves . . . into differently based speaking collectivities . . . Then their languages become both symbolic of as well as a basis for that grouping'.

But he then makes a significant qualification:

> However, just as ethnicity itself is perspectival and situational and therefore variable in saliency, so the link between language and ethnicity is also variable. For some (and in some historical and situational contexts) language is the prime indicator and expression of their own and another's ethnicity; for others, language is both merely marginal and optional (i.e. detachable) vis-a-vis their ethnicity (and that of others as well). (Fishman, 1997, 329–30)

Setting aside this qualification for the moment, and bringing these rather abstruse academic ideas down to the clichés of everyday life, it is often observed when no common ground can be found between two people 'that they are not speaking the same language'; that a meeting of minds is impossible because views are totally incompatible and that the basis lies in the lack of a common language which is the necessary criterion for a common understanding.

At this point it is appropriate to allude to the important linkage between language and ethnicity, and in particular Welsh ethnic identity. Seeking to define ethnicity, Anthony D. Smith writes that:

> it relates mainly to a sense of community based on history and culture, rather than to any collectivity or to the concept of ideology. In this, I follow the emendation proposed by Epstein to the literature of 'situational' ethnicity in which the growth of a sense of the collective self is treated as an important part of a group (especially ethnic) identity and solidarity. Only here, the sense of self is viewed through the prism of symbols and mythologies of the community's heritage . . . The core of ethnicity, as it has been transmitted in the historical record and as it shapes individual experience, resides in this quartet of 'myths, memories, values and symbols' and in the characteristic forms or styles and genres of certain historical configurations of populations. (Smith A. D., 1986, 14/15)

The conclusion from the above discussion is quite clear; that identity, and especially ethnic identity and the culture on which it is based, are dependent on a communality. That communality is derived from an inheritance which is passed on through language. There is an alternative basis in religion, which also generates a unifying view of the nature of the environment and specifies accepted modes of behaviour and patterns of living. It, too, has played its part in Welsh ethnic identity, but the manifest implication of the debate thus far is that to be Welsh, in any meaningful way, a person must speak, or at least understand, Welsh. Otherwise he or she is no more than someone dwelling in a defined area called Wales; and ethnically no more than a version of provincial English, or more tactfully someone who can be called British, like the Geordies or the Cornish, Cumbrians or perhaps even Liverpudlians – all variations on a central theme. To broach these matters is inevitably to enter a field of major controversy. Responses to such assertions are always immediate and angry, for to deny Welshness to non-Welsh-speakers whose families have lived in Wales from time immemorial is to touch a very raw nerve. Moreover, it is possible to cite Celtic countries where language is now of peripheral significance in the definition of identity. The Irish language by now is only a relict feature of being Irish (Hindley, 1992), although it is possible to argue that Lallans is an indicator of being Scottish, much more so than Gaelic. Again, across the Atlantic, American identity is not based on a different language, though the appearance of American English dictionaries might cause some hesitation.

Since it is at least an implicit assumption of this analysis that the Welsh language has a significance over and beyond its role as a means of communication, a role to which at least some would relegate it, it is pertinent briefly to note the assertions and denials of the association of language with ethnic identity. Out of the very many discussions on this

3

topic, it is sufficient to select one which is a good representative, and John Osmond's paper 'The modernisation of Wales' (1989) is as good as any. Moreover, it appeared in a volume appropriately entitled *National Identity in the British Isles* (Evans, 1989). The only reservation to be made at this point is that we are not concerned here with the issue of nationalism, that is whether ethnic identity should be associated with political autonomy (Dofny and Akiwowo, 1980; Smith, 1986; Williams, C. H., 1982, 1991). That is a separate matter, although one which it is difficult to elide.

Osmond's paper develops a critique by Ned Thomas (1988) of the attitudes of Dafydd Elis Thomas (1988), the then President of Plaid Cymru. It is worth a lengthy quotation –

> Part of the focus of the attack was Elis Thomas's *Western Mail* article about Wales's image . . . The argument was over the vexed issue of in-migration and the response to it that is both possible and appropriate. The thrust of Ned Thomas's attack was that Plaid Cymru's leader was seeking a Wales, or perhaps recognising the inevitability of a future Wales where the Welsh speaking community would not be the defining essence of Welsh identity and nationhood, but part of the nation, 'a kind of ethnic substratum'.

Osmond proceeds to quote Ned Thomas as maintaining that there can be no sense of territorial belonging in Wales without the language, and then to provide his own answer.

> But Ned Thomas ignores a number of powerful elements which guide the sensibility of the English-speaking Welsh: primarily a sense of responsibility for their communities, but beyond that other factors like identification with a landscape and a growing structure of institutions that above else . . . define the territory of Wales. (Osmond, 1989, 88)

Clearly, here, Osmond is adopting a position in line with Fishman's qualification referred to above, 'language is both marginal and optional', and the future of Welsh identity lies not in the divisive issue of language but in the unifying role of institutions, primarily now a National Assembly for Wales or *Cynulliad*, even though at the time barely half the population voted in favour of such a body (see Chapter 8).

Another contribution to this debate is that by Giggs and Pattie (1991; 1992 a and b). In an analysis of census data they explore statistical relationships between language, social class and birthplace. Among other revelations, they demonstrate that:

> Welsh-speakers collectively were an important component of the élite service class chiefly in metropolitan south Wales and its industrial hinterland and secondarily in north-east Wales. In contrast, in the Welsh-speaking rural heartland of Wales (i.e. Gwynedd, Dyfed and Powys), Welsh-speakers were actually under-represented in the service class. (Giggs and Pattie, 1991, 27)

It follows from this, and the associated analysis, that contemporary Welsh society is plural rather than homogeneous, divided rather than cohesive. . . 'There are in Welsh society profound internal divisions based on ethnicity, language (with all its attendant cultural manifestations) and class' (p.28).

It is certainly possible that some of these conclusions are no more than the product of statistical analysis at a very crude aggregate scale and would need to be supported by studies at a behavioural level. But the general summary is in line with Osmond's presentation.

> There seems to be evidence of a disquieting preoccupation with cultural élitism among some Welsh-speaking Welsh people. It is heartening that proficiency in Britain's oldest language (hitherto long derided) now provides dignity, social prestige and opportunity in Wales. At the same time it is profoundly disheartening that a few zealots can seriously assert that the English-speaking majority, who constitute 77.6 per cent of the Welsh-born residents in 1981 . . . are 'not *really* Welsh'. Moreover, the problems are not simply those of proficiency in the Welsh language being touted as the essential qualification for Welsh nationality, rather than mere nativity, which is deemed a qualification in the majority of countries: there are attendant cultural, political and economic implications. (Giggs and Pattie, 1991, 29)

The authors go on to quote a letter by Alan Watkins to the *Observer* of 19 February 1989:

> Thus the Welsh establishment is still Welsh-speaking, literary but philistine, Nonconformist (with a bias towards Calvinism), hostile towards Labour and, above all, essentially pacifist. So it is that Welsh school children are asked to admire the works of second rate versifiers while remaining ignorant of the fact that, in the Great War, Wales proportionately sacrificed more men than any other part of the UK. Likewise, children will be told of the exploits, largely made up, of Owain Glyndŵr but not about the very real achievements of the South Wales Borderers and the Welsh regiment. (Giggs and Pattie, 1991, 29–30)

A polemic is necessarily unbalanced, but an appeal to the teaching of imperial history is perhaps the most unlikely part of the letter.

Here, then, is the nub of the debate over the role of language: one which has no easy resolution. At this point, too, as was noted earlier, and as Osmond's and Giggs and Pattie's comments imply, the issues of nationalism as well as ethnic identity enter. On the one hand there is the contention that Welsh identity can rest only on the language, for there is nothing else; all other aspects of separateness having been lost. Thus, there is no distinctive Welsh legal system for the English system was imposed at the time of the Union. But, it could be argued that political separation is a necessary condition for the survival of the language. Against that is set the view that with an enhanced institutional base, both political and economic, a distinctive Wales can be created in which the language would be incidental. It would be a Wales necessarily independent for only under that condition could the essential institutional framework be effectively developed. The USA and Ireland now, apart from its Catholicism, are identified not by language, or indeed by culture, but by the political, social and economic structures which make them different.

This is the view expressed in typical fashion by Gwyn A. Williams. 'Wales is an artefact which the Welsh produce; the Welsh make and remake Wales day by day and year after year . . . It is not history which does this; it is not traditions which do this' (Williams, G. A., 1979, 23). Thus he rejects the role of culture, defined as inherited ideas and traditions and their attached values, in this remaking process, and presumably, if it is what those resident in Wales want as they remake Wales, the language too. Being Welsh, for example, would be possible without having read a single line of the language's literature, even of second-rate versifiers, and being totally ignorant of its traditions for they would be something to make anew. The country's history would be an irrelevance. It is difficult to envisage under such conditions what being Welsh would mean, other than having a government more to the left, and that with no guarantee of permanency, and shouting for the rugby team on international days! But whatever the consequent state, such an ideal is in contrast to that of the language protagonists; it condemns 'a fossilized liberal nonconformist Welsh nationalism with its fixed concept of Welsh identity' and 'the tunnel vision within large swathes of the Welsh-speaking intelligentsia' (Williams, E. W., 1989, 58) and deploys a view of a socialist republic on the land of Wales where the language used would be of incidental significance. The crucial unity would be based on a whole range of institutions which have been developed largely during the twentieth century; a National Library, a National Museum and a Museum of Welsh Life, a national University, in spite of efforts to fragment it, and with the traditional cultural interests in music now represented by a Welsh National Opera and a BBC National Orchestra of Wales. The culmination of all this lies in the creation in government of a Welsh Office with a Secretary of State and the National Assembly or *Cynulliad*. Likewise, in sport there are now Welsh teams in virtually every branch symbolizing a unity in which language has no necessary part. However, it is also apparent that few commercial organizations recognize the unity of Wales. Thus, for example, in the utilities, neither water nor electricity are related to the territory of Wales and in some cases Liverpool and Bristol remain, as they did in the past, the effective northern and southern capitals. The crux of the problem is that there are two bases of national identity, the one called ethnic, the other institutional (McCrone, 1998). But whereas the trend to globalization tends to diminish the latter, as institutions, and especially commercial concerns, become large-scale and transcend political boundaries, in reaction the former – ethnic nationalism – becomes more passionate and intense in its nature. This said, perhaps the essential issue is that there are two ethnolinguistic groups in Wales, the Welsh and the Anglo-Welsh, but with both attempting to claim some form of priority in representative status.

These sorts of problems have achieved a more immediate relevance and a new turn in the postmodern world. Postmodernism has many definitions, but it is crucially marked by the collapse of ordered certainties and of monolithic structures. Nowhere has that been more apparent than in the field of imperial disintegration and political nationalism. The once 'united' systems are breaking apart into older constituent pieces, which are as much defined by their histories and by their languages and religions as by any other criteria. The past and the cultural inheritance do seem to matter as the imposed rigidities dissolve. Certainly in the Baltic republics, as in the break up of the USSR and Yugoslavia, language and religion seem to have played central roles. Freedom from centralized socialist coercion is demanded so that democratic institutions can ensure the survival of language and culture.

The purpose of this introductory section is not to make any contribution to the substantive debate which it has broached. The burgeoning field of ethnolinguistic identity theory (Gudykunst, 1989) is broad in compass and deals with speech accommodation, language attitudes and second language acquisition. The topic has been raised here simply to underline the significance of the relationship between language and ethnicity. If language is solely a means of communication, an alphabetical as opposed to a numerical system, then its loss would mean little. Indeed, it could be conceived as an advantage, a view certainly held by a number of people in Wales. Its disappearance would eliminate one of those divisive elements in Wales, which Giggs and Pattie identified, in favour of an international language of great richness. But as we have endeavoured to demonstrate, language is much more than a means of communication. Not only does it carry a view of the environment, using that word in its proper inclusive sense, but through its vocabulary and its structure, through the associations generated by its literature, through the symbol which it is and the symbols which it transmits, it creates a distinctive identity which is at once a derivative of tradition and an expression of the present. It is difficult to envisage an ethnic identity as defined earlier without an awareness through the language of the myths, memories, values and symbols of Welshness. Indeed, where identity has to be created so does a language; perhaps modern Hebrew is the best example.

If one believes that the salvation of Wales and its language rests on some form of total revolution of society as it is now constituted, then a mere geographical analysis of the patterns of language change (as presented here) will be considered a waste of time. If, however, one associates language with ethnic identity and looks to change as giving insight into the operative processes within and related to that identity, and it would be equally relevant within an independent democratic Wales, then mapping and the interpretation of associated distributions are central to language issues. What this text is designed to present is a great deal more than the distribution of contrasted sounds and grammars.

Much of the foregoing discussion has entered marginally and tentatively into the field of socio-linguistics, whereas this study is essentially a contribution to a parallel field of geolinguistics. As early as 1965 the American Society of Geolinguistics was formed; and the series *Discussion Papers in Geolinguistics*, edited by Colin Williams, has appeared since 1980. In definition of geolinguistics it is appropriate to quote Williams's words:

> Its specific concern is with the relationship between languages and their physical and human settings. Thus it may seek among other things to illuminate the socio-spatial context of language use and language choice; to measure language distribution and variety; 'to assess the relative practical importance, usefulness and availability' of different languages from the economic, psychological, political and cultural standpoints

of specific speech milieux; to understand variations in their basic grammatical, phonological and lexical structure and to measure and 'map their genetic, historical and geographical affiliations and relationships'. (Williams, C. 1984)

The quotations within the above extract are included among the aims of the American Society of Geolinguistics, and are in their turn derived from Mario Pei's book *Invitation to Linguistics* (1971). It is clear that this text can in no way cover the whole field of geolinguistics. It is however firmly set in the speciality of geolinguistics and focuses on the analysis of language patterns, their historical development and contemporary form. Language mapping is more than an academic exercise. It is an enquiry into the identity of a people and how that identity survives.

## Spatial Dimensions of Ethnicity, Culture and Language

Any discussion of ethnic identity of necessity introduces another dimension – territoriality and the spatial context of that identity. World events in the 1990s have brought that relationship to the forefront of political consideration; the drawing of lines on maps has become crucial. But the relationship of ethnicity to land is a very complex one which in its totality is beyond the scope of this discussion. However, three aspects can be abstracted.

*(i) Ethnicity and the nation state*
The nation state is a political entity, but one which in modern history has been more and more correlated with ethnic character, so that nation and ethnic group have almost become synonymous (Gellner, 1983). Certainly that was not true of early empires where hegemony was established over a multiplicity of peoples. But it has been the collapse of imperial systems over the last century which has produced, or in part been produced by, a determination among subject peoples to control their own destinies. Interpretation of these processes has produced an immense literature (Dofny and Akiwowo, 1980; Gellner, 1983; Smith A. D., 1986; McCrone, 1998). As far as Wales is concerned the central issue is the relationship of the Welsh language, as the hallmark of Welsh identity, to Welsh nationalism (Williams C. H., 1982; Evans, 1989). This is a matter of widespread concern and is the crux of a major problem for Plaid Cymru, now called in English The Party of Wales. To associate itself too closely with language issues means association with less than 20 per cent of the voters; to distance itself from the language alienates its basic core of support in Welsh-speaking Wales. Although this has been the most intensely discussed of the territorial relationships, it is not one which this analysis seeks to highlight. That said, even describing basic language distributions inevitably brings it to the fore.

*(ii) Ethnicity, culture and the culture region*
An attempt was made in the previous section to present a brief definition of ethnic identity. The collective tradition there outlined has much in common with the concept of culture, although culture can be taken as a broader, all-embracing term which includes the manifest representations of a way of life, both material and immaterial. Early in the development of

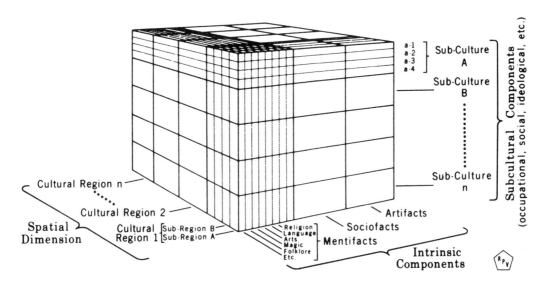

*A schematic, three-dimensional representation of cultural systems.*

**Figure 1.1**

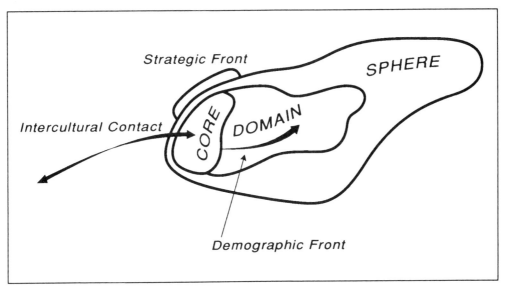

The morphology of a Culture Region  (after D. Meinig)

**Figure 1.2**

anthropology, attempts were made to relate cultures to spatial contexts and the notion of the culture region became an integral part of cultural anthropology, and indeed of human geography. The very use of the word 'region' again introduces as massive a literature as that on the definition of culture. But it is hardly pertinent to develop that theme, rather is it more relevant to consider the idea of the culture region itself. 'The culture-area concept has its origin in the practical exigencies of American ethnographic research, as a heuristic device for mapping and clarifying the tribal groups of North and South America' (Harris, 1968, 374). Its early use was characterized by an emphasis on the linkage with environmental conditions. Perhaps the nearest equivalent in relation to Wales was the late E. G. Bowen's presidential address to the Institution of British Geographers (Bowen, 1959), entitled 'Le Pays de Galles'. Bowen sought to 'study the interrelationships of systematic geographical phenomena in different parts of Wales' and he went on to assert that 'in one area at least, these interrelationships produce a characteristic way of life integrated with the physical setting' (Bowen, 1959, 23). That one area constituted the true 'Pays de Galles', the land of the Welsh-speaking, the area that was later to be called *Y Fro Gymraeg*. However, few now would attempt to argue for a basis in the physical environment.

At this point two further sets of ideas need to be introduced. The first is Wilbur Zelinsky's 'schematic three-dimensional model of cultural systems' (Zelinsky, 1973a, 1973b), which is shown in Figure 1.1. In it three intrinsic components of cultural regions are identified as mentifacts, sociofacts and artifacts. The breakdown of the mentifact component is detailed as religion, language, the arts, magic, folklore, to which rather diverse list a covering 'etcetera' is added. The other two components are not so detailed. Successive divisions into subcultures is envisaged, based on components such as occupations, presumably a surrogate for economic character, social composition and ideological orientation. It must be admitted that in its detail it is not a particularly convincing schema. But in its general representation it is of real value; for it displays the complexity of components which make up a culture and hence the difficulty of turning them into a cartographic form.

It follows that the second set of ideas is directly related to the mapping of the various components of culture. Three basic approaches can be distinguished. The first is usually referred to as a 'cultural block' procedure. Here, components are treated as being mutually exclusive so that their distribution defines the discrete region. That in reality is a most unlikely situation. A second approach is one which can be referred to as 'radial concentric' in that it views a culture as declining in intensity and integrity from a core to a periphery where it is weaker and mixed with neighbouring cultures. The third approach can be termed 'polythetic' for it is one where all the components are seen as having differing, even dissimilar, distribution patterns, but where an area of maximum overlap can be derived and identified as a culture region of sufficient homogeneity to be meaningful, a climax area.

The block procedure has seldom been used, but the other two have been considerably developed. From the outset the polythetic procedure has been the most frequently employed. It was favoured by the doyen of culture region definition, the anthropologist

A. L. Kroeber. His two classic works were, *Handbook of the Indians of California* (1925) and *Cultural and Natural Areas of Native North America* (1939). As Harris writes, 'he approached the construction of cultural areas by means of increasingly elaborate statistical manipulation of disjointed trait-element lists consisting of as many as six thousand items' (Harris, 1968, 339). Harris adds that no one has ever taken up his suggestion 'to measure intensity and climax by counting fragmented trait lists' (p.341). Even so, the development of multivariate statistical methods, especially factor and cluster analyses, have enabled procedures in keeping with Kroeber's concept to be carried out. Such studies have tended not to engage in hypothesis-testing or model-building however; they have usually been inductive exercises using as large a number of variables as possible to establish areas of common character. Needless to say, studies of this type do not escape the criticism as to the choice and relative significance of the variables used. Several typological analyses have been carried out for Wales using language, socio-economic and political (voting patterns) data (Carter and Williams, 1978; Williams, C. H., 1982; Carter and Aitchison 1986).

*(iii) A model of a culture region*

The only attempt to provide a model of a culture region is that proposed by Meinig (1965) in his consideration of the Mormon area of the United States. It is a more specified version of the radial concentric schema and based on one criterion only, in his case membership of the Church of the Latter Day Saints. He contended that it was possible to identify three sections associated with diminishing dominance. The first of them he called the 'core', 'the zone of concentration displaying the greatest density of occupation and intensity of organisation, and the area most representative of the definitive characteristics of the culture'. The second Meinig termed the 'domain', an 'outlying area dominated by the patterns of the culture under study but with less intensity and homogeneity'. There are lower densities and local allegiances. The third part is called the 'sphere' where elements of the culture 'may be apparent but not dominant'. These elements may indeed be in the form of alien influences spreading into local cultures. The model is shown in Figure 1.2 where other features are added. The first is the localization of cultural contact and interaction in terms of a line of 'intercultural contact', which Meinig envisaged as a dominant routeway. The second is a 'strategic front' where the greatest physical threat to a culture is concentrated; 'where that danger is military in type, concentrations of walls and fortresses, garrisons and depots, may be readily apparent; where it is merely political it may be more diffuse and less obvious.' Finally, there is the 'demographic front' where actual population movements involve a physical extension of the core or domain.

It is clear that the model is conceived in terms of an expanding culture region and it is not easily adapted to decline. But the basic ideas are easily identified in the Welsh language context. Thus, for example, the demographic front can in contemporary terms be interpreted as the inflow of non-Welsh-speaking migrants into Wales over the last two decades. In more general terms, the division of Wales, such as that adopted by Rees Pryce, into Welsh-speaking, bilingual and English-speaking zones corresponds to core, domain and sphere (1978a). A major criticism of Meinig's study is that there is no attempt to

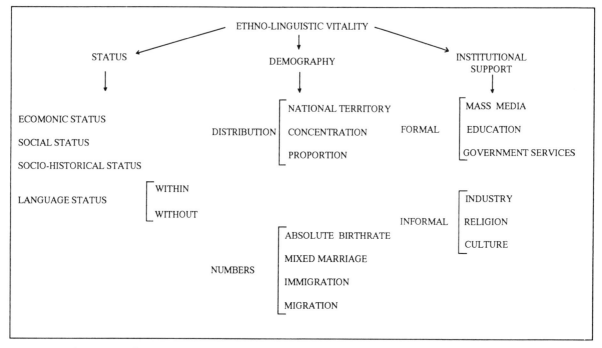

A taxonomy of the structural variables affecting ethno-linguistic vitality (after Giles, Bourhis and Taylor)

**Figure 1.3**

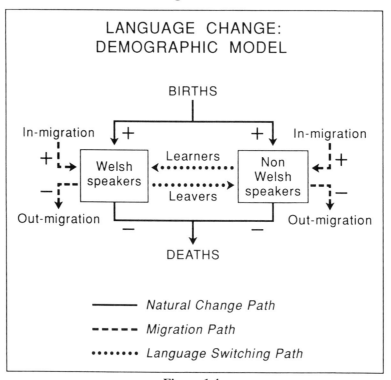

**Figure 1.4**

justify a threefold division. Presumably the implication is that an analysis of relevant data, church membership in his case, would show borders with steeper gradients of change at the boundaries. But no such measures were undertaken and the division into core, domain and sphere is proposed without any attempt at justification. Meinig's work was based simply on church membership but subsequent studies have attempted to add landscape elements (Francaviglia, 1970). The model has been used by Carter (1969; 1976) in his interpretation of the referenda on the Sunday opening of licensed premises in Wales as a criterion of a culture region, and by Pryce in his historical studies of the language. It is a useful heuristic device, and indeed is implicit in most studies of language patterns in Wales; inevitably so perhaps. Thus, E. G. Bowen's inner and outer Wales (1964) are no more than core and sphere, whilst, of course, *Y Fro Gymraeg* is the classic core of a culture region. It is evident that much of the work on Wales has been concerned with only one symbol of culture and that it would be more appropriate to refer to language areas and to keep to the notion of ethnicity as represented by language. There have been few attempts to map other criteria apart from Carter's use of referenda data. But there is no problem in applying Meinig's concept to language alone for, as has been noted, his work was based solely on religion.

## Ethnolinguistic Vitality

Having considered the links between language and ethnic identity and the possibility of deriving some model of the ethnic or culture area, it is appropriate to consider the issue of linguistic vitality (Giles, Bourhis and Taylor, 1977); for it is this concept more than any other that guides the present study of language change in Wales.

Figure 1.3 identifies a set of structural variables which determine degrees of linguistic vitality. Three contributory factors are specified. They are status, demography and institutional support. Status is divided into social status – the degree of esteem a linguistic group affords itself – and economic status – the degree of control a language group has gained over the economic life of its nation, region or community. To these are added socio-historical status or the symbolic value of the language, and the evaluation of the language both from within and from without.

The second set of variables is termed demographic and includes two aspects. The first is the relation of language to territory and the numbers and proportions within that territory. Closely related to those features are the standard demographic processes of population change, including increase or decrease by natural causes (the excess or otherwise of births over deaths), and by in- or out-migration. The only unusual element in this schema is that of mixed marriages which have an obvious consequence on language shift (Harrison, 1978). Figure 1.4 seeks to summarize these demographic movements and their impact on numbers of Welsh-speakers in a simple model. In addition to the population variables noted above, it also takes into account second-language learning and language loss (i.e. subsequent rejection of the language by native speakers or learners), both of which to varying degrees affect numbers of speakers within particular localities.

The third set of variables is related to institutional support and stresses a whole gamut of formal and informal sources of language maintenance. These include the role of government, the media, education, religion and a host of others.

Simple identification of such a set of factors in seeking to explain the process of language change has not been without its critics of course, and there are clearly alternative conceptual and theoretical models that could be structured; for example, approaches based on materialism, political economy or critical socio-cultural theory (Jackson, 1989; Williams, G. 1992). It cannot be gainsaid, however, that the variables included have been (and are) of central significance in shaping the development of the Welsh language; accordingly they figure prominently in the historical review and statistical analyses that form the basis of this study. Before moving on to consider such substantive matters, however, it is necessary to draw attention to a number of technical matters associated with language mapping.

# CHAPTER 2

# Mapping the Welsh Language

Studies of the changing geography of the Welsh language have drawn heavily upon data derived from national population censuses. Other sources of information have been used (e.g., church records, local authority statistics for schools), but it is to successive census enumerations that most researchers of have turned for insights into regional patterns and trends. Unfortunately, the censuses themselves have not assured researchers a consistent set of statistics for purposes of comparative analysis. The questions asked have changed, the population bases have been continually modified, and, most problematic of all, the spatial units (administrative divisions) to which the data relate have varied. Census data need to be treated with care, especially when, as in this study, they are being used to describe patterns and trends over time.

## Censuses of the Welsh Language 1891–1981

The first formal census of the Welsh language was undertaken in 1891. The data collected indicated the numbers of persons aged two years old and over who were monoglot Welsh-speakers and those who had a facility in both Welsh and English. However, as Southall (1895) was soon to point out, the enumeration process was defective on several counts and failed to yield a reliable record of the state of the language at the time. The language statistics were treated in cursory fashion by the census authorities and were presented only for registration districts and counties. These divisions were largely unrelated to existing administrative areas and certainly lacked the fine spatial detail necessary for an appreciation of geographical variations. The fact that certain localities along the Welsh border were excluded from the enumeration, while others actually located in England were included, confused the issue even further (Parry and Williams, 1999).

The population census for 1901 again recorded numbers of Welsh-speakers, but this time data related to persons aged three years and over. This particular threshold has been maintained through successive censuses to the present. In terms of the data themselves Welsh-speakers were categorized according their sex and age characteristics. Statistics were collated for administrative counties, county boroughs, municipal boroughs, urban districts and rural districts. These same conditions also applied to the census of 1911, although with more detailed subdivisions according to age. The most significant feature of the 1921 census was that for the first time data were presented for civil parishes, as well as the administrative divisions used in the two previous censuses. Numbers of Welsh-speakers in urban areas with populations over 50,000 were also detailed.

For each of the first four censuses it is worth noting that variable adjustments were made to the total figures to take account of persons who had failed to make language returns. Inevitably, these adjustments, which were largely based on the language of heads of households (where this was known), introduced a degree of uncertainty into the data. The 1931 and 1951 censuses (there was no census in 1941) were broadly similar in format to that adopted in 1921, but with the Welsh-speaking population in smaller urban areas (20,000–50,000) also being specified in published tabulations. In 1961 the spatial frames for the aggregation of statistics on Welsh-speakers included the small areas or enumeration districts used in the initial compilation of returns. This was a significant advance, although few researchers have taken advantage of the opportunity to explore patterns at such scales.

Responding to pressures for more detailed information on literacy levels the 1971 census requested Welsh-speakers to state whether or not they could read and/or write the language. Not surprisingly, given the complexities of the issues involved, the census did not seek to determine proficiencies in reading and writing. The 1981 census continued with the categorization of Welsh-speakers according to sex, age and ability to read and/or write the language. Interestingly, and for the first time since 1921, language statistics for the 1981 census were not published for the communities (formerly parishes) of Wales. To assure continuity in their analyses of language change, Aitchison and Carter (1985) were obliged to re-create community data by aggregating records for constituent enumeration districts.

**The 1991 Census**

The 1991 Census of Population for Great Britain was taken on 21–2 April. Apart from published tabulations (e.g., county monitors), data have been made available in two datasets – Small Area Statistics (SAS) and Local Base Statistics (LBS). The former contain information for enumeration districts and aggregations thereof (e.g., wards), while the latter refer to wards and higher areal units (e.g., districts). The two datasets also differ in the number of items of information recorded, and in confidentiality restrictions (i.e. the minimum number of households and residents that there must be in an administrative unit before data are released without first being aggregated with other areas). Both datasets contain tables relating to the Welsh language. The tabulation used in this study is Table 67 from the SAS file. This contains 336 separate items of data. As in previous enumerations, the 1991 census details numbers of persons able to speak, read and write Welsh. However, there are differences in form. Firstly, the age-group subdivisions for the 1991 census are more numerous (20 in all); secondly, the categories relating to reading and writing Welsh are more detailed. Thus, in terms of language proficiency, it is possible to differentiate all combinations of ability to speak, read and write Welsh. Interestingly, the 1991 census did not ask whether or not persons were able to speak English. Thus, for the first time the number of Welsh monoglots cannot be determined.

Apart from changes in the precise presentation of the language statistics themselves, a further complication for those concerned with the analysis of language change arises as a result of differences in the definition of the base resident population for enumeration purposes.

The 1991 census considers the resident population to include:

(a)    Present residents
(b)    Absent residents (part of the household present)
(c)    Absent residents (wholly absent household – enumerated)
(d)    Absent residents (wholly absent household – imputed)

Given its treatment of absent households, this definition yields higher population figures than the definitions used in 1971 and 1981. The 1971 census covered those persons actually resident in households (including visitors), whereas in 1981 the base population related to persons 'usually resident' and therefore embraced just categories (a) and (b) above. These differences are of critical significance when it comes to precise calibrations of language trends, for they clearly influence both absolute numbers and the calculation of percentages. For purposes of comparison, it can be noted that the 1991 base population of Wales was 2,835,073. If the data are re-structured to accord with the 1971 and 1981 bases the total figures are 2,766,837 and 2,811,865 respectively. Unfortunately, apart from some limited data contained in the county monitors, the data relating to the Welsh language are only available at the 1991 population base. This makes it impossible to undertake any detailed analyses of language change at other than county level.

As has been noted, language data for the 1991 census are available for counties, districts, wards and enumeration districts. At the time the present analyses were undertaken, language data were not available at community level, although it would have been possible to aggregate constituent enumeration districts to derive such values. While this process was effected by Aitchison and Carter for the 1981 census in order to determine rates of change for the inter-censal periods between 1961 and 1981, such an exercise is not repeated here. The reasons for this are twofold. Firstly, the published data for enumeration districts are at the 1991 population base. As a consequence, direct comparisons cannot be made with previous censuses. This was not the case with the 1981 census; here data were also published at the 1971 base. Secondly, major changes in the boundaries of communities have taken place since the 1981 census, making the derivation of a constant spatial frame for the analysis of language change much more complex. Examination of administrative maps make it abundantly clear that quite major aggregations of communities would have to be made to secure a standard set of divisions (i.e. a spatial frame that could be used for the four censuses 1961–91). Together, these two limitations make it impossible to consider extending the previous the study of language change between 1961 and 1981 (Aitchison and Carter, 1985). Table 2.1 lists the numbers of wards, communities and enumeration districts that are contained in each of the county census files for 1991. Equivalent data for 1981 are also included for reference purposes. The tabulation confirms the major changes that have taken place in the numbers of communities, especially in Dyfed, Powys and Gwynedd. Although the numbers of wards have changed between 1981 and 1991, it is evident that they are not of the same order as for communities.

**Table 2.1**
**Numbers of wards, communities and enumeration districts by counties**

| County | Wards 1981 | Wards 1991 | Communities 1981 | Communities 1991 | Enumeration Districts 1981 | Enumeration Districts 1991 |
|---|---|---|---|---|---|---|
| Clwyd | 134 | 150 | 128 | 127 | 881 | 906 |
| Dyfed | 144 | 163 | 307 | 203 | 955 | 926 |
| Gwent | 93 | 111 | 76 | 98 | 925 | 944 |
| Gwynedd | 142 | 139 | 152 | 122 | 689 | 681 |
| Mid Glamorgan | 95 | 120 | 50 | 85 | 1170 | 1100 |
| Powys | 98 | 96 | 202 | 101 | 434 | 364 |
| South Glamorgan | 39 | 47 | 53 | 54 | 828 | 851 |
| West Glamorgan | 55 | 82 | 41 | 69 | 781 | 789 |
| **Total** | **800** | **908** | **1009** | **859** | **6663** | **6561** |

In this study the Welsh language maps for 1991 are prepared at the ward level. Figure 2.1 shows the spatial distribution of the 908 wards in Wales. The fact that the wards differ in areal size and shape is of some significance for it clearly affects not only the visual structure of the maps that are produced, but also impinges upon the interpretation of regional patterns. Of particular note in this regard are the differences in spatial detail for rural and urban areas. In the former, wards tend to be large in area and to have lower populations; this is especially true in upland regions. Urban areas are normally characterized by clusters of small wards with denser populations. Here it is possible to highlight more detailed local variations. These matters need not be elaborated upon further. Suffice it to say that geographers have long appreciated the importance of the scale issue in

**Table 2.2**
**Wards by population size, 1991**

| Total population | Number of wards | % Number | % Population |
|---|---|---|---|
| Under 1000 | 88 | 9.7 | 2.4 |
| 1000–1499 | 140 | 15.4 | 6.4 |
| 1500–2499 | 278 | 30.6 | 19.1 |
| 2500–3499 | 127 | 14.0 | 13.3 |
| 3500–4499 | 93 | 10.2 | 13.0 |
| 4500–5499 | 65 | 7.2 | 11.4 |
| 5500 and over | 117 | 12.9 | 34.4 |

cartographic analyses of this type. For purposes of reference, Table 2.2 lists the numbers and proportions of wards in terms of resident population size. The statistics serve to underline the degree of variation that exists within the set of Welsh wards. Thus, the 88 wards that have populations of less than 1,000 account for nearly 10 per cent of wards, but

Figure 2.1

only contain 2.4 per cent of the Welsh population. At the other extreme are wards with populations of over 5,000 residents. Such areas (117) comprise 12.9 per cent of all wards, but have over a third of the total population.

While the main body of data presented in this study are derived from SAS files and in particular Table 67, considerable reference is made in Chapter 7 to more recently published census statistics derived from 10 per cent samples of households and 1 per cent samples of individuals in households. These samples are referred to as Samples of Anonymized Records (SARs). Although inevitably subject to sampling errors, such data allow more detailed analyses to be undertaken of the Welsh-speaking community. In particular consideration can be given to migration, family structures and social class attributes. Since these are important variables in seeking to explain language structures and regional patterns they are worthy of detailed analysis.

**Language Mapping**

Language maps can be prepared using a variety of numerical measures. Since these are of significance to the present study it is appropriate to comment on the differing approaches that have been adopted. Of particular relevance in this regard is the distinction between absolute and relative values. Four basic treatments of the data can be distinguished:

*(a) Absolute values*
The raw statistics recorded by the census can be mapped directly as absolute values. In this case, proportional symbols (e.g., circles) can for instance be used to display the size of particular language features (e.g., numbers of Welsh-speakers).

*(b) Relative values*
While absolute values are of interest, it is often appropriate to express such data as percentages or ratios. Maps depicting the percentage of the resident population in an area that are able to speak Welsh are of this type. So too are maps showing densities (e.g., numbers of Welsh-speakers per km$^2$).

*(c) Measures of change*
Absolute and relative values can also be used to capture trends or changes over time. Various possibilities exist here. One approach is simply to determine the differences in absolute values between time t1 and time t2. Needless to say such values can be either positive, negative, or can show no change. Another approach is to chart differences in percentages or ratios (i.e. relative values) between t1 and t2. Finally, it is possible to calculate percentage rates of change over a period of time. In this case, absolute values at t2 can be expressed as ratios of values at t1. When considering these various approaches to the measurement of change it is to be appreciated that they can yield very differing interpretations. A simple example serves to illustrate the point. Table 2.3 records the total resident populations and numbers of Welsh-speakers for 1971 and 1981 in the community of Caron Uwch Clawdd (Tregaron). The figures show that the Welsh-speaking population

20

increased during the decade by 23 or 12.1 per cent (percentage rate of change). However, whereas in 1971 the proportion of the population able to speak Welsh was 92.7 per cent (190 out of 205), in 1981 it had fallen to 81 per cent (213 out of 263). The percentage difference here is -11.7 per cent (92.7 – 81.0). The reason for this seemingly incongruous situation is of course that the percentage differences also take into account changes in the number of non-Welsh-speakers in the area concerned. In this case a high in-migration of English monoglots diluted the relative strength of the language in the community.

**Table 2.3**
**Total population over three years of age and**
**Welsh-speakers in Caron Uwch Clawdd**

|  | 1971 | 1981 |
|---|---|---|
| Total resident population | 205 | 263 |
| Welsh-speakers | 190 | 213 |

One final issue needs to be addressed before moving on to examine more substantive matters, and this is the nature of the questions asked in the census, and the likely quality of responses. Of particular concern here is the basic question on the census form – 'Does the person speak Welsh?' – and associated questions concerning reading and writing. Three problems arise.

Firstly, it is possible, though now, given the publicity which has surrounded the language issue, unlikely, that the question could be interpreted as a request concerning usage rather than fluency. That is the 'does' in the question, rather than the expected 'can', could be interpreted to mean 'What language do you usually use?' rather than 'Can you speak Welsh?'. Significantly, in Scotland and Northern Ireland the census question uses the word 'can'.

A second issue is that there is no measure of the degree of fluency which defines a Welsh-speaker; the interpretation is left to the individual completing the form and a wide variation is possible. The standard response has been to argue that variation will be equally distributed and, therefore, will not affect mapped distributions. But in 1991 a new problem has arisen. A considerable number of monoglot English-speaking parents have completed the census form on behalf of their children. Those children may be attending bilingual schools or be having Welsh lessons at school. There seems little doubt that such parents can easily exaggerate the fluency of their children and return them as Welsh-speakers, even though their grasp of the language may be rudimentary.

Finally, the question 'Do you understand Welsh?' is not asked. Evidence suggests that if this question were to be posed then the numbers would be much higher than those indicating that they are able speak Welsh. Significantly, it is to be asked in the 2001 census.

Unfortunately, the census question relating to the language was only asked in Wales. No information is therefore available concerning the numbers of Welsh-speakers residing in other parts of Great Britain. Given the high and long-standing level of out-migration from traditional Welsh-speaking areas these numbers could be quite significant (relatively speaking). At the 1981 census there were nearly 600,000 people resident in England and Scotland who were born in Wales.

Having elaborated upon these mapping and associated methodological issues the basis has been set for a consideration of the changing geography of the Welsh language. Chapter 3 provides a broad historical introduction and identifies the major forces and trends that affected the status and distribution of the language up until the 1961 census. This is followed by an examination of changes during the critical period 1961–81 (Chapter 4). Chapter 5 looks more closely at the 1980s, drawing heavily on selected case studies of language change in rural and urban Wales. Chapter 6 charts contemporary language patterns through a more detailed, and strongly map-based study of the 1991 census, and highlights more recent trends. Drawing upon data largely derived from the SARs (see above), Chapter 7 examines patterns of in- and out-migration in more detail, and disaggregates Welsh- and non-Welsh-speakers according to social class and types of household formations. Finally, Chapter 8 reflects on the future of the language in the light of more recent developments.

# CHAPTER 3

# The Welsh Language and its Development: A Historical Overview

Although the statistical and cartographic analyses which form the heart of this study are primarily concerned with the period after the Second World War, and especially the three decades 1961 to 1991, it is appropriate to preface the discussion with a brief review of the major forces and events that have shaped the changing geography of the language in Wales up to the beginning of the 1960s. For much more detailed insights into these various forces and events, reference should be made to the highly acclaimed project of the Centre for Advanced Welsh and Celtic Studies of the University of Wales on the Social History of the Welsh Language (Jenkins,1997b, 1998, 1999, Jones, D. 1998).

The Welsh language is derived from what is called by linguists Common Celtic, itself a derivative from an Indo-European root. From their heartland in Central Europe the Celtic peoples spread in pre-Roman times to occupy most of Western Europe. Eventually, however, with the expansion of the Roman Empire, Celtic was replaced in all but the peripheral regions of Europe by Romance languages (Germanic regions apart). In these outlying imperial margins two branches of Celtic emerged – Brittonic (P Celtic) which characterized much of Britain, and Goidelic (Q Celtic) which was the language of Ireland. Presumably Brittonic remained the language of southern Britain during the Roman occupation, but the question as to whether a Celtic or Romance language would have succeeded in that area was pre-empted by the Anglo-Saxon invasions and the introduction of a Germanic language. One consequence of these folk movements was a reciprocal or counter invasion of north-west France from Cornwall and Wales. This was to result in the dominance there of the Breton language – a Brittonic successor.

The eastward press of the Anglo-Saxon peoples eventually led to the isolation of the Celtic-speaking populations, with those living in what is now Wales separated from their counterparts in Cornwall and in the north (Cumbria and Strathclyde). But, as Davies has argued,

> . . .we do not have to subscribe to the old cliché that the battles of Dyrham and Chester, *c.* 577 and 616 respectively, cut off the British of the South from those of the North to recognise that the English settlement over much of south western Britain had a politically and culturally confining effect. (Davies, 1982, 112)

Locked as they were in their remote strongholds, the Celts were called 'the strangers' by the Saxons (W(e)alas or Welsh; see Davies, J. 1990, 70). In their own terminology however they were 'the compatriots' (Y Cymry) and they spoke 'Cymraeg'.

At the end of the eighth century this cultural divide was given formal expression in the landscape when Offa, king of the growing power of Mercia, built the dyke or earthwork which now bears his name. To cross Offa's Dyke was to become in later days the symbol of leaving one's compatriots and entering the land of the English. The boundary which it constituted cannot be taken as a contemporary language divide however, for Welsh is recorded as having been spoken in Hereford and Shropshire even in modern times. Be that as it may, the effect of the dyke must have been greatly to accentuate differences, and it is certainly feasible to adopt it as a starting point for any discussion of language history. It serves as a base line from which to chart the slow and complex westward retreat of the Welsh language.

The first major episode in that retreat, and the one which brought English significantly beyond Offa's Dyke, was the Anglo-Norman invasion of Wales, beginning about 1070. Its ultimate impact is effectively measured by the distribution of one of its introductions, the system of manorial cultivation based on open-field agriculture. This system established itself most intensively along the coastal lowland regions of south Wales – southern Gwent, the Vale of Glamorgan, peninsular Gower and South Pembroke. The whole of the border lowland showed the same pattern of occupation with penetration along the valleys of the Usk, Wye and Severn. In the north the distribution was confined mainly to the east of the river Dee, with but occasional occurrences to the west. Beyond these areas the Anglo-Norman castle towns must also be regarded as forward bases of Anglicization.

The problem central to any investigation of subsequent retreat is not so much the absence of reliable data but the lack of any data at all. The most extensive discussion of the language in the period between the Norman incursion and the Act of Union is to be found in Llinos Beverly Smith's study, *Pwnc yr Iaith yng Nghymru 1282–1536* (Smith, L. B., 1986). She indicates how at the beginning of the period Welsh remained spoken to the limits of Offa's Dyke and, indeed, beyond.

> Ond yn y drydedd ganrif ar ddeg yr oedd acenion y Gymraeg yn berffaith hyglyw ar hyd y ffin â Lloegr. [But in the thirteenth century Welsh speech was clearly to be heard all along the English border.]

and . . .

> Y mae mwy nag un awgrym bod poblogaeth Gymraeg ei hiaith mewn rhanbarth mor ddwyreiniol â swydd Henffordd ar ddiwedd y bedwaredd ganrif ar ddeg ac wedyn. [There is more than one suggestion of Welsh-speakers in an area as far east as Herefordshire at the end of the fourteenth century and later.] (Smith, 1986, 4)

Even so, the inroads of the Anglo-Normans and their followers became more and more significant.

Mae'n bur debyg, er enghraifft, mai'r Saesneg oedd iaith y gwladychwyr a ddaeth yn sgil goresgyniad y Normaniaid cynnar ac mai honno oedd yr iaith a gyflwynwyd ganddynt i Fro Morgannwg a deheudir Penfro. [It is certain, for example, that English was the language of the settlers who followed the early Norman invasion and that English was the language which they introduced to the Vale of Glamorgan and south Pembrokeshire.] (Smith, 1986, 8)

This was particularly significant after the Edwardian conquest of Wales when –

Daeth ton newydd o deuluoedd estron, yn hanu o siroedd Caer a Chaerhirfryn, Caerefrog, Henffordd a Chaerwrangon, i ymsefydlu yn y bwrdeisdrefi newydd ac yn rhai o ardaloedd gwledig y gogledd-ddwyrain, a dichon iddynt hwythau ddwyn eu hiaith hefyd i'r mannau hynny. [There came a new wave of foreign families, from Cheshire and Lancashire, Yorkshire, Herefordshire and Worcestershire, to settle in the new boroughs and in some of the rural areas of the north-east, and probably they too brought their language to those areas.] (Smith, 1986, 8)

Whilst these trends and movements are significant, it does not mean that in the areas affected by Anglicizing influences Welsh was not present, or indeed that it was in decline. Even if the early burgess lists suggest the Anglicization of the towns, later listings indicate that the Welsh reasserted themselves (Carter, 1989). Moreover, as Llinos Smith points out, at no time was there any feeling that Welsh was in peril, and she notes that when the chronicler Ranulph Hegden, in the middle of the fourteenth century, listed the characteristics of the Welsh, there was no need to mention language but rather such things as dress, customs and diet. Again, at the time of the Glyndŵr uprising, only one chronicler refers to the language, namely Adda of Brynbuga who wrote –

. . . ac wedi derbyn pardwn gan y Saeson, bradychwyd Owain gan y Cymry, ac aethant yn ôl i'w cartrefi mewn cyni eithriadol, a chawsant yr hawl i ddefnyddio'r iaith Gymraeg er bod y Saeson wedi penderfynu ei dileu. Ond parodd yr Hollalluog, Brenin y Brenhinoedd, bod yr ordeiniad hwn yn cael ei ddymchwel ar ddeisyfiad y darostyngedig. [And having been pardoned by the English, Owain was betrayed by the Welsh, and they returned to their homes in great sorrow and obtained the right to use the Welsh language though the English had decided to eliminate it. But the Almighty, King of Kings caused this order to be overthrown on the petition of those in subjection.] (Smith, 1986, 26–7)

There was certainly a diminution in the dominance of Welsh in the areas settled by the Anglo-Normans, but perhaps the critical damage was not in the restriction of geographical extent but in the limitation of domain and consequent loss of status. To a great degree a distinctive legal system rather than a language was seen as the symbol of national identity at a time when kingdoms were being formed often out of amalgamations of ethnically contrasted territories. But Welsh law was essentially customary and within Wales the formal language of administration on such documents as treaties or charters was either

Latin or French. With time, however, English was more and more used. Eventually it asserted itself as the language of formal documentation. This had the serious consequence of displacing Welsh from possible use in such transactions and effectively eliminating it from one of the most significant of domains. That, rather than any retreat in distribution, was the major setback for the language and a crucial step on what might have been its degradation to a patois.

> Ai tynged anorfod yr iaith oedd iddi sicrhau ei lle yn gyfrwng llên a diwylliant a bywyd ysbrydol y genedl heb ddatblygu'n iaith ddogfen a threfn ac ai cyn yr Uno y seliwyd ei ffawd? [Was it the inevitable fate of the language to ensure its place as the medium of the literature, culture and spiritual life of the nation but without its developing as the language of documentation and administration, and was its fate sealed before the Union?] (Smith, 1986, 31)

Thus, there ultimately followed from the proscription of Welsh from legal and administration affairs, a growing emphasis on language as the significant criterion of difference. R. R. Davies comments in the introductory chapter to his book *The Age of Conquest. Wales 1063–1415* (1991), that language was becoming one of the badges of national identity:

> Those who did not speak Welsh (W. anghyfiaith) were immediately designated as aliens (W. estron); so it was that the English came to be branded as 'a foreign alien tongued people' (W. estron genedl anghyfiaith). (Davies, 1991, 17)

By the end of the period which the book considers, the failure of the Glyndŵr revolt

> meant that the prospect of unitary native rule and political independence were gone for good. If the Welsh were to survive as a people, they would henceforth have to cultivate and sustain their identity, as in the past, by other means. (Davies, 1991, 465)

The 'other means' became the critical issue, for with the elimination of political identity, and the destruction of legal and administrative systems such as they were (which the Act of Union was finally to consummate), then language, and the literary tradition which was its highest expression, remained as the most significant hallmarks of Welshness. It might well be that one of the explanations of the unexpected survival of Welsh, as compared with Scots Gaelic and Irish, was that the other two Celtic peoples retained elements of separate legal, administrative and political systems as expressions of identity: Wales had nothing but the language.

Professor Rees Davies has described Wales during the Middle Ages as

> an ill-assorted jigsaw of private lordships and royal shires, lacking all unity in law and government. It was treated, in effect, as a collection of colonial annexes dependent on the Crown and the higher aristocracy of England. (Davies, 1991, 461–2)

But once a United Kingdom was being created then that situation was totally unacceptable to the English crown. The Act of Union which ended it had inevitable repercussions on the language which had become the most tangible symbol of difference.

Under the Welsh house of Tudor the formal and complete association of Wales with England was accomplished by 'An Act for Laws and Justice to be ministered in Wales in like form as it is in this Realm' – the Act of Union as it has subsequently, if not properly, been called. The Welsh language was not formally proscribed by the Act, though by implication its demise was seen as something to be desired:

> And also by cause that the people of the same dominion have and do daily use a speech nothing like or consonant to the natural mother tongue used within this realm some rude and ignorant people have made distinction and diversity between the King's subjects of this Realm and his subjects of the said dominion and Principality of Wales. Whereby great discord variance debate division murmur and sedition have grown between his said subjects . . . his highness therefore minding and intending to reduce them to perfect order notice and knowledge of the laws . . . and utterly to extirpate all and singular the sinister usages and customs differing . . . his said country or dominion of Wales shall stand and continue from henceforth incorporated united and annexed to and with his realm of England.

The critical phrase here is 'to extirpate all and singular the sinister usages and customs differing'. Although it applied directly to law, it also unequivocally implied a process of cultural assimilation and hence of language erosion. This was reinforced by the provision that 'from henceforth no Person or Persons that use the Welsh Speech or Language shall have or enjoy any Manner Office or Fees within the Realm of England, Wales or Other the King's Dominion' (Bowen, 1908).

The Act of Union by making the English language the sole language of government and law finally and formally abstracted a domain of use from Welsh which had effectively been lost long before. But to that it is possible to add another and less tangible reduction. If Welsh were not to be used in a significant formal context then it meant, too, that its use in informal contexts would diminish. Inevitably, if the Welsh gentry wished to participate in public life then that participation would be in English and the language of polite society, if such it can be called, would also be English. There followed the conviction that Welsh was the language of the barbarous past, English the language of the civilized future. 'The increasing tendency among churchmen to ascribe a superior status to the English tongue was . . . a growing problem' (Jenkins, 1978, 9). Geraint Jenkins notes that until 'the end of the seventeenth century, the survival of the Welsh language had been largely the result of the efforts of the Welsh clergy and their flocks' but that alliance was under threat. In 1717 an Anglican minister of the diocese of St David's 'claimed that some of his fellow clergy, ensnared in the web of Anglicization, were too haughty and "puffed up" to preach in Welsh to monoglot parishioners' (Jenkins, 1978, 9). Even

. . .the attitude of charitable bodies towards the Welsh language was an open secret: it was, at best, a nuisance, and, at worst, a pernicious relic of barbarism. It is plain that the policy of the Welsh Trust and the SPCK of distributing religious literature in Welsh was essentially a short-term expedient calculated to save the souls of those monoglot Welshmen who were poised on the brink of everlasting damnation; they believed their more enduring function to be the rearing of a new generation of English speakers in the network of charity schools which they had established in the Principality. (Jenkins, 1987, 37)

But religious attitudes that souls were best saved in English were the mirror of those growing in secular society, expressed in their most extreme form by William Richards of Helmdon in his *Wallography* of 1682.

The Native Gibberish is usually prattled throughout the whole of Taphydome, except in their Market Towns, whose Inhabitants being a little raised, and (as it were) pufft up into Bubbles, above the ordinary scum, do begin to despise it . . . 'Tis usually cashier'd out of Gentlemen's Houses . . . the Lingua will be Englishd out of Wales. (Richards, 1682, 63)

In a more balanced summary Geraint Jenkins writes in relation to writers in Welsh –

Authors knew that there had been a time when the gentry's pride included a delight in Welshness and a proper regard for the language; but it was all too evident now that their pride was being shaped and dominated by the values of their English counterparts. (Jenkins, 1987, 260–1)

There can be distilled from these various comments another critical loss of domain. The eighteenth century was the Age of Enlightenment, the time which saw the widespread influence of scholars such as Descartes, Leibnitz and Newton. Not only did natural science experience a major efflorescence, but in all the professions issues were scrutinized free from the trammels of traditional religious orthodoxy. Above all, it was the age of science: the Royal Society had been founded in 1660. But these new ideas were to permeate society through the educated gentry and down the urban hierarchy. In brief, the diffusion of the new ideas was directly related to social standing and to settlement size, and in that way they were bound into social class and the English language. Thus science, too, became a domain in which Welsh took little part, although there were the obvious exceptions, most notably Edward Lhuyd and the Morris brothers (*Cylch y Morrisiaid*).

It is apparent that in the foregoing discussion little has been written about geographical distribution, largely because little can be written. There is no evidence of any clear retreat. Even William Richards of Helmdon referred to the *whole* of Wales in his animadversion. Perhaps the best summary is provided by Prys Morgan, for in considering the distribution in the eighteenth century he writes,

in that sense Welsh was as healthy as any other language in Europe; left in total isolation, its future would be secure. Yet its status was low, hardly more than that of a patois or peasant language, rescued from dissolving into mutually incomprehensible dialects by the excellent Welsh of the Elizabethan Anglican liturgy, the Bible and the supporting homilies and apologetic literature. Welsh was used remarkably rarely as a written language, and it was not taught to more than a handful in any methodical way. (Morgan, 1981, 68)

Further, but not totally unproblematical, insights into the geographical distribution of the Welsh language at this time can be gained from the map of non-Celtic place-names before 1715 (Figure 3.1) constructed by A. J. Parkinson for Peter Smith's *Houses of the Welsh Countryside* (Smith, P., 1975, 340). It serves as one indicator of the strength of the penetration of English throughout the Marcher regions of south Wales and the borderland.

There can be no doubt that the changes taking place during the eighteenth century were to have a major impact upon Wales, upon Welshness and upon the language.

In the Methodist view of Welsh history, the eighteenth century is the century of the Great Revival . . . One of the earliest attempts to define this cultural revival was by William Roberts 'Nefyn' in 1852. In his *Crefydd yr Oesoedd Tywyll* (Religion of the Dark Ages), he called it the *Cyffrawd Cymreigyddol* (Movement of Welshness). (Morgan, 1981, 13)

It was characterized by the abandonment of what had become traditional culture based on the myths of Gildas and Geoffrey of Monmouth, and of 'the rise of a more serious, self-conscious Welshness based on books, eisteddfodau and literary or debating societies' (Morgan, 1981, 13). Many regarded with despair the loss of the past, most notably epitomized in Ellis Wynne's *Gweledigaethau y Bardd Cwsg* (Visions of the Sleeping Bard), but the renaissance of the eighteenth century encompassed a unique revival of things Welsh. As John Davies writes,

Yn wir, llwyddwyd i ailddiffinio Cymreictod gan beri amheuon ynglŷn â hawl y rhai nad anwesent y diwylliant hwnnw i gael eu hystyried yn etifeddion gwir draddodiadau Cymru. [Indeed, they succeeded in redefining Welshness, causing doubt concerning the right of those who did not embrace that culture to be considered heirs of the true traditions of Wales.] (Davies, 1990, 300)

Without question, one of the greatest influences in the preservation and extension of the language during the eighteenth century were the circulating schools initiated by Griffith Jones, Vicar of Llanddowror. His motivation was the saving of souls, not the safeguarding of the language. The scheme was based on itinerant teachers who stayed at a location for about three months to teach reading so that the Bible was made accessible. As John Davies writes,

Yn *Welch Piety* ceir manylion o flwyddyn i flwyddyn am nifer y disgyblion. Gellir eu dehongli i olygu fod dros 200,000 o bobl, bron hanner poblogaeth Cymru, wedi

Non-Celtic Place-Names
before 1715

•   Village

◦   House

0 _____ 20 miles
0 _____ 30 kilometres

**Figure 3.1**

mynychu'r ysgolion erbyn 1771, blwyddyn marwolaeth Griffith Jones. [In *Welch Piety* there are details from year to year of the number of pupils. It is possible to estimate that over 200,000, almost half the population of Wales, attended the schools by 1771, the year of Griffith Jones' death.] (Davies, J., 1990, 295)

David Williams's summary of Griffith Jones's work remains appropriate –

He helped to make the Welsh a literate nation, and his circulating schools were the most important experiment in religious education in the eighteenth century, not only in Wales but in Britain and all the British dominions. (Williams, D. 1950, 147)

But the renaissance was a great deal more than a Methodist movement and was expressed through such aspects as the preparation of dictionaries of the language, the revival of eisteddfodau, the growth of Welsh debating societies, and the rise of scholarly history to replace the old myths. It even generated the inventions of Iolo Morganwg. However, one feature stands out. The movements of the eighteenth century deepened and enriched the domains in which Welsh was already used, and it conserved the language because of that; but it did not extend the domains, and that was to be crucial in the next century.

The earliest map of the distribution of the language is that for 1750 constructed by Rees Pryce (1978a; 1978b). The data on which this is based are derived from the returns of curates, vicars and rectors throughout Wales concerning the use of Welsh and/or English in services. This information allows a distinction to be made between areas where services were Welsh, mainly Welsh, bilingual, mainly English and English. In considering the territorial domination of Welsh, Pryce writes,

Before the early industrialization of north-east Wales and the later growth of metallurgical and mining industries in the south, on the evidence of the visitation returns Wales was overwhelmingly a Welsh speaking country. (Pryce, 1978a, 241)

And again,

In south-east Wales the Welsh-speaking heartland extended right through the western half of the county of Monmouth to reach the River Usk. Moreover, the greater part of Glamorganshire was then an integral part of Welsh Wales. (Pryce, 1978a, 244)

The conclusion from an examination of Pryce's map (Figure 3.2) is that the completely Anglicized areas were very restricted and that no major inroads into Welsh Wales had been made since the Middle Ages. Although Pryce allows for some change in a narrow zone which he characterized as bilingual, he accepts that 'in the county of Radnor, east Monmouthshire, Gower and south Pembrokeshire, even in the mid-eighteenth century English had been the sole language of the people for many generations' (Pryce, 1978a,

Principal language zones
c. 1750

Welsh

Bilingual

English

Welsh–Bilingual divides

Definite

Presumed

Bilingual–English divides

Definite

Presumed

Area
without data

0          20 miles

0          30 kilometres

**Figure 3.2**

After W.T.R. Pryce 1978

247). These were, of course, the Englishries of the Middle Ages. The critical point which emerges, therefore, is not the geographical displacement of Welsh during the long period from the Act of Union to the middle of the eighteenth century, but rather the crucial and progressive limitation of domains in which it was used and the concomitant restriction of status. The domains were never purely domestic, that is confined to the hearth, and the language never suffered from such limitation, largely due to the translation of the Bible and the religious movements of the eighteenth century. But whereas these traditional domains of hearth, chapel, literature and all its associated activities as in eisteddfodau, and it must be added of agriculture, remained secure, the newer domains of what can be called 'polite society', and of science, together with the long-standing domains of law, administration and government remained essentially English. Thus the dilution of language which had occurred largely by the Anglicization of the gentry, and in the towns, together with domain limitation which was intimately associated with it, left the language particularly vulnerable to the massive transformations of the next century.

It is an impossible task to present a brief resumé of language change during the nineteenth century. Fortunately there are two major studies, that by Ieuan Gwynedd Jones on 'Language and Community in Nineteenth Century Wales' which was included in his book of essays on *Mid-Victorian Wales* (Jones, 1992), and that by Hywel Teifi Edwards on 'Y Gymraeg yn y Bedwaredd Ganrif ar Bymtheg' which appeared in Volume 2 of *Cof Cenedl* (Edwards, 1987). In 1999 the volume *Language and Community in the Nineteenth Century* edited by G. H. Jenkins was published. In addition, there is a thorough presentation of all the relevant data in Dot Jones's book, *Statistical Evidence relating to the Welsh Language, 1801–1911* (Jones, 1998). Local studies have become much richer and one of the latest and best is *Oes y Byd i'r Iaith Gymraeg* by Sian Rhiannon Williams (1992), a study of Welsh in the industrial area of Monmouthshire during the nineteenth century. Alongside the richness of those works only a rudimentary review can be undertaken here, but with a continued emphasis on the combined theme of domains of use and social status.

The complexity, which makes a constrained discussion of language change difficult, derives from the massive economic changes associated with industrialization and the related transformation of the population distribution. In simplest terms the total population of Wales increased from 587,245 at the 1801 census to 2,012,876 at the 1901 census, although some boundary changes were involved. Glamorgan returned a population of 70,879 in 1801 but by 1901 this had increased elevenfold to 859,931. In contrast, by 1871 all the rural counties were experiencing actual population loss; the rural depopulation which was to be characteristic for one hundred years had set in. Such change inevitably had a major impact upon language distribution, particularly in the build-up of Welsh-speaking populations in Glamorgan, Carmarthenshire and Monmouthshire, as well as in the counties of Denbigh and Flint. But it is essential to stress one point. Much of the movement was internal migration and, especially in the south, migration from England only became significant at the end of the century. Even so, closely linked to migration was an increasing ease of movement which was brought about by the new railway system. The isolation of Wales, upon which the survival of the language had to a degree been reliant, was being broken down.

Inevitably much of the discussion of the language in the nineteenth century centres on the Report of the Commissioners of Inquiry into the State of Education in Wales of 1847, 'Brad y Llyfrau Gleision' (the Treachery of the Blue Books). Again, there is an admirable exegesis by Ieuan Gwynedd Jones (1992) and an excellent extended review of *The Language of the Blue Books* by Gwyneth Tyson Roberts (1998). The reason for the reaction to the Report is quite clear. Industrialization and the business entrepreneur were creating new opportunities for the generation of wealth; and progress was defined in terms of material wealth. But the language in the domains of technology and business, successors of science and administration, was English. Without fluency in that language Welsh people would remain isolated and poor. But further, as has been already suggested, English was the language of 'polite society', so it was thought the Welsh would also be removed from the civilizing influences of the new bourgeoisie. The commissioners were unable to comprehend that a different culture, possibly with different values, could exist within the bounds of a United Kingdom. Wales was therefore perceived as backward and the reason manifestly rested with the language which isolated the population from the benefits of 'progress'. There is little space here for extended quotation and analysis, but one extract from I. G. Jones's study clearly indicates the central issue:

> In the minds of the Commissioners and of their political masters the two [the Welsh language and Nonconformity] were connected, and it was in the connection that the evil resided. The language was the major isolating factor in the life of the ordinary people: it isolated the Welshman from all influences except those which arose within his class. He lived 'in an underworld of his own', as Lingen [one of the Commissioners] puts it; 'a disastrous barrier to all moral progress', as Symonds [another Commissioner] expressed it. According to Lingen it distorted the class system, by isolating the mass of the people from their natural leaders, and compelled the ordinary man to the life of a helot or labourer; 'they are never masters . . . never found at the top of the social scale', either in town or country, lacking the entrepreneurial spirit, initiating nothing new, no new enterprise or source of profit or means of social advance. (Jones, 1992b, 137)

From the above it is possible to derive two fundamental limitations of the language perceived by Victorian society. The first was the exclusion of Welsh from the new and developing domains of technology, a successor of science, and of business. As David Davies of Llandinam, 'the exemplar of the self-made man', is quoted as saying in *Y Geninen* –

> Os ydych am barhau i fwyta bara tywyll a gorwedd ar wely gwellt, gwaeddwch chwi eich gorau, 'Oes y byd i'r iaith Gymraeg': ond os ydych chwi yn chwennych bwyta bara gwyn a chig eidon rost, mae yn rhaid i chwi ddysgu Saesneg. [If you wish to continue to eat black bread and lie on straw beds, carry on shouting 'Long life to the Welsh language'. But if you wish to eat white bread and roast beef you must learn English.] (Jones, 1992a, 70)

The second perceived limitation is a derivative from the English character of bourgeois society. The nineteenth century was a period when there was a massive extension in the array of social classes, not only due to the development of industrial skills, but also, and in many ways more significantly, due to the growth of clerical work. Each stratum of the class system sought to distance itself from that below and associate itself with that above. There were Pooters in Wales! The language became an integral part of that process, of the way to ape a superior social class. To speak English, preferably with an accent akin to that of genteel English society, became an ideal to be pursued. Welsh became a language which children need not acquire, indeed they were better without it since it carried at least an implication of exclusion from the higher reaches of society. Moreover, time could be devoted to more profitable ends, for Welsh had no apparent economic value. The result was symbolized by the 'Welsh Not' and in practice produced a secular education which was English directed.

But there was also another domain in which the language was to lose relevance, even if only to a degree. The radical reaction of Welsh Nonconformity had been embodied in support for the Liberal Party; Nonconformity and Liberalism were inextricably associated and the Welsh language was the matrix of that association. But by the end of the nineteenth century and the beginning of the twentieth much of radical opinion was turning to socialism, and to a socialism which saw itself as international and cosmopolitan, and so removed from purely Welsh traditions.

> From 1911 onwards socialism and the new miners' union were becoming the new religion. The language of socialism was English . . . To abandon Welsh became not only a valuational but also a symbolic rejection and affirmation. (Jones, 1992a, 78)

That was a rejection of the Liberal/Nonconformist past, an affirmation of a secular and English-based movement. Thus yet another domain was lost to the Welsh language as political philosophy and action became rooted in English. It was in English that the confrontation between Labour and Conservative, the parties of the new era, was to be conducted. So it was in the greatly burgeoning field of local government, partly as a result of the ancient proscriptions, partly because of the new party systems.

The immediate assumption from this catalogue of problems, curtailed as it is, would be one of marked language decline. But, superficially at least, nothing could be further from the truth. The end of the century was the period when the highest *numbers* of Welsh speakers were recorded; the maximum was 977,366 reached in 1911, although a higher *proportion*, effectively half the population, was returned in 1901 when the number was 929,824. Hywel Teifi Edwards adds to these figures the fact that in 1896 there were 32 periodicals and 25 newspapers published in Welsh and that in 1886–7 Hughes and Son (publishers at Wrexham) gave evidence before the Cross Commission (on elementary education) that at least £100,000 was spent annually on literature in Welsh. He adds, 'dyna le i gredu, mae'n rhaid, fod diwedd y bedwaredd ganrif ar bymtheg yn Oes Aur yn hanes Cymreictod', (There is room to believe, certainly, that the end of the nineteenth century was a golden age in the history of Welshness), (Edwards, 1987, 122). This is the traditional view clearly set out by Professor K. O. Morgan in what is the definitive history of Wales at this period:

> Welsh in the 1880s was securely based in terms of daily intercourse . . . Whatever its aesthetic or technical limitations, it had a clear capacity for growth – and as a medium for a significant mode of cultural expression, not merely as a peasant patois . . . Most important of all, Welsh was the language of contemporary argument and discussion. (Morgan, 1981, 21)

And again, during the 1880s 'dramatic transformations swept through the land which added up to a kind of national renaissance' which

> expressed itself at the most popular grass roots level. The Welsh language in some ways proved more vigorous than ever in the years after 1880. It had new status and protection. In 1885 a group of cultured patriots . . . founded a Society for the Utilization of the Welsh Language. (Morgan, 1981, 95)

Moreover, all this was backed by, indeed was part of, what Morgan uses as his chapter heading – 'The growth of national consciousness'. It is usually symbolized in the founding of a national movement, Cymru Fydd, in 1866; a Young Wales movement parallel to those on the continent.

Given the general opinion of the time, and the characterization by historians since, that the turn of the century marked a 'Golden Age', then two basic questions arise. The first is, why was the condition of the language regarded so optimistically when all the evidence which has been presented would suggest the opposite? The second is, why did the twentieth century witness such an immediate and, indeed, drastic collapse?

Before seeking to answer these questions, one word of caution needs to be introduced. After referring to a Golden Age, Hywel Teifi Edwards adds:

> Nid dyna'r gwir, wrth gwrs. Gwyddom, er bod nifer y Cymry Cymraeg rhwng 1871 a 1901 yn fwy nag y buasai erioed, ei fod fel canran o'r boblogaeth gyfan wedi gostwng yn gyson trwy gydol y ganrif. Amcangyfrifodd Thomas Darlington fod rhyw 587,245 yn byw yng Nghymru ym 1801 a bod 80% yn siarad Cymraeg. Erbyn 1841, yn ôl amcangyfrif Syr Thomas Phillips, roedd y boblogaeth yn 1,046,073 a 67% ohoni a siaradai'r iaith, ac er i Ernst Georg Ravenstein faentumio ym 1879 fod 71.2% o boblogaeth o 1,312,583 yn medru'r Gymraeg, erbyn troad y ganrif, fel y nodwyd roedd y canran wedi disgyn i 49.9. Buan y peidia ystadegau'r Gymraeg ar derfyn Oes Victoria â bod yn foddion llawenydd pan wynebir y caswir am dwf y boblogaeth rhwng 1801 a 1891.
>
> [That was not true, of course, we know that although the number of Welsh-speakers between 1871 and 1901 was more than ever, the percentage had steadily declined during the century. Thomas Darlington estimated that 587,245 people lived in Wales in 1801 and

that 80 per cent spoke Welsh. By 1841, according to the estimate of Sir Thomas Phillips, out of a population of 1,046,073, some 67 per cent were Welsh speaking, and although Ernst Georg Ravenstein maintained that in 1879 out of a population of 1,312,583 there were 71.2 per cent who spoke Welsh, by the end of the century, as has been noted, the percentage had fallen to 49.9. The statistics concerning the Welsh language at the end of the Victorian age soon cease to be a cause for rejoicing when faced with the unpalatable truth regarding the growth in population between 1801 and 1891.] (Edwards, 1987, 122)

Professor Edwards proceeds to demonstrate how rising numbers of Welsh-speakers constituted a falling proportion of the rapidly growing population. He notes the conclusion of J. C. Southall that whereas the 'clientele' of Welsh had risen by some 25 per cent between 1841 and 1871 it had remained much the same between 1876 and 1891, and that while Southall considered the century to be not 'wholly against Welsh', 'all the while . . . the nineteenth century was sharpening its knives, and gradually gathering strength, to dispute further advances' (Edwards, 1987, 123).

In Edwards's summary lie the answers to the two questions which were set out above. The growth of population had meant simply and directly the growth of the Welsh-speaking population. Moreover, until the end of the century most of the migrants to the coalfields of north and south came from the rural Welsh-speaking areas of Wales, rather than from England. And the main generator of growth was natural increase. In the five decades of the latter half of the nineteenth century, natural increase in Wales registered percentage gains of 12.3, 13.52, 14.73, 13.73 and 14.06 respectively. For the same decades migration actually registered percentage losses of 1.67, 3.82, 3.67, 1.13 and 0.53. The succeeding decade 1901–11 recorded a migration gain of 4.84 per cent, marking the late major phase of in-migration from England (Williams, J. 1985, 68). But a natural increase over most of the century, largely of Welsh families, produced the growth of Welsh-speaking numbers.

The consequence of internal migration and natural increase was one of the major phenomena of the nineteenth century, urban growth (Carter and Lewis, 1991). Certainly in their early stages these towns, and especially the urban villages, were predominantly Welsh-speaking. This is one of the reasons why Gwyn A. Williams called Merthyr Tydfil the first Welsh town (Williams, 1966, 2). It is also the reason why Brinley Thomas has so cogently argued that industrialization and urbanization saved the Welsh language by giving it a new vitality as against decline, like Irish, to a remote western Gaeltacht (Thomas, 1987). In these towns and villages the stereotype of the chapel-going, choir-singing, and in the south, rugby-playing, Welshman (it was a time when stereotypes were male-derived) was founded. But it was the numbers that were the real basis for the optimism which sustained the idea of a Golden Age, especially perhaps amongst an élite which was somewhat removed from the realities of Anglicization. The most optimistic expression was that of D. Isaac Davies who published a book of essays in 1885 under the title *Yr Iaith Gymraeg, 1785, 1885, 1985! neu Tair Miliwn o Gymry Dwy-iaethawg mewn Can Mlynedd* (The Welsh Language, 1785, 1885, 1985! or Three Million Bilingual Welsh People in a Hundred Years). But as Southall was foresighted enough to realize, 'the knives were being sharpened'. All the problems of the loss of domains and the associated decline of social prestige were already apparent. Brinley Thomas was, of course, quite right when he argued

> that a major cause of the decline of the Welsh language was the collapse of the Welsh economy after World War I . . . Because of the dazzling heights reached just before World War I, the subsequent fall was all the more disastrous. The class war in the coalfields intensified, and the clarion call was Marxist not Methodist. What the potato famine did to the Irish economy, the great depression did to the Welsh economy. In the twentieth century, economic and demographic contraction, the decline of nonconformity, severe unemployment and emigration . . . have been a curse to the language. (Thomas, 1987, 437)

But all these forces, to which rural depopulation must be added, were acting upon a condition which had been established and developed over the long period since the Anglo-Norman incursion; they acted upon a context long prepared and their impact was great because of that.

By the end of the nineteenth century the process of monitoring language change became possible following the first formal enumeration of Welsh-speakers in the census of 1891. Significantly, a pioneering study of the data contained in the enumerators' books for this census has recently been published by Parry and Williams (1999). It is not appropriate here to enter into a discussion of their findings; suffice it to say that access to such disaggregated information yields detailed insights into language patterns for individuals and households. Personalized, micro-level information of this type is confidential for a hundred-year period following the census. There can be no doubt that, as they are released, similar data for subsequent censuses will add significantly to the body of statistics available for the analysis of language trends and associations.

Drawing upon two sets of data Pryce (1978a) has mapped the distribution of the Welsh language at 1900/1 (Figure 3.3). The first set is derived from the 1901 census and records the percentage of the population able to speak Welsh in rural and urban districts. The second is the Welsh–bilingual–English divides which Pryce derived from the language used in Anglican Church services, and which he took to represent core, domain and sphere. Even by 1901 it is apparent that the significant lineaments of decline which have characterized the twentieth century were already evident. But before identifying them, and possibly overstressing them, it is pertinent to emphasize the strength of the core. There is a dominant and extensive area, virtually all of Wales, except for South Pembrokeshire, west of a line running north–south from the Conwy estuary to that of the Tawe, where over 90 per cent of the population spoke Welsh. The core was clear, unmistakable and strong.

Strong as it was, however, the core was also clearly being eroded at its edges. The whole of the classic Marcher area, along the English border to the east, and in the Vale of Glamorgan, Gower and South Pembrokeshire to the south revealed the considerable impact of an ancient Anglicization which was progressive in its character. As Pryce observes, 'the figures for Brecnockshire display the classic stages of language change . . . Welsh in 1801, bilingual in 1851 and substantially Anglicized by 1881'. The crucial zone was that

Principal language divides c. 1900

—— Welsh–Bilingual

—— Bilingual–English

% Welsh Speaking 1901

90 and over

0          20 miles

0          30 kilometres

**Figure 3.3**                                    After W.T.R. Pryce 1978 identified by Pryce as bilingual, where the two languages were in contact. 'In effect, therefore, it seems that bilingualism was merely a stage in the process of Anglicization. Once a community became bilingual, the next generation failed to retain Welsh as a spoken language' (Pryce, 1978a, 5). This same pattern has been identified by Philip N. Jones by using *Baptist chapels as an index of cultural transition in the South Wales Coalfield before 1914* (1976). His work identifies three chronological phases 'during which the coalfield was transformed from a uniformly Welsh cultural area before 1860, through an intervening phase of linguistic heterogeneity, to a situation in the final phase after 1890, when the dominance of Welsh was restricted to the western section only'. He proposes a progressive 'rolling back' of Welsh from east to west, 'a rapid and regular process in which bilingualism was only a transient resting-place' (Jones, P. N. 1976, 347). And that was during the 'Golden Age' of the language.

The forces at work are difficult to identify from aggregate data. However, standard linguistic processes would suggest stages where codes are mixed, that is, English words or structures are used in Welsh speech, followed by code switching, where speakers of a minority language change for a variety of reasons into another language. But the bases of switching have been evident. These were largely related to motivation which was in turn linked to the loss of domains and status which this survey has traced. The young or their parents saw no advantage in the language and it was gradually lost. At the same time the predominant English bias of the education system meant that formal learning, too, diminished.

> There seems little doubt that in the promotion of English for supposedly secular needs, state education soon began to reflect what was then considered to be a popular aspiration. The policies adopted during the later decades of the nineteenth century meant that the children of Wales were to be eventually divorced from a close experiential knowledge of the language and culture of previous generations. (Pryce, 1987a, 28)

At this point it is necessary to observe that all the processes which were inimical to Welsh were at their most virulent where Welsh and English were in daily contact. Isolation had always been one of the major sustainers of Welsh. Industrialization, by increasing the mobility of populations (just as the railway provided the means), broke down that isolation, as did social upheavals like the First World War. But even so, until the coming of the mass media, direct contact had a strong geographical limitation and the pattern of language change can be discussed in the terms of a retreating frontier. But all this was beginning to change.

If the westward retreat of the language divide, albeit leaving some outliers, was apparent, so too was the characteristic pattern within the south Wales coalfield. Anglicization was greatest lower down the valleys, and to the east. It was spreading up-valley and westward, a process to be accelerated during the century. Even the incipient Anglicization of the north Wales coastline is apparent, revealed both by the church service data and the census figures. The beginnings of the axis of decline across Snowdonia from Conwy to Porthmadog is again suggested, as are fragments of diminution along the west coast. In brief, the great fault lines which were later to break up the core are just perceptible.

Over 80 percent Welsh Speaking 1931
(after D.T. Williams)

Over 80 percent Welsh Speaking 1951
(after J.G. Thomas)

**Figure 3.4**

The basic features of the ensuing period of retreat are apparent in Figure 3.4 which maps the areas in which over 80 per cent of the population spoke Welsh in 1931 and 1951. Perhaps one aspect is unexpected in that there had been no significant westward retreat of the eastern 'frontier' with English. After the retreat in the nineteenth century there appears to have been a period of some stability with only marginal shifts. But that was probably as much a reflection of the very thinly inhabited mountain backbone on which the divide eventually came to rest. As that happened so the crucial areas of conflict switched to those

**Table 3.1**
**Percentage of population able to speak Welsh, 1901–1951 (pre-1974 counties)**

|                   | 1901 | 1911 | 1921 | 1931 | 1951 |
|-------------------|------|------|------|------|------|
| Anglesey          | 91.7 | 88.7 | 84.9 | 87.4 | 79.8 |
| Breconshire       | 45.9 | 41.5 | 37.2 | 37.3 | 30.3 |
| Caernarfonshire   | 89.6 | 85.6 | 75.0 | 79.2 | 71.0 |
| Cardiganshire     | 93.0 | 89.6 | 82.1 | 87.1 | 79.5 |
| Carmarthenshire   | 90.4 | 84.9 | 82.4 | 82.3 | 77.3 |
| Denbighshire      | 61.9 | 56.7 | 48.4 | 48.5 | 38.5 |
| Flintshire        | 49.1 | 42.2 | 32.7 | 31.7 | 21.1 |
| Glamorgan         | 43.5 | 38.1 | 31.6 | 30.5 | 20.3 |
| Merioneth         | 93.7 | 90.3 | 82.1 | 86.1 | 75.4 |
| Monmouthshire     | 13.0 | 9.6  | 6.4  | 6.0  | 3.5  |
| Montgomeryshire   | 47.5 | 44.8 | 42.3 | 46.7 | 35.1 |
| Pembrokeshire     | 34.4 | 32.4 | 30.3 | 30.6 | 26.9 |
| Radnorshire       | 6.2  | 5.4  | 6.3  | 4.7  | 4.5  |
| **Wales**         | **49.9** | **43.5** | **37.1** | **36.8** | **28.9** |

locations which have caused the greatest concern in more recent times, parts within the north and west, or *Y Fro Gymraeg* as that Welsh-speaking core came to be called. This is clearly seen in the mapping of the 1951 census returns by J. G. Thomas (Thomas, 1956, 1975). The area with over 90 per cent speaking Welsh, which had been a continuous block in 1901, had by the mid-century been broken down into a series of separated extents, and the area with over 80 per cent was attenuated and barely continuous. Some reservation is needed, however, since the larger units on which the data were available in 1901 might have exaggerated the solidarity of this western block.

The extent of the decline of the language in the first half of the twentieth century is shown in Table 3.1. As has been demonstrated, a whole nexus of socio-economic changes had reacted with domain limitation and status loss to produce a fifty-year period of catastrophic decline, all the more hurtful since it had followed so closely on what had been perceived as a golden age of renewal and opportunity. By 1961 the situation appeared parlous – it was to deteriorate even further in the decade that followed. Urgent action was needed – it was eventually forthcoming.

CHAPTER 4

# The Critical Years: Language Change 1961–1981

Of all the events relating to the recent history of the Welsh language none is of more pivotal significance than the radio broadcast by Saunders Lewis in 1962. Entitled 'Tynged yr Iaith' (The Fate of the Language), it was an apocalyptic and trenchant lecture, designed to bring home to the people of Wales the full severity of the crisis facing the language. The celebrated polemic was an attempt to raise the Welsh from what he saw as apathy and an acceptance of inevitable loss.

> I shall presuppose that the figures which will shortly be published [the 1961 census] will shock and disappoint those of us who consider that Wales without the Welsh language will not be Wales. I shall also presuppose that Welsh will end as a living language, should the present trend continue, about the beginning of the twenty-first century. (Lewis, 1973)

Lewis's greatest condemnation was not of the external English but of the neglect, indeed the clear opposition, by Welsh people themselves –

> Naturally there would be a few muttered curses from clerks looking for a dictionary and from girl typists who were learning to spell, but the Civil Service has long since learned to accept revolutionary changes in the British Empire as part of the daily routine. The opposition – harsh, vindictive and violent – would come from Wales. (Lewis, 1973, 137)

And again –

> In my opinion, if any kind of self-government for Wales were obtained before the Welsh language was acknowledged and used as an official language in local authority and state administration in the Welsh-speaking parts of our country, then the language would never achieve official status at all, and its demise would be quicker than it will under English rule. (Lewis, 1973, 141)

Lewis set out no coherent policy, other than a demand for Welsh in public life, but his lecture led directly to the founding of Cymdeithas yr Iaith Gymraeg in 1962 (Tudur, 1989) and opened up a new era in the struggle to maintain and advance the language.

As it turned out the results of the 1961 census were not as cataclysmic as Lewis had feared. Certainly, the decline continued, but given what had happened previously it could hardly be described as dramatic; the proportion of Welsh-speakers having fallen from 28.9

per cent in 1951 to 26.0 per cent in 1961. In their study of language patterns based on the 1961 census Emrys Jones and Ieuan Griffiths noted the maintenance of the 'sharp division between Welsh Wales and English Wales', and suggested that 'little can be added to what has previously been said [by Williams, 1937 and Thomas, 1956] about the Anglicized area of Wales'. They concluded, 'The distribution emphasizes that there is a predominantly Welsh Wales, fairly sharply divided from a highly Anglicized area, and yielding territorially only reluctantly to the peripheral advances of the latter' (Jones and Griffiths, 1963, 195). That said, they also noted that rural depopulation had greatly reduced the actual numbers speaking Welsh in the heartland and that consequently territorial resistance should not be mistaken for linguistic strength. Perhaps they should also have stressed the clear development of the fault lines within Welsh Wales; the fractures along which the incipient breakdown of that core was already apparent.

Recognizing perhaps that the future of the language was critically poised on a cusp of change, a whole series of movements, inquiries and initiatives were launched during the following decades. Concern about the health of the language had of course been voiced throughout the first half of the twentieth century, but it was during the 1960s that major efforts were made to strengthen its position. Most notable were developments in the field of education (Williams, Jac L., 1973). Since many of these built on earlier programmes, a brief historical digression is appropriate.

The Welsh Department of the Board of Education was set up in 1907, and in 1927, recognizing the importance of the language issue, a departmental committee published its widely cited report entitled *Welsh in Education and Life*. In similar fashion, a quarter of a century later, the Central Advisory Panel (Wales) completed its report on *The Place of Welsh and English in the Schools of Wales* (1953). It took a firm stance as to the relationship between language and Welsh ethnic identity.

> We cannot support the view that the culture and the ways of life of Wales have no relationship to the language, or that it is quite possible for the non-Welsh-speaking child to partake of the tradition, and the culture of Wales, without a knowledge of the language. There is a close relationship between our language and our culture; the one cannot fully or even adequately be understood without the knowledge of the other. . . '. (Welsh Department, Ministry of Education, 1953, 16)

A firm recommendation followed, that –

> having due regard to the varied abilities and aptitudes of pupils, and of the varied linguistic patterns in which at present they live, the children of the whole of Wales, including Monmouthshire, should be taught Welsh and English according to their ability to profit from such instruction. (p.17)

In 1939 the first Welsh-medium primary school had been established at Aberystwyth, although it was independent and did not come under the Local Education Authority until

1951. The first local authority school was actually opened at Llanelli in 1947. In 1952 the Welsh-medium Schools Movement (Mudiad Ysgolion Cymraeg) was established, and by the time of the 1953 Report there were in addition single schools in Caernarfonshire, Denbighshire, Cardiff and Swansea, and four in Glamorgan and five in Flint. Almost a thousand pupils attended these schools, and such was the demand that further expansion was carefully considered. Thus, in 1956 the Flintshire Education Authority established the first Welsh-medium secondary school, Ysgol Glan Clwyd at Rhyl. A second followed in 1961, and in 1962 Glamorgan set up their first Welsh-language secondary school at Rhydfelin.

It might be added that the first primary school at Aberystwyth owed its founding to the enthusiasm of Sir Ifan ap Owen Edwards. Earlier he had made an equally significant contribution to the promotion of the Welsh language amongst the young in the establishment of Urdd Gobaith Cymru (The Welsh League of Youth) in 1922. Its membership eventually rose to some 50,000 and, as Dafydd Glyn Jones wrote of it –

> All in all, Yr Urdd's. . . history constitutes an impressive feat in combining idealism, enthusiasm, and ambition with careful planning and skilled manipulation of resources. Of all the different branches of the Welsh language movement today [1972], it must be accounted the one most immediately successful. (Jones, D. G., 1973, 288)

But perhaps most significant of all from the viewpoint of the development of the language was the determination of parents, especially in urban areas of south Wales, to set up Welsh-medium nursery schools. The movement began in 1949 in Maesteg with the creation of Welsh-medium pre-school groups (Cylchoedd Meithrin). Similar groups quickly followed in Cardiff and Barry. By 1970 there were some sixty *ysgolion meithrin* and at the 1971 Eisteddfod at Bangor an organization was set up to promote their growth. Mudiad Ysgolion Meithrin Cymraeg (The Welsh-medium Nursery Schools Movement) has been in recent times one of the most influential sustainers of the language (see below).

These developments embraced the full spectrum of education from nursery school to university and college, and even included provision for Welsh-medium adult education. Together they constituted a combined attempt to restore a key language domain – one that had been all but lost at the turn of the century.

Other developments during the 1960s focused attention on the status of the language in Wales. Thus, in 1963 the Council for Wales and Monmouthshire published its *Report on the Welsh Language Today* (Council for Wales and Monmouthshire, 1963). It was primarily a 'state-of-affairs' report and its conclusions were modest. Even so, its wide review of the use of Welsh in most of the domains of living included discussions on government and administration, working life, leisure, religious worship and education. Recognizing the urgency of the situation, Cymdeithas yr Iaith began to take a more dominant and radical role. Its campaigns, though never specified in such a manner, amounted to a succession of attempts to restore Welsh fully to all the domains of Welsh life. The first was the comparatively minor one of road signs (Tudur, 1989), but subsequently the more central themes of the law, bureaucracy (official forms), administration and government were approached.

As was demonstrated earlier, the major effect of the Act of Union of 1536 had not been universally to proscribe Welsh but to banish it from all official use in law, government and administration. To use modern jargon, the language was marginalized. Over the years efforts were made to change that condition (Lewis, R. 1973; Rees, I. B., 1973). The Welsh Courts Act of 1942 allowed anyone who could demonstrate disadvantage to use Welsh, although the decision remained with the Court not with the individual. As a result of agitation, however, the Hughes-Parry Committee was set up in 1963 'to clarify the status of the Welsh language' and its report – *Legal Status of the Welsh Language* – was published in 1965 (HMSO, 1965). The consequence was the Welsh Language Act of 1967 which effectively gave the unrestricted right to use Welsh in the courts, although practice was to prove rather different (Lewis, R. 1973).

The feeling that little had been accomplished by the 1967 Act led to the establishment of The Council for the Welsh Language and the preparation of yet another report, *A Future for the Welsh Language*. In that report it was stated categorically that

> We find the concept of 'equal validity' totally inadequate to the needs of the Welsh language today. Nor do we share the Hughes-Parry concept of bilingualism. To us, bilingualism means that throughout Wales every individual should be enabled and encouraged to achieve sufficient facility in both Welsh and English to choose which of the two languages to use on all occasions and for all purposes in Wales. (The Council for the Welsh Language, 1978)

This describes the system usually known as the 'personality principle' by which any person can use one of two, or indeed more, official languages according to choice at any time. Not all of the report's recommendations were acted upon, but it helped to maintain the momentum of debate.

In reviewing the efforts that have been made to help revitalize the language, one further domain requires reference – the media. The Anglicizing impact of television became a major concern (Rees, 1973) and the demand for a Welsh-medium channel grew rapidly throughout the 1970s. The report *A Future for the Welsh Language* highlighted the urgency for such a provision. In its seventh recommendation it stated that

> . . . in the case of Welsh, the most powerful external influence affecting the home is broadcasting. . . We recommend that the government in the very near future, should make funds available to enable the fourth television channel in Wales to be established and maintained. (The Council for the Welsh Language, 1978, 21/2 and 63/4)

Not without drama, S4C (Sianel Pedwar Cymru – the Welsh Fourth Channel) was established in 1982. In considering the media it is also important to mention the support for the written word through the rapid expansion of Welsh publications. The roles of the Welsh

Arts Council, and particularly of the Welsh Books Council, which was established in 1962, have been particularly important in this regard.

Despite all of these efforts to promote the use and status of the language, the situation deteriorated alarmingly during the 1960s and early 1970s. In no small measure this was due to powerful demographic forces. Out-migration, especially of the young, continued apace while in-migration of non-Welsh-speakers overwhelmed many communities within the heart of *Y Fro Gymraeg*. The problem of rural depopulation was long-standing of course and characterized all except the most prosperous parts during the first half of the century. Inevitably, depopulation was a prime concern of academic analysis and government action. The reasons for the long phase of population loss are well known and were well treated in the Beacham Report – *Depopulation in Mid Wales* (HMSO, 1964). They need not be repeated here. What is more problematic, however, is the impact that depopulation had on language; such matters were not part of the remit of the group that produced the 1964 report. A simple loss of population on its own, unless it is language specific, will not alter the proportion of Welsh-speakers in individual communities. That this was the case is attested by the stability exhibited in the spatial patterns for 1961. It will have an effect, however, on the absolute numbers of speakers. Furthermore, the process would disturb age structures, since those moving out were primarily the younger and more active sections of the population. The consequences of rural depopulation were therefore not necessarily a fall in the proportion of Welsh-speakers or an apparent diminution in the Welshness of *Y Fro Gymraeg*, but a very considerable loss in language vitality.

Such a loss became all the more significant with the demographic changes which followed after 1961. Without entering into statistical detail it can be noted that most districts of rural Wales between 1961 and 1981 showed a gain in population, largely due to a turnaround in migratory flows. For the Welsh language in-migration became a major issue. The reasons for this reversal have again been widely analysed, and are commonly associated with the processes of rural retreating and counterurbanization (Champion, 1987). The majority of incomers were those who felt moved to reject urban lifestyles and who, with capital often gained from the sale of metropolitan property, were able to settle in more congenial environments, both physical and social. As was widely publicized, the inflow also included other social groupings (hippies, drop-outs, artists etc.); less wealthy perhaps, but also in search of alternative life-styles. The critical point as far as the well-being of the language was concerned was that this in-migration was of a sufficient order even to hide the continued out-migration of young people from the rural heartland.

In contrast, during this critical twenty-year period, there were signs of a continuing resurgence of the language in selected parts of urban and sub-urban south-east Wales and in parts of the borderland. This development is of major consequence and will be developed more fully later; it can partly be explained by the emergence of the transactional city during the latter part of the twentieth century.

> The twentieth century has inverted the old profile of the division of labour. In the past most workers were occupied in the production of goods, that is in agriculture, mining and

manufacture. . . A small minority of white-collar workers served in the management of public and private affairs. . . In our century this minority has grown enormously while the other sectors of the labour force have shrunk. (Gottmann, 1987)

It is a process which is often referred to as de-industrialization. But it also impacts upon agriculture where the demand for labour, too, is limited. The city is now essentially a centre of transactions of all varieties, a manipulator of information flows based on electronic information technology. The main protagonists are the administrators, the bankers and financiers, and those working in marketing, advertising and the media.

These trends, which have been common throughout the western world, have had a significant effect in Wales. De-industrialization, symbolized by the elimination of the coal-mining industry, has led to significant population loss. This in turn meant the undermining of coalfield communities where if Welsh was no longer central it was still a distinctive element, especially in those areas of the anthracite coalfield where the largest numbers of Welsh-speakers in Wales were to be found. Likewise, agriculture was not able to sustain employment and it too saw a diminution of the labour-force. In complete contrast, the administrative towns, such as Carmarthen or Mold have experienced increases, if not within their boundaries then within their commuting areas. But the epitome of the transactional city in Wales is Cardiff (Aitchison and Carter, 1987). Characteristically, the development of Cardiff Bay symbolizes the role and functions of the transactional city – administration, banking and finance, leisure, together with gentrification in the provision of housing. But in Wales, with the new attention to language which this and the previous chapter have traced, facility in Welsh, if not an essential, is certainly seen as a great advantage; less so in the business world, more so in administration, and especially so in media where S4C obviously must demand proficiency. There has, therefore, been a clear migratory flow from rural Wales to the administrative towns, that is of Welsh-speakers from *Y Fro Gymraeg* to the early Anglicized and urban areas of Wales. There they have demanded Welsh-medium schools for their children and the right to use Welsh in daily life – that is for the operation of the personality principle.

Since an appreciation of these critical regional shifts is essential to an understanding of the contemporary situation, as depicted in the 1991 census, it is appropriate at this juncture to present a series of map distributions for the period 1961–1981. They summarize the main findings of a previous study undertaken by Aitchison and Carter (1985).

**Relative Dominance of Welsh-speakers**

Figures 4.1, 4.2 and 4.3 record the percentages of the total population (aged 3 and over) who claimed to be able to speak Welsh for the years 1961, 1971 and 1981. Each of the maps is based on a consistent set of class intervals and can therefore be directly compared and contrasted. Together they offer a generalized visual impression of the changing strength or concentration of the language at community level. Again it must be stressed that these maps reveal nothing of the change in actual numbers but are indicative of the

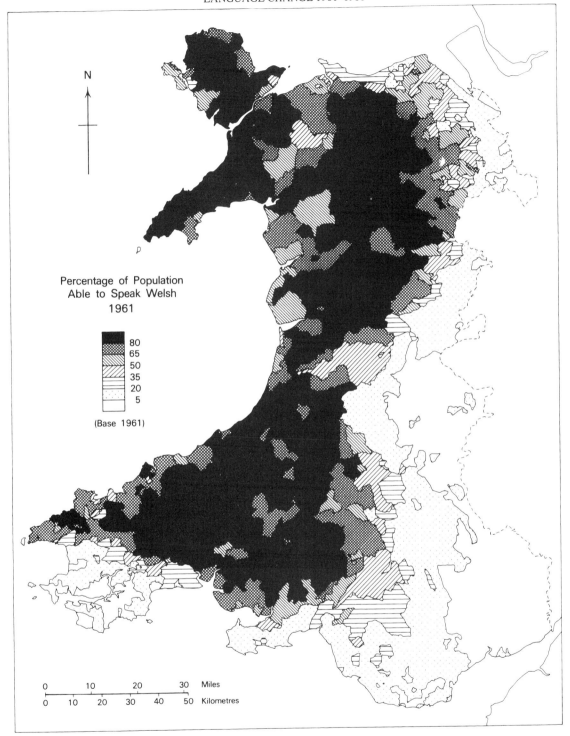

N

Percentage of Population
Able to Speak Welsh
1961

80
65
50
35
20
5

(Base 1961)

| 0 | 10 | 20 | 30 | Miles |
| 0 | 10 | 20 | 30 | 40 | 50 | Kilometres |

**Figure 4.1**

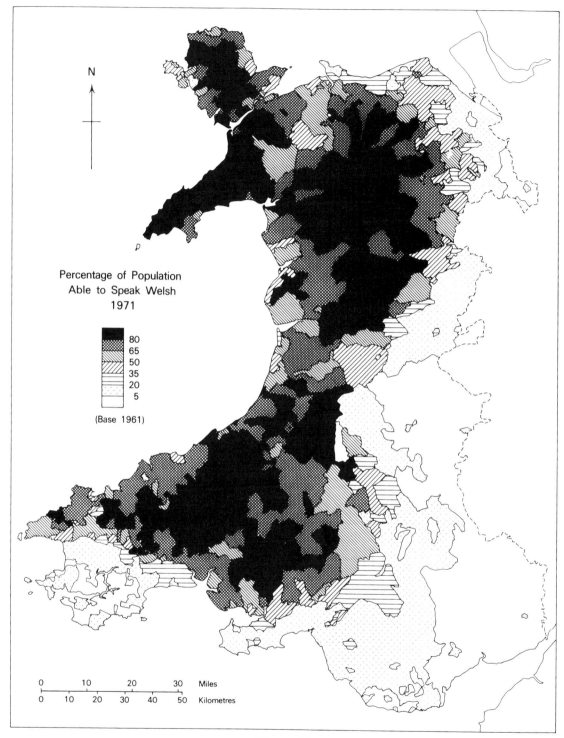

N

Percentage of Population
Able to Speak Welsh
1971

| | |
|---|---|
| ■ | 80 |
| | 65 |
| | 50 |
| | 35 |
| | 20 |
| | 5 |

(Base 1961)

0    10    20    30    Miles
0    10    20    30    40    50    Kilometres

**Figure 4.2**

relative status of the language within the regions concerned. Changes in the proportion of Welsh-speakers at county level (pre-1974 counties) for the same period are recorded in Table 4.1.

**Table 4.1**
**Percentage of population able to speak Welsh, 1961–1981**

| County (pre-1974) | 1961 | 1971 | 1981 |
|---|---|---|---|
| Anglesey | 75.5 | 65.7 | 61.0 |
| Breconshire | 28.1 | 22.9 | 19.3 |
| Caernarfonshire | 68.3 | 62.0 | 59.7 |
| Cardiganshire | 74.8 | 67.6 | 63.2 |
| Carmarthenshire | 75.1 | 66.5 | 60.0 |
| Denbighshire | 34.8 | 28.1 | 24.2 |
| Flintshire | 19.0 | 14.7 | 13.5 |
| Glamorgan | 17.2 | 11.8 | 10.0 |
| Merioneth | 75.9 | 73.5 | 68.2 |
| Monmouthshire | 3.4 | 2.1 | 2.7 |
| Montgomeryshire | 32.3 | 28.1 | 24.0 |
| Pembrokeshire | 24.4 | 20.7 | 18.1 |
| Radnorshire | 4.5 | 3.7 | 5.0 |
| **Wales** | **26.0** | **20.8** | **18.9** |

It has been noted earlier that in their study of the language situation in 1961, Jones and Griffiths wrote of a resilient 'Welsh Wales' yielding only slowly to forces of Anglicization. The extent and strength of that heartland is well delineated in Figure 4.1. As Tables 4.2 and 4.3 show, in 279 of the 993 communities Welsh-speakers accounted for over 80 per cent of the total population over the age of three. Furthermore, in terms of area these same communities claimed a notable 37 per cent of the national territory. Welsh was the dominant language (percentages in excess of 50) in 454 communities. Together, these covered almost 57 per cent of Wales. Such was the continued hold of the language in 1961 that it was still possible to traverse Wales from Llanfairynghornwy at the north-western extremity of Anglesey to Kidwelly on the Carmarthen coast of south Wales, without having to leave a community (at that time parish) in which over 80 per cent of the population was able to speak Welsh. Perhaps more surprisingly, it would almost have been possible to do the same in a west–east direction – from the tip of the Llŷn peninsula to very near the English border at the south-eastern limit of the parish of Llanrhaeadr-ym-Mochnant in the former county of Montgomeryshire.

There were inevitably temporary local anomalies which disturbed the continuity of the pattern. The largest of them was caused by the influx of workers into Trawsfynydd during the construction of the nuclear power plant, whilst, less spectacularly, a similar impact was made by the building of the hydro-electric project at Cwm Rheidol, near Aberystwyth. But, taking these exceptional developments into account, the overall picture is one of a compact and relatively extensive heartland in which the Welsh language was pre-eminent. Having said that, however, it is necessary to recall that the geography of the situation, as it expressed itself in 1961, was but a phase in the long-standing and persistent retreat of the language which was traced in Chapter 3. Already the indications of fault lines within the core were apparent and they were to become the major features of change in the succeeding decade.

**Table 4.2**
**Percentage of population able to speak Welsh**
**by numbers of communities**

| Classes | 1961 | 1971 | 1981 |
|---|---|---|---|
| Under 5 | 194 | 224 | 209 |
| 5–20 | 239 | 243 | 278 |
| 21–35 | 59 | 51 | 66 |
| 36–50 | 47 | 60 | 76 |
| 51–65 | 61 | 76 | 114 |
| 66–80 | 114 | 148 | 184 |
| Over 80 | 279 | 191 | 66 |

**Table 4.3**
**Percentage of population able to speak Welsh by areas of communities**

| | 1961 | | 1971 | | 1981 | |
|---|---|---|---|---|---|---|
| | Area (km²) | % | Area (km²) | % | Area (km²) | % |
| Under 5 | 2973 | 14.3 | 3353 | 17.0 | 3139 | 15.2 |
| 5–20 | 3846 | 18.5 | 3870 | 18.6 | 4615 | 22.2 |
| 21–35 | 1055 | 5.1 | 1028 | 5.0 | 1552 | 7.5 |
| 36–50 | 1145 | 5.5 | 1228 | 5.9 | 1700 | 8.2 |
| 51–65 | 1276 | 6.2 | 1828 | 8.8 | 2557 | 12.2 |
| 66–80 | 2830 | 13.6 | 3579 | 17.3 | 5193 | 24.9 |
| Over 80 | 7637 | 36.8 | 5694 | 27.4 | 2006 | 9.7 |

A comparison of Figures 4.1 and 4.2 suggests that the Welsh-speaking heartland had by 1971 been quite heavily eroded. As Table 4.2 reveals, the number of communities with over 80 per cent of their population able to speak Welsh had fallen to 191. That is, 88 of the 279 communities of 1961 had fallen below that level. Those communities covered only 27.4 per cent of the national territory compared with the 36.8 per cent in 1961. The contraction manifested itself most dramatically in the apparent break up of the previously compact core. Although there were indications at earlier dates, it was clear by 1971 that five separate Welsh-speaking nuclei had devolved from the once discrete and consolidated *Bro Gymraeg* (Bowen and Carter, 1975). The main fracture lines had been the Menai

Straits (Afon Menai), the line across Snowdonia from Conwy to Porthmadog, the Severn Valley and the break that divided rural and industrial Dyfed. These will be discussed below when the 1981 pattern is analysed.

Although it was in evidence before 1961, the Anglicization of coastal margins in the former counties of Anglesey, Caernarfonshire, Denbighshire, Merioneth and Cardiganshire, as well as of the lowland valleys penetrating the interior, was particularly intense throughout the 1961–71 decade. But whereas the interior fault lines continued to deepen, the line of the eastern frontier remained fairly stable, with quite sharp gradients dividing the Welsh and English-speaking areas. One surprising exception was the 'landsker' zone in Pembrokeshire, a divide which had remained virtually unmoved for many centuries, but which now showed clear signs of retreat (see below p. 54).

Given the fact that the fall in absolute numbers of Welsh-speakers between 1971 and 1981 was of a much lower order than that recorded during the previous decade, the differences in the pattern of percentages for the two censal years as shown in Figures 4.2 and 4.3 respectively, was both unexpected and disturbing in its extent. The statistics in Tables 4.2 and 4.3 vividly demonstrate that the period 1971 to 1981 witnessed a major collapse in the number of communities with over 80 per cent of their population able to speak Welsh. In 1981 only 66 communities were in that category compared with 279 in 1961. Together they accounted for a mere 9.7 per cent of the total area of Wales in contrast to the 36.8 per cent of 1961. Whilst that development was of major significance it must be tempered by the fact that in 364 communities, covering 47 per cent of the land surface of Wales, Welsh-speakers were still in the majority.

In terms of their spatial expression, the patterns of change suggested an exacerbation of the movements which had been apparent in the previous decade. But there were some new developments which can be enumerated.

(i) In Anglesey the growth of tourism and the popularity of the region for retirement contributed significantly to the Anglicization of the coastal communities, with a subsequent encroachment on the strong central Welsh-speaking core area. Between 1961 and 1981 such communities as Llanbadrig, Llaniestyn Rural, Llaneilian, Llanfair Mathafan Eithaf, Pentraeth, Llanddona, Llandegfan, Llangeinwen and Llanynghedl, all experienced major reductions in the proportions able to speak Welsh, that is percentage differences between the two dates of over 20 per cent.

(ii) Anglicizing influences continued to operate throughout the period along the coast of north Wales. This was effectively a continuing westward ripple effect, associated once again with retirement and tourism, although locally modified by suburbanization. During the twenty years the proportion speaking Welsh in Conwy fell from 42.0 per cent to 30.4 per cent, that of Llanfairfechan from 58.1 per cent to 42.0 per cent and that of Llanllechid from 87.0 per cent to 67.8 per cent.

(iii) In Snowdonia, the wedge of Anglicization which entered the massif from the lower Conwy valley, and which was observed as early as 1931, both widened and deepened. The

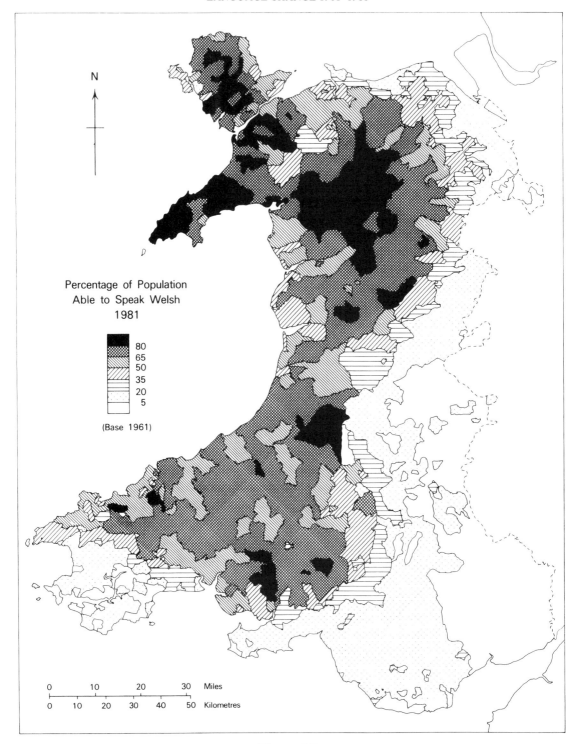

Figure 4.3

percentage of Welsh-speakers in the community of Capel Curig, for instance, fell very sharply from 45.7 per cent to 28.6.

(iv) The proportions of Welsh-speakers in many communities along the coast of west Wales, from Harlech in the north to the St David's Peninsula in the south, fell very considerably. Whereas in 1961 quite extensive areas returned percentages in excess of 80, by 1981 such was the pace of relative decline that not a single community on the coast sustained percentages of that order of magnitude. So significant were the inroads into the Welsh-speaking cores of Meirionnydd and Ceredigion that it became possible to consider this coastal fringe as giving rise to a new frontier of language dilution, parallelling the long-standing divide within the border counties to the east. The possibility of two frontiers inexorably moving towards each other and pinching out the interior core, constituted a major threat to the traditional language heartland.

(v) At various points along the eastern edge of the Welsh-speaking heartland there were clear signs of a softening of the once sharp language gradients. Whilst the map distributions alone suggest a quickening of the pace of change between 1971 and 1981, it is evident that the process extended over the whole of the twenty years under review. This can be illustrated by considering a line of communities across the eastern edge of Mynydd Hiraethog. Thus in the west, within *Y Fro Gymraeg*, the percentage of Welsh-speakers in Cerrig-y-drudion fell from 90.8 in 1961 to 89.6 in 1971 and 86.8 in 1981, a discernible but minor retreat. However, further to the east the three decadal percentages for Clocaenog were 88.9, 75.0, and 61.4; for Llanynys 79.4, 72.8 and 64.2; for Efenechtyd 74.4, 69.8 and 57.6. The sharper falls in the later decade are quite evident and indicate a retreat of that frontier which in 1961 had been described as strongly resistant to Anglicization.

(vi) In central Wales, the wedge of Anglicization which followed the upper sections of the Severn had clearly gained in strength, penetrating almost to the coast. With the declining community percentages in the hinterland of Aberystwyth, the Welsh-speaking areas of Meirionnydd and Dyfed, which were effectively continuous in 1951, were being prised further apart.

(vii) Writing of the 'Landsker' in 1972, John stated that 'the present-day divide is a cultural feature of surprising tenacity; it is quite as discernible, and only a little less strong, than the divide of four centuries ago. In the landsker we have a unique cultural heritage' (John, 1972, 7). The evidence of the map distributions, however, would suggest that in terms of the Welsh-speaking proportions the landsker was suffering the fate of the other language bulwarks, and was retreating. Thus, if a band of nine communities is taken across Pembrokeshire from Llandeloy in the west through Puncheston and Castleblythe to Llandissilio in the east, then it will be seen that in 1961 all nine, apart from Llandeloy (77.2) and Letterston (71.0) recorded percentages of Welsh-speakers over 80. In 1981 none of them did; and only one was over 75. Llandeloy had fallen to 43.7 per cent from 77.0, and Letterston to 55.2 from 71 per cent.

(viii) Along the southern and eastern edges of the main Welsh-speaking core area of Dyfed similar patterns of relative decline were apparent. In the parish of Llanelli Rural, for example, the percentage of Welsh-speakers fell from 69.2 to 46.7 in 1981. Similar figures could be cited for other communities skirting the fringes of this region with its large population of Welsh-speakers.

This part of the analysis has considered changes in percentages of Welsh-speakers. Since the relationship between relative and absolute values is not necessarily direct or positive, consideration now needs to be given to regional variations in the actual number of Welsh-speakers.

## Absolute Change in Numbers of Welsh-speakers

In 1961 the total number of Welsh-speakers enumerated in Wales stood at 656,002. During the decade which followed that figure fell to 542,425. As Figure 4.4 vividly demonstrates, losses were greatest in the industrial valleys of south Wales. By 1971 Rhondda had 11,938 fewer Welsh-speakers, Merthyr Tydfil 5,224 and Aberdare 5,039. Further west the Welsh-speaking population of Swansea declined by 6,517 and of Llanelli by 5,035. These are in part due to direct population loss as major restructuring programmes for the coal, iron and steel and tinplate industries had an enormous impact upon the well-being of the region and forced many to leave it in search of work. This pattern of industrial decline and out-migration repeated itself in the coal-mining areas of north-east Wales. Between 1961 and 1971 the community of Rhosllannerchrugog, for instance, lost 1,778 Welsh-speakers. Communities bordering the Dee estuary recorded similar, if less dramatic decreases. There were also falls in settlements along the north Wales coast, Bangor recorded a decrease of 1,328 and Llandudno of 530.

One point which needs to be considered when reviewing the fall in numbers in areas such as the old industrial centres and the retirement settlements along the coasts, is the age structure of the population. The high ratio of elderly naturally leads to greater declines.

Absolute decreases in other rural areas were inevitably less spectacular, although Denbigh fell by 924 and Ffestiniog by 669. While small, such decreases were of considerable significance to the communities concerned. The explanation here, too, lies in the frailty of the local economies. The problems faced by small family farms, especially in the upland and marginal areas, and of small businesses in general, were critical. They contributed to a steady depopulation of the countryside and a concomitant loss of Welsh-speakers.

Whilst the overwhelming impression is one of decline, it is interesting to note that between 1961 and 1971 a number of communities actually recorded increases in their Welsh-speaking populations. As Figure 4.5 demonstrates, however, absolute increases were confined to communities in the more Anglicized parts of Wales, for example suburban Cardiff, the Alyn and Deeside District of north-east Wales and South Pembroke. Within the main Welsh-speaking areas, isolated but notable increases were recorded by such communities as Llangefni, Llanfairpwll and Amlwch on the island of Anglesey,

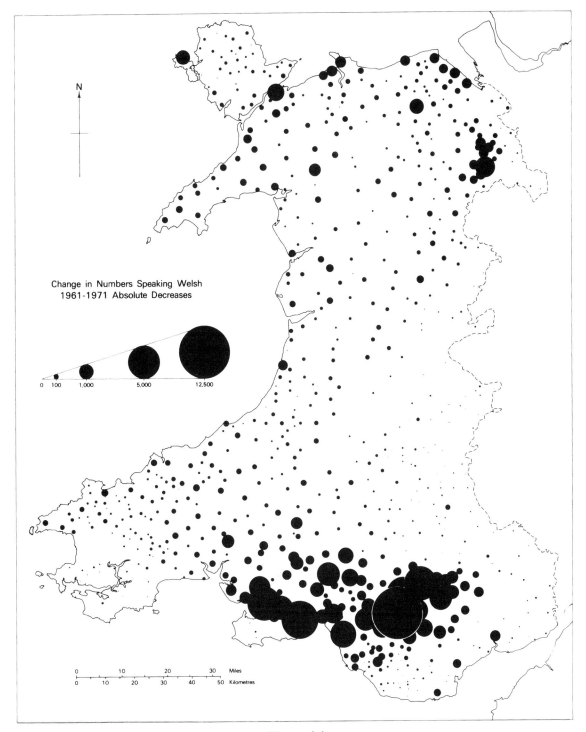

Change in Numbers Speaking Welsh
1961-1971 Absolute Decreases

0   100   1,000      5,000        12,500

0          10          20          30   Miles
0     10     20     30     40     50   Kilometres

**Figure 4.4**

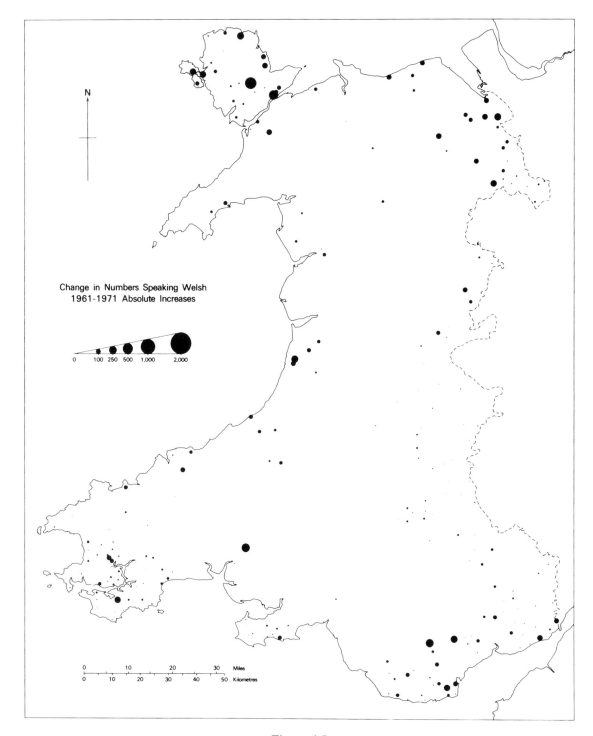

Change in Numbers Speaking Welsh
1961-1971 Absolute Increases

0   100  250  500  1,000        2,000

0        10        20        30    Miles
0    10   20   30   40   50  Kilometres

**Figure 4.5**

Llangunnor (Llangynnwr) to the east of Carmarthen, and Upper Vaenor near Aberystwyth. It is difficult to offer a general explanation, but certainly most of these were in suburban locations.

Between 1971 and 1981 the total population of Welsh-speakers enumerated in Wales continued to decline, but at a much reduced rate. With a fall of 6.3 per cent for the decade, the total in 1981 was 508,207 (using the 1971 population base). Figure 4.6 shows the pattern of decline at the community level. In broad terms it repeats that described for the period 1961–71. The old industrial heartlands of south and north-east Wales once again account for the bulk of the national loss, although the numbers are reduced. Throughout rural Wales, falls in the numbers of Welsh-speakers are also noticeably lighter. Interestingly, relatively high losses were recorded for the two university towns of Aberystwyth (-775) and Bangor (-951). This anomaly is partly explained by the timing of the censuses in relation to student vacations, but it certainly does not explain the whole situation.

Again, many communities showed increases (Figure 4.7), the dominant growth points being Cardiff with its surrounding communities in the District of Taff-Ely and the southern parts of the Rhymney Valley, as well as the Newport, Cwmbran and Pontypool axis. Significant increases were also in evidence in north-east Wales around Mold and Connah's Quay, and on Anglesey. During the seventies, a number of these areas benefited from the expansion of job opportunities in national and local government, in various administrative and commercial organizations, and in the mass media and entertainment sector, especially television. For employment in many of those, the ability to speak Welsh was either essential or highly advantageous. The establishment of bilingual secondary education also undoubtedly contributed to a resurgence of interest, a point which will be taken up later as it becomes particularly apparent in the next decade. The immediate import of these areas of increase is that they highlight a very significant revival of the language beyond the traditional heartland and point the way to crucial changes in process.

## Percentage Rates of Change in Numbers of Welsh-speakers

Between 1961 and 1971 the number of Welsh-speakers fell by a massive 17.3 per cent, from a total of 656,002 to 542,425. Table 4.4 shows that decreases in excess of 10 per cent were recorded in all but three of the pre-1974 counties. The pace of decline slackened somewhat between 1971 and 1981, but the Welsh-speaking population still contracted by 6.3 per cent. Notable proportionate increases were, however, returned in the areas of the former counties of Radnor and Monmouth, whilst Anglesey and Flint experienced more marginal gains. Elsewhere, Welsh-speaking populations declined, and most dramatically in the old county of Glamorgan

Figures 4.8, 4.9 and 4.10 focus on patterns of relative change in the number of Welsh-speakers for the intercensal periods 1961–71 and 1971–81. Figures 4.8 and 4.9 show percentage change, whilst Figure 4.10 categorizes communities according to trends during

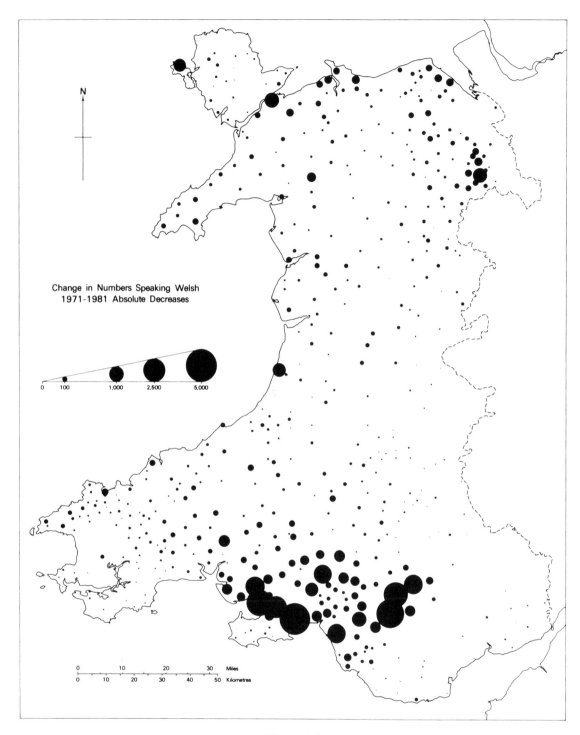

Change in Numbers Speaking Welsh
1971-1981 Absolute Decreases

0    100    1,000    2,500    5,000

0        10        20        30    Miles
0    10    20    30    40    50    Kilometres

**Figure 4.6**

60

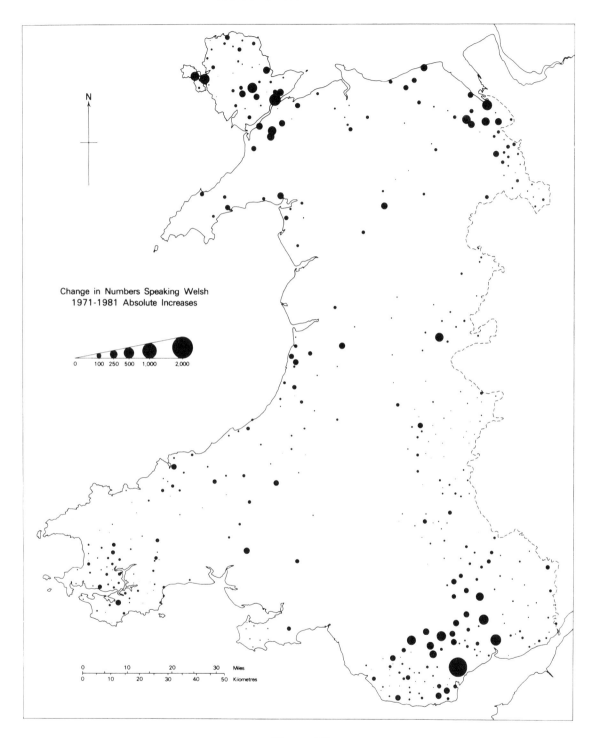

**Figure 4.7**

**Table 4.4**
**Percentage change in numbers able to speak Welsh**

| County (pre-1974) | 1961–1971 | 1971–1981 |
|---|---|---|
| Anglesey | -0.03 | 5.98 |
| Breconshire | -21.18 | -10.30 |
| Caernarfonshire | -8.49 | -2.28 |
| Cardiganshire | -7.10 | -1.79 |
| Carmarthenshire | -14.15 | -10.27 |
| Denbighshire | -14.45 | -6.99 |
| Flintshire | -10.22 | -4.48 |
| Glamorgan | -14.96 | -29.79 |
| Merioneth | -10.37 | -4.77 |
| Monmouthshire | -35.85 | 27.78 |
| Montgomeryshire | -14.80 | -3.74 |
| Pembrokeshire | -10.74 | -2.98 |
| Radnorshire | -17.09 | 58.17 |
| **Wales** | **-17.31** | **-6.34** |

the two intercensal periods. To aid comparison, the scales adopted for Figures 4.8 and 4.9 have been standardized. The frequency of communities within each of the eight categories used in these maps is given in Table 4.5. It will be noted that the total number of communities referred to in this tabulation varies for the two periods concerned. This is because it is not possible to calculate rates of change for those communities with no Welsh-speakers in either of the base years.

**Table 4.5**
**Change in numbers able to speak Welsh:**
**numbers of communities by percentage classes**

| Percentage Classes | 1961–1971 | | 1971–1981 | |
|---|---|---|---|---|
| | Numbers of Communities | % Total | Number of Communities | % Total |
| Over 50 | 78 | 8.1 | 107 | 11.5 |
| 21 to 50 | 55 | 5.7 | 82 | 8.8 |
| 0 to 20 | 101 | 10.4 | 210 | 22.6 |
| 0 to -10 | 165 | 17.0 | 198 | 21.2 |
| -11 to -20 | 213 | 22.0 | 135 | 14.5 |
| -21 to -30 | 154 | 15.9 | 89 | 9.6 |
| -31 to -50 | 111 | 11.5 | 69 | 7.4 |
| Over -50 | 91 | 9.4 | 41 | 4.4 |
| **Total** | **968** | **100.0** | **931** | **100.0** |

**Figure 4.8**

**Figure 4.9**

**Figure 4.10**

Table 4.5 shows that between 1971 and 1981 a total of 399 communities recorded increases in their number of Welsh-speakers, and that in 107 of them the increases were in excess of 50 per cent. Admittedly, many of the high increases were returned by communities with rather low Welsh-speaking populations, for example in the borderlands and Pembrokeshire. Nevertheless, that represented a distinct improvement on the situation between 1961 and 1971. Then, only 234 communities showed a positive rate of change.

The data also indicate that, whilst the number of communities recording negative rates of up to -10 per cent increased, 165 in 1961–71 as against 198 in 1971–81, there was a substantial fall in the number with the greater relative decreases. Thus, 91 communities experienced a loss of Welsh-speakers in excess of 50 per cent for 1961–71 as against only 41 for the following decade.

In order to present a clearer picture of the changes detailed in Figure 4.8 and 4.9, an attempt has been made to draw together both sets of information in a single classification of communities. Figure 4.10 presents a six-fold categorization of communities according to the direction and rates of change over the two periods. The nature of each of the six categories is described in the key to the map, and Table 4.6 lists the associated number of communities, together with mean rates of change for the two periods.

**Table 4.6**
**Numbers of Welsh-speakers: change categories**
**1961–1971 and 1971–1981**

| Categories | Number of Communities | Mean % 1961–71 | Mean % 1971–81 |
|---|---|---|---|
| 1 | 143 | -15.6 | -28.1 |
| 2 | 277 | -24.1 | -12.6 |
| 3 | 87 | 58.2 | -34.5 |
| 4 | 260 | -24.1 | 40.1 |
| 5 | 80 | 100.5 | 24.3 |
| 6 | 82 | 19.5 | 55.4 |

*(See Figure 4.10 for category definitions)*

Category 1 is made up of those communities (143 in all) where the number of Welsh-speakers declined continuously over the two decades, but where the pace of decline increased between 1971 and 1981. These are the major problem regions for the language. It is evident from Figure 4.10 that they are scattered throughout Wales. Significant clusters covered substantial areas of land in western and central Montgomery, and in central parts of Brecknock. The large number of communities belonging to this category in central parts of Dyfed, and their highly fragmented distribution, underlines the complexity and often localized character of language decline in these most vulnerable areas. Even so, it is possible to associate them in very general terms with the main areas of loss as identified in the earlier section on trends in differences. Certainly there seems to be a link with the main frontier of retreat; hence the representation in Montgomery and Brecknock. Between 1961 and 1971 the average rate of decline was -15.6 per cent, whilst for 1971–81 it was -28.1.

Category 2 contains the greatest number of communities (277) and extends over a large part of south-west Wales (excluding South Pembrokeshire), Gwynedd and Clwyd. The majority of communities within the main Welsh-speaking area belong to this category. It is defined by continuous decrease, but one which slackened during the second of the two decades. Average statistics suggest a decline of 24.1 per cent, followed by one of 12.6 per cent. The fact that categories 1 and 2 dominantly characterize both urban and rural regions of Welsh-speaking Wales is clearly indicative of the crucial problems which those areas faced in terms of language survival.

Category 3 includes those communities that experienced an increase or stability in numbers of Welsh-speakers between 1961 and 1971, but a decline in the decade that followed. This applies to a scattering of communities, mainly located in borderland regions. With the small numbers involved it is difficult to assess the precise significance of this sharp, and seemingly anomalous, reversal of fortunes.

In contrast, comfort could be derived from the presence within the heartland of a sizable number of communities which registered increases in their Welsh-speaking population between 1971 and 1981, after having experienced losses in the previous decade. These communities make up category 4. They are seen to be concentrated in more westerly locations, especially in Ceredigion and Gwynedd, but are patchy in nature. The majority, however, are situated in south-east Wales. The most extensive grouping includes communities in the Vale of Glamorgan, southern parts of Mid Glamorgan, Gwent and south-east Brecknock. Developments in these areas have already been noted as a distinctive feature of the 1971–81 decade. Their potential significance for the future of the Welsh language is further emphasized by the presence within the areas they cover of many communities which fall into categories 5 and 6. As Table 4.6 indicates these categories define areas where there was continuous growth in the numbers of people able to speak Welsh. Away from the south-east, there were marked concentrations of this type in South Pembrokeshire, in Anglesey and in north-east Wales where Mold seemed to be the focus.

## Conclusion

This chapter has attempted to highlight the major forces that impressed on the geography of the Welsh language during what must be seen as a particularly critical period in its history. By the beginning of the 1960s the language appeared to be entering a deep spiral of decline from which it would not be able to extricate itself. Although major new initiatives were launched to help retrieve matters, the situation deteriorated markedly between 1961 and 1971. However, despite continuing pressures in the decade that followed, signs of a slackening in the pace of decline were in evidence as the efforts to improve the status and use of the language began to assert themselves. That said, it is clear that conditions in the main rural heartlands were still a cause for concern, while the full significance of the seemingly positive developments taking place in certain urban areas needed to be treated circumspectly. It is to these matters, and their implications for the language during the 1980s, that the discussion now turns.

# CHAPTER 5

# The Welsh Language in the 1980s:
# A Decade of Mixed Blessings

During the 1980s many of the positive and negative forces that have been alluded to previously continued to impact on the Welsh language. There were, however, new developments of considerable significance for the long-term future of the language at national and local levels. Added to these were countervailing trends of an international order which also figured prominently. It is not possible here to elaborate in detail on these initiatives and tendencies, the more limited intention is to provide a very broad overview and then to capture some of the main changes taking place during the decade through two detailed case studies. The one examines language patterns in an archetypal Welsh-speaking rural area (centred on the settlements of Tregaron and Llangeitho in Ceredigion), the other explores recent developments in Cardiff and its environs.

To set the context for these case studies, it is appropriate to make a number of broad observations on some general changes of relevance to the condition of the language in rural and urban regions of Wales. Firstly, there is the demographic situation. Table 5.1 records absolute and relative trends in the resident populations of rural districts between 1981 and 1991. The statistics show that during the 1980s numbers increased in all areas, although with significant variations between districts. Thus, growth rates in excess of 8 per cent were recorded for Colwyn (13.4%), Ceredigion (10.4%), Radnor (9.7%), South Pembrokeshire (8.8%) and Montgomeryshire (8.1%), while in Brecknock, Preseli Pembrokeshire and Ynys Môn (Anglesey) they were less than 2 per cent. It is evident from Table 5.1 that the increase in population totals was mainly due to in-migration, although in some instances natural increases also contributed to the expansion. The process of counter-urbanization that began in the previous decade continued to assert itself, albeit at a reduced pace. The origins of those moving into rural Wales are difficult to ascertain for the entire period, but it is likely that significant percentages emanated from England. The situation in Ceredigion demonstrates the point. Here, for the year preceding the 1981 census, there was an inflow of 5,598; of these 1,357 (24%) came from England, with nearly 42 per cent of these being from the South-East. This movement, which affected many parts of rural Wales, clearly maintained pressure on the language, and not only at its geographical margins, but at its very heart. The situation was further exacerbated by the fact that the out-migration of young, and often well qualified, people from the rural heartland still continued in the 1980s, hidden beneath the net migrational increase.

**Table 5.1**
**Rural Wales: population change, 1981–1991**

| Districts | 1 | 2 | 3 | 4 | 5 | 6 |
|---|---|---|---|---|---|---|
| Colwyn | 47283 | 53622 | 6339 | 13.4 | -6.9 | 20.3 |
| Glyndŵr | 38947 | 40855 | 1908 | 5.0 | -2.1 | 7.1 |
| Carmarthen | 50839 | 53920 | 3081 | 6.1 | -2.4 | 8.4 |
| Ceredigion | 55353 | 61109 | 5756 | 10.4 | -2.3 | 12.7 |
| Dinefwr | 36606 | 37798 | 1192 | 3.3 | -3.2 | 6.5 |
| Preseli Pembrokeshire | 67688 | 68638 | 950 | 1.4 | 1.6 | -0.2 |
| South Pembrokeshire | 37593 | 40896 | 3303 | 8.8 | 0.7 | 8.1 |
| Aberconwy | 49621 | 51262 | 1641 | 3.3 | -5.4 | 8.7 |
| Arfon | 50295 | 51461 | 1166 | 2.3 | 1.6 | 0.7 |
| Dwyfor | 25409 | 26419 | 1010 | 4.0 | -5.2 | 9.2 |
| Meirionnydd | 30458 | 31963 | 1505 | 4.9 | -3.3 | 8.2 |
| Ynys Môn | 66496 | 67371 | 875 | 1.3 | 1.9 | -0.5 |
| Brecknock | 39536 | 40206 | 670 | 1.7 | -2.2 | 3.9 |
| Montgomeryshire | 47649 | 51527 | 3878 | 8.1 | -0.3 | 8.4 |
| Radnor | 20940 | 22982 | 2042 | 9.7 | -1.9 | 11.7 |

*KEY*

*1. Resident Population 1981*
*2. Resident Population 1991 (1981 base)*
*3. Absolute Population Change*

*4. % Population Change*
*5. % Natural Change*
*6. % Migrational Change*

(Source: OPCS County Monitors)

Also reinforced during the 1980s was the process of de-industrialization and the dominance of Cardiff as a transactional city. Both of these trends had impacts on the geography of the language. The loss of population from the mining valleys of south Wales negatively affected numbers of Welsh-speakers, most especially in the anthracite coalfield where large concentrations of speakers were to be found. However, contrary trends were operative in many small administrative towns and in their associated suburban areas. Here, growth in residential populations was often accompanied by an increase in numbers of Welsh-speakers (e.g., Mold and Carmarthen). Most dramatic of all, however, was the increase in employment opportunities for Welsh-speakers in the Cardiff region. Positions in administration and the media continued to attract upwardly mobile people to the area, many of whom came from *Y Fro Gymraeg*. Here, in this long-Anglicized urban setting, they demanded even further provision of Welsh-medium schools for their children, and a Welsh-speaking social environment steadily established itself.

While these various demographic developments had mixed impacts on the language, some negative and some positive, more planned initiatives to support its development continued to flourish. Formally, the most noteworthy was the creation in 1988 by the Secretary of State of yet another body with special commitment to the needs of the language – The Welsh Language Board. Its remit was to advise on language matters in general, and to promote wider use of Welsh in both public and private spheres. The Board outlined a strategy for the period 1989–94 which recognized the need to 'improve the infrastructure of the Welsh language' and ensure 'ways in which the two languages in Wales can live side by side' (Welsh Language Board, 1989, 5). Although the Board placed emphasis on the notion of a 'community of languages' and 'bilingualism', this 'does not mean that everything has to be done bilingually in every part of the country. Political, social and resource constraints are going to have a very strong influence on the pattern of services that will be provided when the strategy is interpreted at local level' (Welsh Language Board, 1989, 5). A further notion to be given emphasis was that of 'normalization', a concept similar to that of the personality principle. The term, which is widely used in the European arena of lesser-used languages, is construed by the Welsh Language Board to mean ensuring that 'it is possible, convenient and normal for everyone, in every situation where a public service is provided, to choose which language he or she wishes to use' (Welsh Language Board, 1989, 5). But since the Board itself only published its strategy in 1989 its impact on Welsh language figures in the 1991 census must be minimal. Accordingly, further discussion of such matters is left to the conclusion.

As has been noted, it is not possible or appropriate in this geolinguistic study to enter into a detailed review of the many initiatives that were launched in support of the language during the 1980s. A wide-ranging and accessible summary of these is available in the report *Language Strategy 1991–2001* drawn up and published by the National Language Forum (1991), itself a body with an extensive representation, and characteristic of the determination to advance the language. In this strategic report there are sections on the statutory status of the language, of its employment in education, local and central government, health and social services, the economy and industry, publishing and the media, the churches, societies and voluntary bodies, as well as the relationship to housing and migration. Of these, two of the most important are education and the media – they warrant further comment for they figure in the case studies that follow.

During the 1980s considerable advances were made in Welsh-medium education at all levels. The Welsh-medium Nursery Schools Movement continued to expand and by 1990 there were 553 nursery groups and nearly 345 'mother and child' groups throughout Wales. Together they catered for nearly 13,000 children. Significantly, 60 per cent of these came from non-Welsh-speaking homes. During this period there was also a steady expansion in the number of Welsh-medium primary schools, most notably in Mid Glamorgan and South Glamorgan. That said, statistics for 1988 suggested that throughout Wales just 13 per cent of primary school children spoke Welsh fluently. A further 74 per cent had no Welsh whatsoever. As far as secondary education is concerned the picture was very variable. The fact that in 1988 over 80 per cent of pupils received Welsh lessons in their first year of secondary school is significant; less so is the fact that for the fourth year this figure stood at 28 per cent.

Although it does not influence the results of the 1991 census, it is appropriate at this point to note that in 1988 the Education Reform Act came into force. This Act is of immense importance to the future of the language since it ensures that all children aged between 5 and 16 will be introduced to the language at school. This is because the Act accords Welsh the status of a core subject in Welsh-medium schools and a foundation subject in all others.

Advances in the provision of Welsh-medium courses in colleges of further education were not as impressive as in the primary and secondary sectors, although there was a notable increase in opportunities for certain vocational courses (e.g., business, catering). Progress in higher education was also exceedingly slow, at least within the constituent University Colleges of Wales. It was only in 1979 for instance that a Board was established to oversee the promotion of teaching through the medium of Welsh. Greater support for the language came from the training colleges, in particular those at Bangor and Carmarthen. It has to be said, however, that within the University of Wales problems of finance have certainly hampered developments in the field of Welsh-medium education.

The second area of support for the language worthy of special reference is that of the media. It is now widely recognized that the establishment of Radio Cymru in 1979 was a most significant development and contributed greatly to the promotion of the language. However, it was the long-awaited decision to set up Sianel 4 Cymru (Broadcasting Act 1981) that was of pivotal import. Its significance cannot be exaggerated. Not only does it offer instruction in the language, an instruction which was once provided by chapel and Sunday school; more crucially, it serves as a base on which to build sentiment. It is a revealing feature of postmodern Wales that an element of the mass media has to be substituted for the chapel, and the synthetic communities of soap operas have replaced community in the real world. But in the decade of the 1980s the gradual evolution of S4C into such a role has been manifest, especially as it takes steps to adapt its language to everyday usage.

While an appreciation of these various specific developments are central to an understanding of the forces at work within the language domain, others of a more global and contradictory nature entrenched themselves during the 1980s. If universal movements of modern times have been generally threatening to the language, the nature of the postmodern world can be considered as very different. Postmodernism can be defined as the ultimate in eclecticism, and if that is inadequate as a definition it at least gives some indication of what has characterized the last decade. The western world has been marked by the decline of large scale certainties and a break down into movements and ideas which are far more ragged and less dominated by overriding notions. Perhaps the rise of what has been called the 'single-issue fanatic', one who devotes total effort to a single issue which is not necessarily related to any standard or coherent philosophy, is the clearest symptom. Animal rights, anti-smoking or environmental issues of all sorts are examples.

All this does have implications for language. It could well be argued, for instance, that Cymdeithas yr Iaith (the Welsh Language Society) was one of the first of the single-issue organizations. And as the old universalist philosophies of the right and left, of both Thatcherite Conservatism and pure socialism, both declined into a form of pragmatism, so Cymdeithas yr Iaith was able to exert more influence. It succeeded in placing the language firmly in the centre of the political agenda in a way that it could not have hoped to have done when monolithic parties and their philosophies dominated the political scene.

More important than the changes in political philosophy, at least in everyday terms, has been its concomitant in terms of political reality. It is perhaps an exaggeration to write of the collapse of the nation state, though not of the questioning as to its relevance as a late medieval structure at the beginning of the twenty-first century when new associations are being sought, both at higher and lower levels of territorial identity. Many contemporary states came into being during the early modern period through conquest or dynastic means, many before the association of ethnic identity with political entity was common. Now the constituent parts of these aggregations are asserting their own rights to separate or devolved government. At the heart of the matter is an appropriate territorial hierarchy, where the old nation state no longer takes unquestioning priority and where each level from federal union to state and the components of the state, to region and to locality, has its proper and appropriate function. It is a difficult process to enable, especially where ethnic groups are intermixed or have mingled over a period of time. It is even more difficult where ethnic groups claim the same territory. Many of these problems were created by the application by western colonialism of the principle of the nation state in Africa and Asia, regardless of tribal areas or traditional territorial systems. But the general contemporary theme is quite clear: these so-called regional conflicts have replaced the old imperial confrontations. The present is not witnessing 'the end of history' but a different post-modern history. Internal colonization as a concept has been long out of fashion, but it might be possible to argue that the post-war decolonization of the external pieces of empire is now being followed by internal decolonization.

If Wales is considered in relation to these tendencies then superficially there are considerable advantages for the language. A clear continent-wide trend to devolution and regionalism must seem to the good; a Europe of the 'Regions' greatly appealing. Certainly its representation in such organizations as The European Bureau for Lesser-Used Languages is indicative of a European movement to reinvigorate the minority languages. It is also symbolic of postmodern trends. But an automatic assumption that in a separate or devolved Wales language would be greatly advantaged needs to be questioned, as a reference back to the statement by Saunders Lewis in 1962 and quoted in the introduction to Chapter 4 would suggest, and as some of the discussion in Chapter 1 indicated. Nevertheless, the operation of these trends during the 1980s has undoubtedly made the language issue widely significant. No longer were large-scale movements entirely inimical to the language: a turnaround in values and ideologies that could prove to be of considerable importance in the long term.

Having traced broad trends and movements of relevance to an understanding of the process of language change, it is apposite at this point to explore the situation, as it manifested itself at the local level during the 1980s. Two case studies are considered; together they capture the extremes of change that characterized the period. The studies themselves are based on behavioural and attitudinal surveys of schoolchildren and their parents, firstly in a traditional Welsh-speaking rural community (Aitchison, Carter and Rogers, 1989), and secondly in an urban area experiencing a resurgence of interest in the language (Aitchison and Carter, 1988).

### The Tregaron Region

The first locality to be examined (henceforth referred to as the Tregaron region) comprises a set of twelve communities that lie within the catchment area of Ysgol Uwchradd Tregaron (Tregaron Comprehensive School). Questionnaire surveys of pupils at this school and of their parents generated data on family backgrounds and use of the Welsh language in differing domains.

The demographic characteristics of the region are displayed in Table 5.2 . They confirm that the area experienced a significant loss of population between 1961 and 1971, but then, in common with other parts of rural Wales, witnessed the impact of a turnaround during the decade that followed. For the two inter-censal periods however it is noteworthy that numbers of Welsh-speakers continued to decline, although the pace slackened considerably between 1971 and 1981. In 1981 nearly 77 per cent of the resident population were able to speak Welsh. This is a high figure and would appear to suggest that all was well with the language in the region. In fact this was far from being the case, for in 1961 nearly 92 per cent of the local population were Welsh-speakers. It is evident that heavy in-migration had significantly transformed social and linguistic structures in the area. The situation varied from community to community, but the severity of the change in the community of Llangeitho was most remarkable, for there the percentage of Welsh-speakers fell from 82.9 in 1971 to just 54.2 in 1981.

Questionnaires for the language survey were completed by 301 pupils (88% of the school population). Virtually all of these were Welsh-speakers, and most (78%) had attended Welsh-medium primary schools. Some 48 per cent of the Welsh-speaking pupils had learned the language at home, the remainder had received their first introduction to it at school. Whilst these figures appear encouraging, the situation is more critically poised when reference is made to the relative standing of Welsh vis-à-vis English, and to the use that is made of the language in different domains. Just over half the pupils indicated that they were able to speak Welsh either better than English (34%), or at least as well as English (17%). For the rest, English was their favoured language. This relatively even split can partly be explained by reference to the home backgrounds of the pupils, for although 47 per cent came from households where both parents were able to speak Welsh, a notable 38 per cent indicated that neither parent could speak the language. The remaining 15 per cent (including some single-parent families) stated that just one parent could speak Welsh. Given this situation it is hardly surprising that a high proportion of pupils (41.7%) claimed that they never spoke Welsh at home (Table 5.3).

That said, Welsh is still seen to be the dominant medium of communication in homes where both parents were able to speak the language, although it is noteworthy that nearly 19 per cent of such homes made little or no use of Welsh.

Tables 5.4, 5.5 and 5.6 record the use of Welsh relative to English in the school playground and outside school, both absolutely and in relation to parents' language abilities.

**Table 5.2**

**The Tregaron area: change in population over the age of three.**
**Welsh-speaking population and proportion born in Wales**

| Community | Population % Change | | Welsh-speaking % Change | | Welsh-speaking 1981 | Welsh-born 1981 |
|---|---|---|---|---|---|---|
| | 61–71 | 71–81 | 61–71 | 71–81 | | |
| Blaenpennal | 7.8 | 1.7 | -4.9 | -2.6 | 79.5 | 73.7 |
| Caron is Clawdd | -6.4 | 4.6 | -7.8 | -0.4 | 84.4 | 82.8 |
| Caron u. Clawdd | -17.7 | 28.3 | -19.5 | 12.1 | 80.9 | 71.4 |
| Gwnnws Isaf | -14.1 | 13.9 | -24.0 | -1.5 | 68.1 | 69.7 |
| Gwynfil | 7.1 | 3.3 | -4.5 | -1.2 | 77.4 | 70.6 |
| Llanbadarn Odwyn | -24.3 | 29.6 | -28.0 | 14.4 | 69.1 | 58.3 |
| Llanddewibrefi | -12.9 | 6.9 | -19.9 | -7.4 | 76.6 | 72.0 |
| Llangeitho | -4.5 | 17.9 | -13.7 | -22.6 | 54.5 | 54.2 |
| Lower Lledrod | 4.3 | 40.0 | -0.9 | 21.4 | 74.3 | 72.4 |
| Upper Gwnnws | -15.5 | -9.3 | -13.9 | -18.8 | 85.7 | 84.8 |
| Upper Lledrod | -18.8 | 4.8 | -26.8 | 6.7 | 73.3 | 68.8 |
| Ysbyty Ystwyth | -19.4 | 15.1 | -25.3 | -10.3 | 67.6 | 65.8 |
| **Tregaron region** | **-9.1** | **10.1** | **-14.0** | **-2.4** | **76.7** | **70.4** |

**Table 5.3**

**Use of Welsh at home by linguistic status of households**

| | Number of parents able to speak Welsh | | |
|---|---|---|---|
| Percentage speaking Welsh | Both | One | Neither |
| More than English | 75.4 | 9.3 | 0.0 |
| Same as English | 6.0 | 11.6 | 0.0 |
| Only a little | 11.2 | 34.9 | 15.6 |
| Never | 7.4 | 44.2 | 84.4 |

**Table 5.4**

**Use of Welsh in the playground and outside school**

| Percentage speaking Welsh | Playground | Outside school |
|---|---|---|
| More than English | 27.0 | 29.1 |
| Same as English | 17.8 | 14.2 |
| Only a little | 17.1 | 17.6 |
| Never | 38.1 | 39.1 |

**Table 5.5**
**Use of Welsh in playground by linguistic character of household**

| | Number of parents able to speak Welsh | | |
| Percentage speaking Welsh | Both | One | Neither |
| --- | --- | --- | --- |
| More than English | 54.1 | 11.6 | 0.0 |
| Same as English | 27.8 | 18.6 | 5.5 |
| Only a little | 2.8 | 27.9 | 18.1 |
| Never | 5.3 | 41.9 | 76.4 |

**Table 5.6**
**Use of Welsh outside school by linguistic character of household**

| | Number of parents able to speak Welsh | | |
| Percentage speaking Welsh | Both | One | Neither |
| --- | --- | --- | --- |
| More than English | 58.1 | 11.9 | 0.0 |
| Same as English | 25.0 | 11.9 | 1.8 |
| Only a little | 11.8 | 28.6 | 20.7 |
| Never | 5.1 | 47.6 | 77.5 |

Given the significant number of pupils who had moved into the area from outside Wales (see below), the figures indicate a higher level of social use than might perhaps have been expected. Even so, just over a third of all pupils claimed that they never communicated with their friends in Welsh. But it is also evident that pupils from dominantly Welsh homes maintained a relatively strong hold on the language, despite the obvious pressures which might have obliged them to make more extensive use of English. In both domains nearly 85 per cent of pupils from Welsh-speaking homes used the language at least as frequently as English, with the majority actually speaking it to a greater extent. Those pupils from non-Welsh-speaking backgrounds inevitably used Welsh to a much smaller degree, but even there a quarter did say that they made some use of the language beyond the classroom.

The pupils of Tregaron school professed a high degree of literacy, with over 70 per cent stating that they had little difficulty in reading and writing Welsh. But a high proportion admitted to reading only a very limited amount of literature written in Welsh outside school. This again was clearly related to the language of the parents; an impressive 68.9 per cent of pupils from Welsh-speaking homes read books and newspapers in Welsh either 'often' or 'quite frequently'. Recognizing the important role that television can play in the promotion of the language, it is significant that 79.4 per cent of those questioned watched Welsh-language television 'often' or 'quite frequently', though the percentage fell to 25.6 where only one parent was Welsh-speaking. Radio was by no means as popular, and only

41.9 per cent from households where both parents spoke Welsh listened 'often' or 'quite frequently', with 58 per cent returning 'hardly ever' or 'never'.

An important cultural feature of the Tregaron area is the access that pupils have to clubs and societies where Welsh is spoken regularly. That these groups play a key role in helping to promote and consolidate the language was confirmed by the high proportion (45%) of pupils who actually attended meetings and events organized by such bodies as the Urdd, YFC (Young Farmers Clubs) and others. More significantly, 70 per cent of pupils from Welsh-speaking homes participated in such societies.

Another finding of considerable interest was the attitude of children to the 'value' of Welsh in finding employment. Where both parents spoke Welsh, 99.2 per cent thought that the ability to speak Welsh was an advantage in seeking work, but even more surprisingly 93.5 per cent of those where neither parent spoke Welsh were of the same opinion. Such responses are not unrelated to the fact that just over two-thirds confirmed a wish to live and work in Wales after leaving school.

Finally, given the centrality of the in-migration issue to the changes taking place in the region, it is of relevance to note that only 62 per cent of the pupils were actually born in Wales; of those the great majority (90%) were born in Ceredigion. Birthplaces of the remainder included the South-East of England (21%), the West Midlands (6%) and the North-West of England (5%). Equally revealing was the fact that many of the school children had moved into the area only recently, 28 per cent having done so within the previous five years.

Having ascertained the behaviour and attitudes of pupils to the Welsh language it was appropriate to deepen the analysis through a survey of parents. Just over 200 responded to the questionnaire, and of these some 40 per cent were born outside Wales. Intermarriage between locals and incomers was of a relatively low order. Thus, out of the 95 respondents born in Ceredigion, 67 had married someone from the same area. In fact, there were only 7 marriage partners born in England. Certainly at this stage 'mixed' marriages do not seem to be a problem for language maintenance and the key issue is the general impact of 'pure' English families on the standing and use of the language. However, the limited degree of intermarriage is probably a consequence of the recency of the in-migratory movement. In that respect there were significant findings, for a goodly proportion of those born outside the area claimed to speak Welsh. Of the 160 respondents and spouses born outside Wales, nearly 44 per cent indicated that they could speak Welsh. Put in another way, of the 283 parents able to speak Welsh nearly a quarter had been born outside Wales. It is also notable that whilst the majority of Welsh-speaking parents came from homes where both their parents were able to speak Welsh, a significantly high proportion, some 24 per cent, came from homes where neither parent was able to speak the language. The latter were predominantly incomers who first learned to speak Welsh by attending beginners' courses. Nearly 13 per cent of the Welsh-speakers had been able to speak the language for less than five years; another 6 per cent had been speaking it for between 5 and 10 years.

**Table 5.7**
**Parents use of Welsh in different domains**

| Respondents' use of Welsh: | Percentages speaking Welsh | | |
| --- | --- | --- | --- |
| | In the home | At work | Socially |
| More often than English | 59.1 | 53.7 | 59.9 |
| About the same as English | 5.4 | 19.4 | 10.6 |
| Hardly ever | 22.8 | 16.4 | 19.7 |
| Never | 12.7 | 10.5 | 9.9 |

The data presented in Table 5.7 suggest that for the parents Welsh was the dominant medium of communication in all language domains, with over 50 per cent stating that they used Welsh more often than English. Thus a strong core of adults had maintained a positive commitment to the language in their everyday activities. On the other hand, about 30 per cent of Welsh-speakers made very little use of the language, though a significant percentage of these were Welsh learners. Again, nearly 70 per cent claimed that they could both read and write Welsh. Some 60 per cent stated that they watched Welsh-language television regularly or fairly often. In contrast to the schoolchildren, a high number also listened to radio in Welsh, just over 30 per cent regularly and a further 19 per cent often.

The parents, like their children, saw real economic advantage in being able to speak Welsh. Almost 66 per cent of the respondents thought it a 'great' help and 32.3 per cent 'some' help in securing employment. Even more encouraging from the point of view of the language was the fact that 72.5 per cent of the respondents and 72.2 per cent of their spouses considered it important that their children should be able to speak Welsh. The fact that over 70 per cent of respondents hoped to stay in the region at least for the next ten years, boded well for increased cultural integration.

It is evident from the two sets of surveys that the Tregaron region experienced a major social and linguistic re-structuring during the 1980s. A typically Welsh environment was radically transformed as a result of the steady flow of in-migrants from urban parts of England. This influx, coupled with the continuing out-migration of young Welsh-speakers, had a major impact on the absolute and relative standing of the Welsh language in the area. Although in-migration could clearly be viewed as a major threat to the language at this time, it has to be noted that a substantial number of incomers had made efforts to learn Welsh, and, furthermore, were happy to see their children become part of the Welsh-speaking community. In general the investigation suggested that the Tregaron region was poised at a critical threshold. Cultural and linguistic continuity clearly depends on the relation between the strength of the host population and numbers of incomers. There is a level where in-migrants can be integrated, and indeed fall under pressure to integrate, and where they can add vitality to a community. But there is also a level where, because of the relatively high numbers, absorption does not take place, nor is it seen as necessary. There is

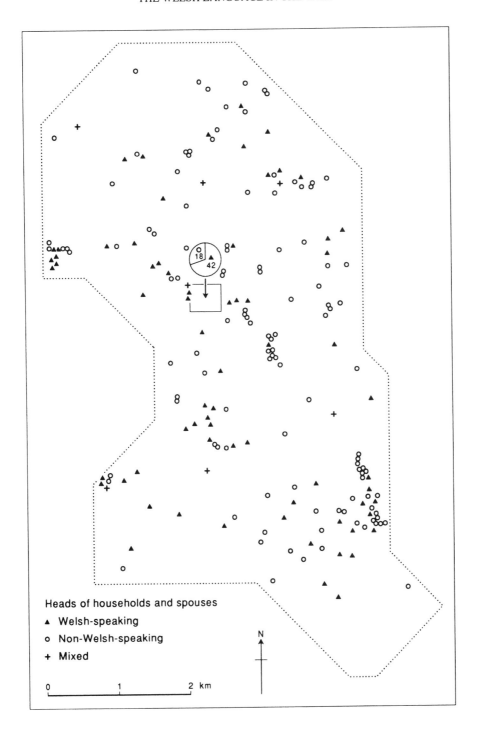

**Figure 5.1**

a 'tipping point' where the domains of language use become restricted, the supporting cultural environment becomes attenuated and Anglicization intensifies. In the mid-1980s that point had not quite been reached in the Tregaron region. The Welshness of the area was sufficiently robust, and the educational system both for children and adults, sufficiently supportive, to have prevented it. Even so, the area appeared to be moving close to a situation where irreversible trends could assert themselves.

This possibility was reinforced by a detailed study of the language of households in two communities within the hinterland of Tregaron (Aitchison, Baptiste and Edwards, 1990). Relating to the period 1970–90 and based on an analysis of electoral registers, the investigation revealed quite dramatic changes. Figure 5.1 shows the location of Welsh- and non-Welsh-speaking households in the area in 1990 and captures the enormity of the language shifts which had taken place over a twenty year period. In 1971 a very high proportion of the households in the area (some 84%) were able to speak Welsh. Evidence gained in the field surveys suggested that this had fallen to nearly 40 per cent by the late 1980s. The swarm of English-speaking homes in what was only a short time ago a community dominated by a population of isolated and dispersed farmsteads, where traditional Welsh values and the language were safeguarded, is graphically representative of the changes which have taken place in many other parts of rural Wales. The dwindling number of children from Welsh-speaking homes attending the local schools, and the size of congregations in the chapels, are but two manifestations of a deep-seated cultural transformation; some would say malaise.

**The Cardiff Region**

The nature of urban growth in the post-industrial period and its implications for the Welsh language have already been broadly summarized. The intention of the study undertaken in the Cardiff region was to examine in more detail the significance of these developments for an area deemed to be experiencing a 'quiet' language revolution (Aitchison and Carter, 1987). Adopting the same questionnaires as those used in the Tregaron region a series of school communities was investigated. Given their crucial significance to language developments in the region special consideration was given to Welsh-medium schools.

The promotion of Welsh-medium teaching in Cardiff and its environs is not a recent phenomenon. As early as 1897, for instance, the Cardiff School Board passed a resolution in favour of teaching the language. In the same year a survey of over 6,000 parents yielded a massive 81 per cent return in support of Welsh-language provision within the schools of the city. In 1907, another survey of parents generated less positive responses, but even so it showed some 40 per cent in favour of their children being taught Welsh. Be that as it may, it was only in 1949 that the first Welsh-medium primary school was established – the Ninian Park School. That was some ten years after a special committee had been set up to consider Welsh-language provision. In its deliberations, the committee was somewhat belatedly responding to the highly influential 1927 Report to the Board of Education entitled *Welsh in Education and Life* (see Chapter 4).

In 1952 the City of Cardiff Education Committee published a comprehensive report on the teaching of Welsh in the city's schools. It placed pupils into three language classes: those for whom Welsh was a mother tongue (5%); those who could understand Welsh (10–15%); and those unable to speak Welsh (80–85%). The report also noted the increasing number of pupils taking Welsh as a subject, the proportion rising from 60 per cent in 1940 to 72 per cent in 1952, a period during which Welsh was not compulsory. At the same time, growth in the number of children attending the Ninian Park primary school necessitated a move to a new site at Highfields in Llandaf, with the school changing its name to Ysgol Gymraeg Bryntaf. It was to prepare children for entry into that new school that the first *ysgol feithrin* in Cardiff was established in the vestry of Capel Heol y Crwys in May 1951.

In March 1961 an application was made to the Education Authority for a Welsh primary school to serve Rhiwbeina and Whitchurch. The application was refused, but a Welsh-medium unit was opened at Ysgol Llanishen Fach in 1965. Meanwhile, 1962 saw the creation of Ysgol Gyfun Rhydfelen, the first Welsh-medium secondary school in the then county of Glamorgan.

In 1972 yet another Welsh language survey was launched, with parents of six to ten year olds being asked to indicate whether or not they wished their children to learn Welsh. The results identified nine schools where there appeared to be significant support for a bilingual stream – Birchgrove, Llanedeyrn, Baden Powell, Moorland, Eglwys Newydd, Springwood, Hawthorn, Ton yr Ywen and Lansdowne. Accommodation problems created difficulties for certain of these schools, but bilingual units were eventually established at the infant and junior schools in Rhiwbeina, Ton yr Ywen, Cefn Onn, Lansdowne and Eglwys Newydd. Following further growth in numbers, and difficulties experienced in the transport of pupils to and from school, there were again calls for a restructuring of Ysgol Gymraeg Bryntaf. It was expected that the school would be split into three separate schools, but in the end the decision was taken to move the site to the Parade, a step which many considered detrimental to the development of Welsh-medium education.

In 1976 the Director of Education for the newly constituted county of South Glamorgan recommended that three Welsh-medium primary schools be established: Coed Glas (Llanishen) in 1977, Eglwys Wen (Whitchurch) and Peter Lea School (Fairwater) in 1978. With the change in the county structure, increasing pressure developed for South Glamorgan to provide its own secondary education through the medium of Welsh rather then relying on Ysgol Rhydfelen, now in Mid Glamorgan. At the time some 100 pupils were receiving secondary education either at Rhydfelen or at Llanhari, also in Mid Glamorgan and established in 1974. Indeed, with growing demand Mid Glamorgan Education Authority made it known that it would not be able to accept pupils from South Glamorgan after 1978. As a result, though not without some local dissent, Ysgol Gyfun Gymraeg Glantaf was opened in 1978 with 100 pupils.

At the time of the survey, and following the closure of Bryntaf in 1983, there were within the City of Cardiff five Welsh-medium primary schools – Ysgol Gymraeg Melin

Gruffydd at Whitchurch (Yr Eglwys Newydd), Ysgol Coed y Gof at Pentrebane (Pentrebaen), Ysgol Bro Eirwg at Llanrhymni, Ysgol y Wern at Llanishen (Llanisien) and Ysgol Gymraeg Radnor Road in Canton (Cantwn). Within the main settlements of Cardiff's commuting hinterland there were other Welsh-medium primary schools, as well as the two important secondary schools at Rhydfelen and Llanhari.

This review of the growth of Welsh-medium education in Cardiff affirms the response made to a growing demand from parents and reflects the pattern of in-migration into Cardiff from the Welsh-speaking heartland. To evaluate the situation in more detail a sample of five primary and four secondary schools was selected for study. From a preliminary survey of all headmasters and headmistresses it was evident that Welsh-medium schools claimed virtually all the young Welsh-speaking population in the region. A highly polarized and asymmetric structure prevailed, with the vast majority of schools having no fluent Welsh-speakers at all. It appeared from this introductory survey that little basis existed in the education system for a movement to a bilingual city. This being the case, it was pertinent to ask to what extent the Welsh-medium schools, as products of the economic and social changes in progress in Wales, provided more than a tenuous hope for the future in a context which is regarded by many as quite crucial. It was to shed some light on that question that a series of surveys were undertaken.

For the surveys three separate questionnaires were administered. One was directed to pupils in the fifth and sixth forms of four secondary schools; the second was completed by parents of the secondary school children; the third was distributed to parents of children attending primary schools. Given that the vast majority of Welsh-speaking children attended Welsh-medium schools, it was to those that the bulk of the questionnaires inevitably had to be directed.

The survey of the four secondary schools yielded a total of 856 responses. For purposes of reference it should be noted that in the tabulations that follow schools 2, 3 and 4 were official Welsh-medium schools; almost all of the pupils in these schools answered the questionnaire in Welsh.

**Table 5.8**
**Cardiff secondary schools: ability to speak Welsh**

|  | Schools | | | |
| --- | --- | --- | --- | --- |
|  | 1 | 2 | 3 | 4 |
| Percentage able to speak Welsh: | | | | |
| Better than English | 0.6 | 17.8 | 10.4 | 6.0 |
| As well as English | 0.7 | 40.2 | 36.4 | 55.0 |
| Not as well as English | 23.0 | 41.5 | 50.9 | 39.0 |
| Only a little | 75.7 | 0.4 | 2.3 | 0.0 |

A feature of Table 5.8, which records ability in speaking Welsh, is the relatively high percentages of pupils in all the Welsh-medium schools who stated that they could not speak Welsh as well as they could English. The figure was as high as 51 per cent in school 3. On the other hand some 61 per cent in school 4 indicated that their Welsh was as good as their English. The questionnaire revealed that the great majority of pupils had learned Welsh at school rather than at home, the 'at school' percentages for the four schools being 91.9, 50.2, 75.0 and 86.0 respectively. That was to be expected given the relatively low proportion of homes where both parents were Welsh-speaking. As reported by the pupils, the relevant percentages for the four schools were 7.4, 39.2, 23.0 and 10.2. Not surprisingly, this situation affects responses relating to the actual use of Welsh in the home (Table 5.9).

**Table 5.9**
**Cardiff secondary schools: use of Welsh in the home**

| | Schools | | | |
| | 1 | 2 | 3 | 4 |
|---|---|---|---|---|
| Percentage speaking Welsh: | | | | |
| More often than English | 1.3 | 30.4 | 11.7 | 6.0 |
| About the same as English | 0.7 | 11.2 | 9.3 | 8.6 |
| Only a little | 8.7 | 30.4 | 31.3 | 44.2 |
| Never | 89.3 | 27.9 | 48.0 | 41.1 |

Given the limited use of Welsh at home, it is perhaps not surprising that use of the language in the playground and outside the home should be of an equally low order. Thus, 92.6, 23.9, 52.0 and 39.5 per cent of pupils stated that they never used Welsh outside of the school. Similar responses emerged in relation to viewing television and listening to the radio in Welsh, and reading Welsh books. Thus, the 'hardly ever' and 'never' categories for the use of Welsh-language television and radio were 90.2, 43.1, 58.6 and 56.0 and 100, 79.7, 88.0 and 89.2, respectively. The equivalent figures for the four schools for reading books and papers were 94.7, 61.8, 59.8 and 59.2 per cent. Again, the percentages attending clubs and societies where Welsh was regularly spoken were low: 10.7, 32.8, 14.6, 15.3. It is evident from these figures that in this growth area it is difficult for the Welsh language to move out of the domain of the schools for the whole of the economic, social and cultural environment is predominantly Anglicized. Even so, there was a general feeling on the part of pupils that an ability to speak Welsh was an advantage in seeking employment. Only 37.9 per cent thought it of no help at all in the non-Welsh-medium school, while the figures in the Welsh-medium schools were, as might be expected, very low at 6.2, 7.3, and 8.0. Interestingly, the great majority of pupils in the Welsh-medium schools stated that they wished to stay in Wales after leaving school.

The associated survey of parents generated responses from 409 families. The results need not be considered in detail here, but two general observations are worth noting. Firstly, parents' estimates of their own ability to speak Welsh differed from that of their children. It has been mentioned above that the proportion of homes with Welsh-speaking parents was relatively low (based on the returns made by pupils). The responses from the parents themselves, however, yielded a set of proportions that suggested a higher level of competence in the language (Table 5.10). Overall 67 per cent of parents claimed to be able to speak Welsh. Various reasons could be cited to account for this discrepancy, but it is of interest to note that a third of those parents who stated they could speak Welsh actually came from non-Welsh-speaking homes and had made efforts to learn the language (Table 5.11). The second observation is that the use of Welsh by parents was highly circumscribed in the main domains (at work and socially). Here, only between 30 and 50 per cent of Welsh-speakers used the language 'more often than' and 'about the same as' English.

**Table 5.10**
**Ability of parents to speak Welsh by households**

| Percentage of households: | Schools | | | |
|---|---|---|---|---|
| | 1 | 2 | 3 | 4 |
| Both parents | 10.0 | 67.7 | 55.1 | 29.3 |
| One parent | 19.3 | 25.8 | 20.2 | 37.8 |
| Neither parent | 70.7 | 6.5 | 24.7 | 32.9 |

**Table 5.11**
**Ability to speak Welsh: respondents and parents of respondents**
**(Welsh-medium schools only)**

| | Parents of respondents | | |
|---|---|---|---|
| | Both | One | Neither |
| Respondents: | | | |
| Welsh-speaking | 252 | 97 | 181 |
| Not Welsh-speaking | 15 | 31 | 212 |

The survey of primary schools was limited to five schools, the questionnaires being completed by parents in 181 households. Schools 1, 2, 4, and 5 were Welsh-medium. Table 5.12 shows the recorded ability of parents to speak Welsh.

**Table 5.12**
**Ability of primary school parents to speak Welsh**

| Percentage of parents: | Schools | | | | |
|---|---|---|---|---|---|
| | 1 | 2 | 3 | 4 | 5 |
| Both | 28.0 | 38.0 | 16.1 | 62.5 | 25.7 |
| One | 56.0 | 52.0 | 12.9 | 15.6 | 68.5 |
| Neither | 16.0 | 10.0 | 71.0 | 21.9 | 5.8 |

The figures reveal a high proportion of households where only one parent was able to speak Welsh, suggesting a rather frail basis for the promotion of the language in the home. This was confirmed by the extent to which Welsh was spoken in the home (Table 5.13).

**Table 5.13**
**Use of Welsh in the home: primary school parents.**
**Percentages of Welsh-speaking parents**

|  | Schools | | | | |
|---|---|---|---|---|---|
|  | 1 | 2 | 3 | 4 | 5 |
| More often than English | 33.3 | 43.7 | 0.0 | 14.3 | 39.6 |
| About the same as English | 16.7 | 22.5 | 0.0 | 14.3 | 27.6 |
| Hardly ever | 38.9 | 28.2 | 30.8 | 53.6 | 31.0 |
| Never | 11.1 | 5.6 | 69.2 | 17.8 | 1.7 |

The results of the survey indicate that the language has only a weak hold on the life of the Welsh-speaking community, with Welsh failing to achieve a dominant position even in the households where the children attended a Welsh-medium school. The same pattern is repeated in the other language domains investigated, with the least use again being in the workplace. Since the influence of the chapel has been stressed as one of the preservers of the language and the decline of attendance as a factor in the decline of the language, it is of interest to consider the responses recorded in Table 5.14. The data are unambiguous, and confirm that only small percentages of respondents attend chapels and churches where the services are in Welsh on a regular basis – yet another negative feature of the language situation in the study area. To this can be added the low degree of interest in Welsh-language television and radio.

**Table 5.14**
**Attendance at church/chapel where services are held in Welsh.**
**Percentage of Welsh-speaking parents**

|  | Schools | | | | |
|---|---|---|---|---|---|
|  | 1 | 2 | 3 | 4 | 5 |
| Regularly | 25.0 | 23.8 | 0.0 | 17.7 | 29.3 |
| Occasionally | 43.2 | 20.2 | 7.7 | 10.7 | 34.5 |
| Never | 31.8 | 55.9 | 92.3 | 71.4 | 36.2 |

In sharp contrast, when questions were asked directly about their children the responses from parents were far more encouraging, with high proportions being returned for speaking Welsh 'better' or 'as well as' English, reading material in Welsh, and attending clubs and societies where Welsh was the medium of communication. Percentages ranging between 50 and 60 applied in all of the Welsh-medium schools.

Having briefly summarized the results of these various surveys, it is appropriate to draw a number of conclusions concerning the condition of the language in the Cardiff area. Firstly, it is clear that the use of Welsh is not widely diffused through the region. Welsh-speaking pupils are overwhelmingly concentrated in the Welsh-medium schools. This 'oasis' condition clearly poses problems for the wider promotion of the language.

Whilst the Welsh-medium schools were playing an important role and satisfying a burgeoning demand, the results of the surveys point to underlying and background conditions which are generally not favourable as far as the use of the language is concerned. These relate in the main to the place of the language in domains that lie beyond the classroom – the home, the social environment of both pupils and parents, and their contact with Welsh literature and the media.

Attention has been drawn throughout the analysis to the rather limited use which is made of Welsh in day-to-day communication. This is partly related to the fact that in many households neither, or, at best, only one of the parents was able to speak Welsh. The same could be said in regard to households in their more extended form. To underline this latter point, extended households were classified according to the number of Welsh-speakers. The maximum score was 6 where the two parents and four grandparents spoke Welsh. The results are shown in Table 5.15.

**Table 5.15**
**The Cardiff region surveys: extended households.**
**Percentage of households**

| Score | Secondary schools | Primary schools |
|-------|-------------------|-----------------|
| 0 | 32.5 | 18.7 |
| 1 | 13.7 | 19.2 |
| 2 | 13.4 | 14.3 |
| 3 | 13.7 | 16.5 |
| 4 | 8.1 | 15.4 |
| 5 | 5.9 | 3.3 |
| 6 | 12.7 | 12.6 |

There are of course various ways in which the different scores can be obtained, but the overall conclusion is that the home foundation on which the Welsh-medium schools are seeking to build is not very deep or strong. That said, the situation could be expected to slowly change as the Welsh-speaking children build their own families: always assuming of course that they stay in the area.

A related weakness, as far as the entrenchment of the language is concerned, is the very limited and seemingly superficial use that was made of Welsh in the playground and in the wider social arena by the pupils of the Welsh-medium schools. Domain limitations also applied to Welsh-speaking parents. There were variations, but generally Welsh was not used to a great extent in the workplace, which would be expected, or in social communication. Equally surprising was the limited interest in Welsh-language television, radio and literature. The reasons offered by way of explanation varied, but often appeared to be mere rationalizations (e.g., comments on the quality of productions and publications).

Somewhat more encouraging findings were related to motivation and future intentions. For there to be a real revival of the language in the Cardiff region there must be a continued build up in the numbers of speakers. The increased provision of Welsh nursery and primary education is fundamental, but equally important is the need to hold young speakers in the region. Responses to questions relating to future intentions indicate that many Welsh-speaking pupils felt that they were likely to seek employment in the local area. Similarly, most parents seemed satisfied with their immediate surroundings. A related and particularly positive development was the large number of parents who had taken steps to learn the language.

An overarching conclusion that can be drawn from these surveys is that as in the Tregaron region, but for different reasons, the language situation in Cardiff is critically poised. There must be doubts as to whether or not there is sufficient momentum for a sustained regeneration of the language. From the predominantly Anglicized environment of the city, and the influences in daily life which are overwhelmingly English, there emerges not even the outline of a strongly identified subculture. Outside very limited domains, indeed outside the school, the use of Welsh at home, at work and at play seems greatly constrained. Without a strong cultural focus, one which was once provided by the chapel, the significant educational efforts are in danger of being seriously dissipated when that special environment is left.

In the region there appeared to be no real wish to have immersion as deeply and as continuously as possible in a Welsh cultural milieu. That particular language subcultures can exist in urban environments is well attested. But the 'urban village' in which such cultural survival takes place needs two attributes – sufficiently large numbers of people and a degree of isolation. Neither of these seems to be apparent in Cardiff.

An interesting and consistent feature from the surveys in both the Tregaron and Cardiff regions is the view that an ability to speak Welsh is a positive attribute when it comes to seeking employment. If this be so, then it represents a complete reversal of the long-standing perception of Welsh as being significant in cultural terms but of no economic value. Whilst such a view may be understandable in Cardiff as a response to the transactional role of the city, it is sadly near the conception of a language as a series of characters for communication, rather than as the matrix of a culture, and it might explain the low ratios for the use of Welsh outside limited domains. Even so, it offers tangible reasons for learning Welsh which did not exist so clearly in the immediate past.

Reflecting on the results of the surveys, Aitchison and Carter (1988, 30) observed that

> At present . . . the Welsh language within Cardiff and its environs is a plant that has grown vigorously but without a deep or extensive root system. The evidence . . . would suggest that, given the pressures in the urban environment at large, it is not yet robust enough to gain a truly meaningful hold and to move out of the 'hot-houses' of the Welsh-medium schools.

This conclusion may be valid, but it cannot be gainsaid that the efforts being made in the area on behalf of the language have been most impressive.

It will be apparent that these detailed local surveys have confirmed many of the conclusions drawn from a consideration of the aggregated data for the period leading up to the 1981 census. Clearly, in the rural areas there have been major problems generated by the forces of counterurbanization. As has been shown, however, the response has been significant, mainly through advances in the educational system. Endeavours to offer language instruction to adults have also been important, and the number of in-migrants willing to learn Welsh during the 1980s was far from insignificant. In Cardiff the growth of the numbers speaking Welsh has been a distinct feature of the recent history of the language, although the bases and infrastructural context for its fuller and deeper development would appear to be somewhat limited. But before offering a final judgement on these matters and on future prospects for the language, it is necessary to bring the statistical record up-to-date with an analysis of the results of the 1991 census.

# CHAPTER 6

# The Welsh Language in 1991

In a study of language patterns and trends in rural Wales, Aitchison and Carter (1989) forecast that while the number of Welsh-speakers would continue to decline between 1981 and 1991, the pace of change would be much reduced when compared with previous intercensal periods. It was further proposed that by the year 2001 there would be a turnaround of great historic significance, with numbers of Welsh-speakers actually increasing for the first time since 1911. Given the major efforts that have been made over the past three decades to secure a stronger future for the language the results of the 1991 census have been eagerly awaited.

Unfortunately, as has already been noted (Chapter 2), differences in the definition of households, in the form of published tabulations and, most critically, in the boundaries of administrative areas (both wards and communities) make detailed quantitative analyses of patterns of change extremely difficult, if not impossible. Certainly, the standard series of community maps generated for the period 1961–81 (Chapter 4) cannot be extended. Be this as it may, in the discussion that follows an attempt is made, wherever possible, to identify what appear to be meaningful trends in language patterns for the period 1981–91. Although it is not feasible to calculate absolute and relative changes and to prepare associated maps, it is in certain instances worth comparing ward distributions for 1981, with those for 1991. It is the ward that constitutes the basic areal unit of study in the main map analyses that follow. Data relating to numbers and percentages of Welsh-speakers for the 908 wards of Wales are included for reference purposes in the Appendix on p. 159. It is to be appreciated that the tabulations presented here relate to administrative divisions (counties and districts) as they existed at the time the census returns were first published. Some data is however presented in Chapter 8 that is based on the new unitary authorities.

## The Welsh-speaking Population

The 1991 census records a total Welsh-speaking population of 508,098. This represents 18.6 per cent of the total resident population aged three years and over (2,723,623). Table 6.1 shows the distribution of Welsh-speakers at county level. The counties of Dyfed and Gwynedd are seen to be the main strongholds of the language; they account for over half of all Welsh-speakers, with a combined total of 283,411 (55.7%). At the other extreme are the counties of Gwent, Powys and South Glamorgan where resident Welsh-speaking populations are in each case less than 25,000. This regional pattern of absolute figures complements a similar pattern for the percentages of the resident county populations (aged three and over) that are able to speak Welsh. Table 6.1 reaffirms the dominant position of Gwynedd and Dyfed. Here 61.0 and 43.7 per cent of the respective populations are Welsh-speakers. In marked contrast are the counties of Gwent, South Glamorgan and Mid Glamorgan where less than one in 10 people speak the language.

**Table 6.1**
**Population and language statistics (1991)**

| County | 1 | 2 | 3 |
|---|---|---|---|
| Clwyd | 392812 | 71405 | 18.2 |
| Dyfed | 331528 | 144998 | 43.7 |
| Gwent | 423794 | 10339 | 2.4 |
| Gwynedd | 226862 | 138413 | 61.0 |
| Mid Glamorgan | 511656 | 43263 | 8.4 |
| Powys | 113335 | 22871 | 20.2 |
| South Glamorgan | 375857 | 24541 | 6.5 |
| West Glamorgan | 347779 | 52268 | 15.0 |
| **Wales** | **2723623** | **508098** | **18.6** |

*KEY*
*1. Resident population aged 3 years and over*
*2. Population able to speak Welsh*
*3. Percentage population able to speak Welsh*

Table 6.2 records the same information for the 37 districts of Wales. Five districts have more than 30,000 Welsh-speakers; in order these are Ynys Môn (Anglesey), Arfon, Ceredigion, Llanelli and Carmarthen. It is noteworthy that the districts dominated by the two main cities of Wales – Swansea and Cardiff – also record quite high figures (in excess of 17,000 in both cases). The lowest totals (less than 3,000 Welsh-speakers) are returned by all of the districts in the county of Gwent.

The proportions of the district populations that speak Welsh vary greatly, from a high of 75.4 per cent in Dwyfor to a mere 1.9 per cent in Monmouth. In addition to Dwyfor, six other districts have Welsh-speaking percentages in excess of 50 per cent – Arfon, Dinefwr, Meirionnydd, Ynys Môn, Ceredigion and Carmarthen. Of all the districts, however, 18 actually returned percentages of less than 15. These include the main urban districts of south and north-east Wales, certain rural districts in the borderland, South Pembrokeshire and the Vale of Glamorgan.

A more detailed appreciation of regional patterns is provided in Figures 6.1 and 6.2. Here, the absolute numbers of Welsh-speakers at ward level are recorded, together with associated densities per $km^2$. Concerning these maps it is important to emphasize once again that urban regions tend to be depicted by dense clusters of small wards, while in rural regions of Wales (especially in the central uplands) the wards tend to be much more extensive in area. This bias in spatial detail clearly needs to be taken into account in appraising the resultant map distributions.

**Figure 6.1**

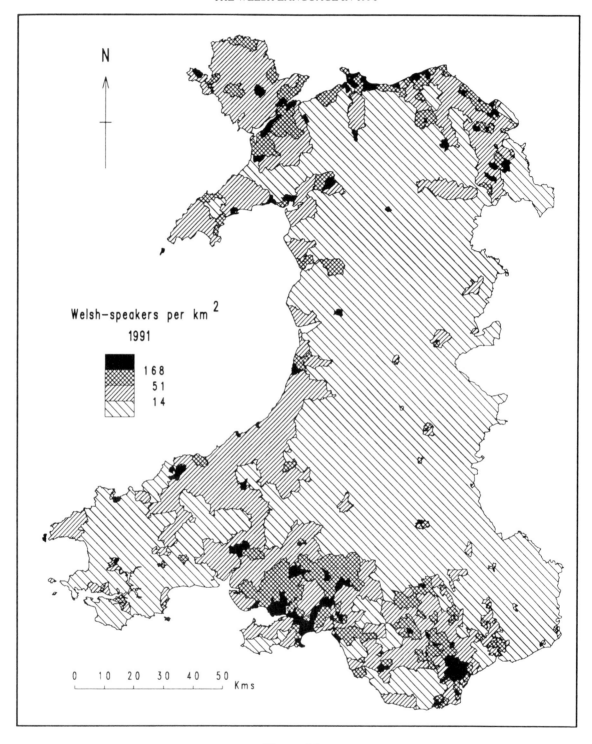

**Figure 6.2**

As is to be expected, the regional pattern of absolute numbers of Welsh-speakers is very similar to that described previously for 1981 (although in this latter instance the base reference was communities). Briefly, Figure 6.1 confirms that the majority of Welsh-speakers are located in two main areas. The first, and the most dominant concentration, covers the urban and old industrial heartland of south-west Wales. Wards in and around the towns of Llanelli, Ammanford and Swansea are seen to return particularly high figures (often in excess of 2,000 Welsh-speakers). Examples include Tumble (2,770), Morriston (2,755), Gorslas (2,602), Gwauncaegurwen (2,204), Ystalyfera (2,110) and Pontardawe (2,093). To the east of this core, a dense swarm of wards with relatively small numbers of Welsh-speakers merges into a much stronger cluster in the immediate hinterland of Cardiff.

The second main zone with relatively high concentrations of Welsh-speakers extends along the coast of north Wales, from Caernarfon in the west to Flint in the east. The wards that make up the towns of Caernarfon, Bangor and Conwy–Llandudno have significant numbers of Welsh-speakers. At its eastern end this coastal zone extends inland and takes in the urban areas of Wrexham and Ruabon. Along the coast of west Wales concentrations of Welsh-speakers are to be found in the towns of Holyhead, Pwllheli, Porthmadog, Ffestiniog, Dolgellau, Aberystwyth and Cardigan. Relatively high figures are also associated within selected inland market towns; for example, Carmarthen and Llandeilo in the Vale of Tywi, Denbigh and Ruthin in the Vale of Clwyd, Llanrwst in the Vale of Conwy, Llandysul and Lampeter in the Vale of Teifi, and finally Newtown and Welshpool in the Vale of Powys.

**Table 6.2**
**Population and language statistics (1991)**

| Districts | 1 | 2 | 3 |
|---|---|---|---|
| Alyn and Deeside | 70502 | 6779 | 9.62 |
| Colwyn | 53220 | 13572 | 25.50 |
| Delyn | 65431 | 11620 | 17.76 |
| Glyndŵr | 40338 | 16076 | 39.85 |
| Rhuddlan | 52546 | 8492 | 16.16 |
| Wrexham Maelor | 110775 | 14866 | 13.42 |
| Carmarthen | 53318 | 30919 | 57.99 |
| Ceredigion | 60980 | 36026 | 59.08 |
| Dinefwr | 37297 | 24811 | 66.52 |
| Llanelli | 72048 | 33483 | 46.47 |
| Preseli Pembrokeshire | 67571 | 16454 | 24.35 |
| South Pembrokeshire | 40314 | 3305 | 8.20 |
| Blaenau Gwent | 72937 | 1696 | 2.33 |
| Islwyn | 63440 | 2183 | 3.44 |
| Monmouth | 73301 | 1458 | 1.99 |
| Newport | 127356 | 2874 | 2.26 |
| Torfaen | 86760 | 2128 | 2.45 |
| Aberconwy | 51184 | 18440 | 36.03 |
| Arfon | 51092 | 38119 | 74.61 |
| Dwyfor | 26246 | 19798 | 75.43 |

(Table 6.2 continued)

| Districts | 1 | 2 | 3 |
|---|---|---|---|
| Meirionnydd | 31815 | 20816 | 65.43 |
| Ynys Môn | 66525 | 41240 | 61.99 |
| Cynon Valley | 62409 | 5933 | 9.51 |
| Merthyr Tydfil | 56662 | 4237 | 7.48 |
| Ogwr | 127087 | 10544 | 8.30 |
| Rhondda | 75085 | 6123 | 8.15 |
| Rhymney Valley | 98936 | 7531 | 7.61 |
| Taff–Ely | 91477 | 8895 | 9.72 |
| Brecknock | 39836 | 9175 | 23.03 |
| Montgomeryshire | 50676 | 11796 | 23.28 |
| Radnor | 22823 | 1900 | 8.32 |
| Cardiff | 266758 | 17171 | 6.44 |
| Vale of Glamorgan | 109099 | 7370 | 6.76 |
| Lliw Valley | 60588 | 22369 | 36.92 |
| Neath | 63051 | 8177 | 12.97 |
| Port Talbot | 49178 | 4222 | 8.59 |
| Swansea | 174962 | 17500 | 10.00 |
| **Wales** | **2723623** | **508098** | **18.65** |

KEY

1. *Resident population aged 3 years and over*
2. *Population able to speak Welsh*
3. *Percentage population able to speak Welsh*

The proportional circles associated with wards in the rural heartlands of Dyfed and Gwynedd confirm the presence of high numbers of Welsh-speakers, but they are widely dispersed in distribution. Finally, Figure 6.1 shows that the Welsh-speaking population is particularly sparse in the uplands of central Wales, the central borderland and South Pembrokeshire.

Figure 6.2 is of interest in this regard, for it displays the density of Welsh-speakers per km$^2$. The distribution is based on quartiles, with the lower, middle and upper limits being 14, 51 and 168, respectively. Because of the sizes of wards in upland regions, and the low absolute numbers of speakers in much of the borderland, densities of less than 14 per km$^2$ are to be found over an extensive area. Wards falling into the second quartile, with densities between 14 and 51, are mainly located either in lowland rural regions of west Wales (e.g., Ynys Môn, Dwyfor and Ceredigion) or on the peripheries of the major urban areas in north and south Wales. Fifty per cent of wards have densities of Welsh-speakers in excess of 51 per km$^2$. By and large these include the two zones of high absolute values identified above, together with isolated urban settlements along the western coast and inland.

A general feature that emerges from Figures 6.1 and 6.2 (and one that has already been alluded to) is that in terms of absolute numbers and densities the majority of Welsh-speakers are associated with dominantly urban and suburban areas. Given the trends that have been identified previously, it is to be expected that the urbanization of the Welsh-speaking population is likely to continue, and at an increased pace.

**Figure 6.3**

While these latter tendencies are significant, it is evident from Figure 6.3 that in terms of relative proportions, the main strongholds of the language are still to be found in rural Wales. Before commenting on these patterns in more detail it is perhaps worth reiterating that past censuses have all drawn attention to the gradual break-up of a once discrete and distinctive core area (*Y Fro Gymraeg*). Whereas the notion of a westward-moving frontier of Anglicization initially sufficed to define the encroachment on the Welsh-speaking heartland, the situation eventually became more complex as a variety of internal fracture lines established themselves.

The sequence of geolinguistic change in terms of the core area can be summarized thus:

1901   A clear and dominant core could be identified  where over 90% of the population spoke Welsh.

1931   The situation was as it was in 1901, but the qualifying proportion for the core had to be reduced to 80%.

1951   The core area was still identifiable, but the qualifying threshold was nearer 75%. Internal fracture lines were becoming more and more evident.

1961   In order to justify a clear core the qualifying proportion had to be reduced yet again, this time to 65%. Four main fracture lines could be discerned :

   (i)     the Menai Straits
   (ii)    the Conwy–Porthmadog 'trench' across Snowdonia
   (iii)   the Severn–Dyfi break
   (iv)    the 'depression' between rural and industrial Dyfed

1971   The fracture lines had become so apparent that, to retain the 65% threshold, it was necessary to recast interpretation in the form of a series of separated sub-cores. They were :

   (i)     Ynys Môn (Anglesey)
   (ii)    Llŷn and Arfon
   (iii)   Meirionnydd–Nant Conwy
   (iv)    Rural Dyfed, north of the Landsker
   (v)     Industrial east Dyfed and western parts of West Glamorgan

1981   The processes which had been evident since 1951 continued apace, and the heartland was now deeply severed. The sub-cores of 1971 had become a series of peaks rising from a low ridge.

Although not on the same spatial or population bases a comparison of the patterns depicted in Figures 6.3 and 6.4 suggest that the process of change maintained its momentum between 1981 and 1991. The four rural sub-cores continued to retract and decline in strength. In north Wales, central parts of Ynys Môn, and much of Dwyfor and Arfon are still seen to be the main centres of concentration for the language, with more

**Figure 6.4**

than 65 per cent of the population in many wards being able to speak Welsh. That said, the sub-core that centres on the uplands of Gwynedd and western Clwyd is weaker than it was, and is evidently being attenuated. Increased Anglicization of the coastal fringes and along the eastern margins is constraining this once highly resistant bastion of the language. The process of fragmentation is most clearly manifest, however, in the uplands of rural Dyfed. In 1981 large parts of this area recorded percentages of Welsh-speakers in excess of 65; now such values apply to much reduced islands along the main rim of the Cambrian Mountains. Figure 6.4 indicates that the final, fifth, core area associated with industrial south-east Dyfed (with an extension into West Glamorgan) is still in evidence, although less sharply delineated.

Beyond the main areas of concentration the percentage of Welsh-speakers falls away rather rapidly, with gradients being at their steepest in south and central Wales. In the districts of Radnor, eastern Brecknock, Gwent, South Glamorgan and much of Mid Glamorgan less than 20 per cent of ward populations are able to speak Welsh. However, it is evident that percentages in these areas are slowly rising as the measures to promote Welsh-language teaching take effect.

Before moving on to consider other language distributions, it is worth making reference to county statistics that allow more precise specifications of rates of change in numbers of Welsh-speakers for the period 1981–91. Derived from the County Monitors and using the 1981 population base (see Chapter 2), the data in Table 6.3 show that, while the overall decline in the number of Welsh-speakers was 1.4 per cent (cf. 6.3% for the previous intercensal period), changes at the county level varied greatly. The high proportionate increase in South Glamorgan (14%) was to be expected (given the developments described previously), but it did little more than compensate for the major losses (absolute and relative) in West Glamorgan (-11%), and to a lesser extent Dyfed (-2.7%). Elsewhere movements in the number of speakers were marginal, with some reductions and some advances. At the time of writing, comparable (1981 base) data had not been published for the districts of Wales.

**Table 6.3**
**Numbers of Welsh-speakers, 1981–1991 (1981 base)**

| County | 1981 | 1991 | % Change |
|---|---|---|---|
| Clwyd | 69578 | 69945 | 0.5 |
| Dyfed | 146213 | 142209 | -2.7 |
| Gwent | 10550 | 9936 | -5.8 |
| Gwynedd | 135067 | 135366 | 0.2 |
| Mid Glamorgan | 42691 | 42150 | -1.3 |
| Powys | 21358 | 22355 | 4.7 |
| South Glamorgan | 20684 | 23593 | 14.0 |
| West Glamorgan | 57408 | 50976 | -11.2 |
| **Wales** | **503549** | **496530** | **-1.4** |

## Literacy

The 1991 census contains a range of information relating to language skills. Table 6.4 shows that, in all, 546,551 persons are able *either* to speak, read or write Welsh. It should be noted that this figure is significantly higher than the total number of Welsh-speakers detailed above, and suggests a stronger representation of the language. Of this total, just over two-thirds (67.6%) are fully literate and can speak, read and write the language (369,609). Although no indication is given as to the degree of proficiency on these three fronts, the figure is still very high. It is even more so if related solely to the Welsh-speaking population; in this case the percentage value increases to 72.7 per cent (cf. 72% for the 1981 census). The published statistics also indicate that a further 38,191 residents (6.9%) are able to speak and read Welsh, but not write it. Just over 100,000 people could speak, but not read or write Welsh. Nearly 37,000 maintained that they could read the language but did not speak it; a small number (1,678) even indicated that they could write but not speak Welsh. These latter statistics appear bizarre but can no doubt be partly explained as arising from variations in the interpretation of the census question 'Does the person speak Welsh?'. As has been mentioned elsewhere, this can be interpreted to mean do you 'normally' or 'habitually' speak Welsh, rather than are you able to. If this explanation is correct then it is to be expected that there will be people who, in completing the census questionnaire, legitimately claim that they do not speak the language but do read or write it. The fact that reading and/or writing can take place without social discourse is also of some relevance.

Table 6.5 specifies the proportion of Welsh-speakers within each of the counties that are (i) only able to speak Welsh, (ii) able to speak and read but not write Welsh, (iii) able to speak, read *and* write Welsh. The results are very revealing. They show that there are distinctive regional differences in patterns of literacy. Thus, it is evident that the main Welsh-speaking county of Gwynedd is characterized by a high level of literacy, with nearly 83 per cent of the Welsh-speaking population being able to read and write the language. Somewhat lower percentages apply in Dyfed (72.9%), largely because of internal regional differences in language skills (see below). Interestingly, similar proportions of the population are able to read and write Welsh in the counties of South Glamorgan (71.7%) and Clwyd (71.0%). The explanation here lies of course in the growth in the number of young Welsh-speakers who have been educated in Welsh-medium schools and, especially in South Glamorgan, the generally high socio-economic status of Welsh-speaking families. As has been demonstrated, attitudes to Welsh in these areas have changed dramatically over recent years.

Language skills are at their lowest in West Glamorgan. Here just 57.7 per cent of the Welsh-speaking population is able to read and write the language. Part of the reason for such a low rating lies in the age profiles for the area (see below). Interestingly, this county does however return the highest proportion of speakers (13.1%) who are able to speak and read Welsh (but not write it). The county of Gwent also records a high figure for the percentage of the Welsh-speaking community who are not able to read and write the language. Again, as in West Glamorgan, the age structure of the population is relevant here, but not for the same reasons.

Finally, it is worth drawing attention to the unusually high number of people in Mid Glamorgan who are apparently able to read Welsh, but who do not speak or write the language (Table 6.4).

**Table 6.4**
**The Welsh language in 1991: literacy categories**

| County | 1 | 2 | 3 | 4 | 5 | 6 |
|---|---|---|---|---|---|---|
| Clwyd | 50696 | 5364 | 15345 | 5779 | 351 | 77535 |
| Dyfed | 105756 | 11576 | 27666 | 4573 | 242 | 149813 |
| Gwent | 6326 | 855 | 3158 | 1492 | 75 | 11906 |
| Gwynedd | 114238 | 5558 | 18617 | 1981 | 87 | 140481 |
| Mid Glam. | 29373 | 4272 | 9618 | 11057 | 332 | 54652 |
| Powys | 15495 | 2014 | 5362 | 1886 | 98 | 24855 |
| South Glam. | 17582 | 1704 | 5255 | 3505 | 208 | 28254 |
| West Glam. | 30143 | 6848 | 15277 | 6502 | 285 | 59055 |
| **Wales** | **369609** | **38191** | **100298** | **36775** | **1678** | **546551** |

*KEY*

1. *Able to speak, read and write Welsh*
2. *Able to speak and read, but not write, Welsh*
3. *Able to speak, but not read or write Welsh*
4. *Able to read, but not speak or write Welsh*
5. *Able to read and write, but not speak, Welsh*
6. *Either able to speak, read or write Welsh*

**Table 6.5**
**Literacy categories: percentage of Welsh-speaking population by county**

| | 1 | 2 | 3 |
|---|---|---|---|
| Clwyd | 21.5 | 7.5 | 71.0 |
| Dyfed | 19.1 | 8.0 | 72.9 |
| Gwent | 30.6 | 8.2 | 61.2 |
| Gwynedd | 13.5 | 4.0 | 82.5 |
| Mid Glamorgan | 22.2 | 9.9 | 67.9 |
| Powys | 23.4 | 8.8 | 67.8 |
| South Glamorgan | 21.4 | 6.9 | 71.7 |
| West Glamorgan | 29.2 | 13.1 | 57.7 |

*KEY*

1. *% only able to speak Welsh*
2. *% able to speak and read, but not write Welsh*
3. *% able to speak, read and write Welsh*

Table 6.6 lists percentages for these three literacy categories at district level. To highlight more detailed regional patterns of variation Figure 6.5 records the proportions of the Welsh-speaking population that are able to read and write Welsh at the ward level. The map

100

Percentage of Welsh-speakers
Able to Read and Write Welsh
1991

85
75
65
55
45

0  10  20  30  40  50 Kms

**Figure 6.5**

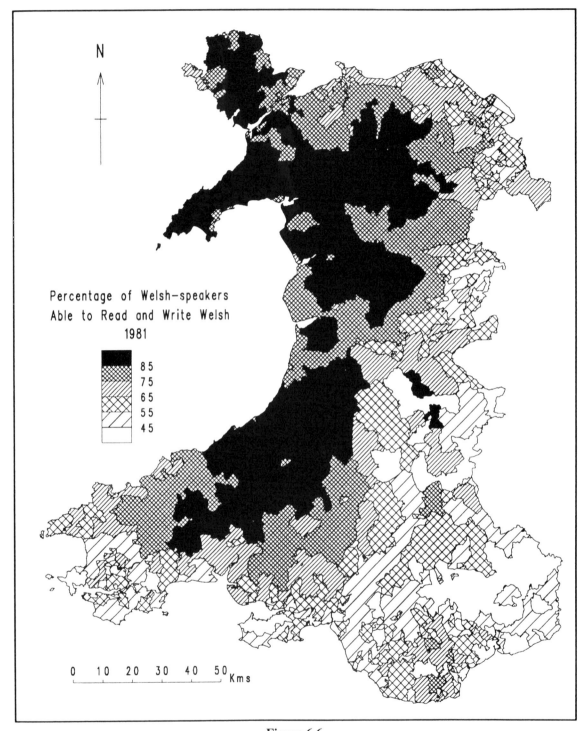

**Figure 6.6**

102

confirms the strength of the language throughout much of Gwynedd, with literacy rates exceeding 85 per cent in many areas. Central parts of Ynys Môn, much of Dwyfor, and the central core of Meirionnydd (in association with neighbouring areas such as the Mynydd Hiraethog region of Clwyd) form a solid and very dominant cluster. Together they define what might be termed the 'articulate heartland' of the language. Similar values obtain in parts of Dyfed, but it is worth noting that the position here has changed dramatically since 1981 (Figure 6.6). The maps are not directly comparable because of boundary changes, but the reduction in the number of wards where over 85 per cent of the Welsh-speaking population are able to read and write the language is significant. In 1981 the greater part of Ceredigion and northern Carmarthen returned literacy percentages of over 85. By 1991 such areas had contracted to just three fragmented blocks. Elsewhere in Wales the figures indicate a significant increase in literacy ratios. The advance in numbers of young, and literate Welsh-speakers in many eastern and southern regions of Wales (especially in the hinterland of Cardiff) is a feature of some significance.

Table 6.6
**Literacy categories: percentage of Welsh-speaking population by district**

| District | 1 | 2 | 3 |
|---|---|---|---|
| Alyn and Deeside | 24.33 | 6.15 | 69.52 |
| Colwyn | 18.49 | 6.01 | 75.49 |
| Delyn | 22.81 | 8.38 | 68.81 |
| Glyndŵr | 19.02 | 6.66 | 74.33 |
| Rhuddlan | 22.83 | 8.02 | 69.15 |
| Wrexham Maelor | 23.81 | 9.46 | 66.73 |
| Carmarthen | 16.39 | 6.91 | 76.70 |
| Ceredigion | 13.60 | 5.04 | 81.36 |
| Dinefwr | 18.63 | 8.47 | 72.90 |
| Llanelli | 25.42 | 11.30 | 63.29 |
| Preseli Pembrokeshire | 21.35 | 8.79 | 69.86 |
| South Pembrokeshire | 31.83 | 8.93 | 59.24 |
| Blaenau Gwent | 35.38 | 6.66 | 57.96 |
| Islwyn | 30.74 | 6.41 | 62.85 |
| Monmouth | 28.46 | 12.48 | 59.05 |
| Newport | 29.40 | 8.70 | 61.90 |
| Torfaen | 29.46 | 7.99 | 62.55 |
| Aberconwy | 20.10 | 6.57 | 73.33 |
| Arfon | 12.89 | 3.76 | 83.35 |
| Dwyfor | 8.13 | 2.12 | 89.76 |
| Meirionnydd | 10.28 | 3.40 | 86.33 |
| Ynys Môn | 15.15 | 4.33 | 80.52 |
| Cynon Valley | 26.77 | 13.01 | 60.22 |
| Merthyr Tydfil | 26.81 | 12.72 | 60.47 |
| Ogwr | 22.93 | 11.24 | 65.83 |

(Table 6.6 continued)

| District | 1 | 2 | 3 |
|---|---|---|---|
| Rhondda | 22.52 | 11.68 | 65.80 |
| Rhymney Valley | 20.36 | 6.98 | 72.66 |
| Taff–Ely | 17.58 | 6.01 | 76.40 |
| Brecknock | 28.05 | 11.49 | 60.46 |
| Montgomeryshire | 19.46 | 6.89 | 73.65 |
| Radnor | 25.95 | 7.74 | 66.32 |
| Cardiff | 21.01 | 6.85 | 72.14 |
| Vale of Glamorgan | 22.36 | 7.15 | 70.49 |
| Lliw Valley | 28.17 | 12.54 | 59.29 |
| Neath | 29.31 | 13.55 | 57.14 |
| Port Talbot | 29.80 | 15.37 | 54.83 |
| Swansea | 30.40 | 13.06 | 56.54 |

*KEY*

*1. % only able to speak Welsh*

*2. % able to speak and read, but not write Welsh*

*3. % able to speak, read and write Welsh*

## Age Structures

The age structure of the Welsh-speaking population has long been recognized as being of crucial importance to the survival of the language. The dangers of an age pyramid dominated by elderly speakers are obvious. It is therefore appropriate to examine age profiles for 1991 in some detail. Table 6.7 shows that 22 per cent of Welsh-speakers are under 15 years of age, as compared with 21.7 per cent for those aged over 65. The highest percentages for the 3–15 age group are seen to be associated with those counties that have experienced a growth in the number of young speakers following a significant expansion of Welsh-language education. In Gwent, Mid Glamorgan and South Glamorgan more than 30 per cent of Welsh speakers are under 15. This contrasts with the situation prevailing in West Glamorgan and Dyfed where the age group accounts for less than 20 per cent of the Welsh-speaking population. West Glamorgan is also distinguished by the very high proportion of speakers that are over 65. With such an age profile the prospects for the language in this region, at least in the short term, are not promising.

The dramatic nature of the changes currently taking place in the age structure of the Welsh-speaking population is revealed in Table 6.8. The data presented here are at the 1981 base and record numbers, percentages and percentage rates of change for Welsh-speakers under the age of 15 years. They show that between 1981 and 1991 numbers of young speakers increased by a remarkable 22.8 per cent. The advances in Gwent, Mid Glamorgan and Powys are of a particularly high order, but of course relate to relatively small numbers. Interestingly, of all the counties only Gwynedd showed a decrease (-3.1%) in its number of young Welsh-speakers. Table 6.8 also indicates that in addition to widespread gains in absolute numbers, the relative proportions of the 3–15 age group able to speak Welsh also increased in all counties. Despite falling total numbers, the county of Gwynedd stands out as the main hearth area for the language; here nearly 78 per cent of the 3–15 age group are able to speak Welsh. In Dyfed, the second most important county, the figure is much lower at 47.7 per cent. Given the relatively large numbers of Welsh-speakers in the county, a figure of 15 per cent for West Glamorgan must be regarded as particularly disappointing. The scope for an expansion in the number of young Welsh-speakers in this, and the other counties of south Wales, is clearly considerable.

**Table 6.7**
**Welsh-speakers: age profiles**

|  | Under 15 | | Over 65 | |
|---|---|---|---|---|
|  | Numbers | % | Numbers | % |
| Clwyd | 18335 | 25.7 | 15187 | 21.3 |
| Dyfed | 26086 | 18.0 | 33820 | 23.3 |
| Gwent | 3558 | 34.4 | 1456 | 14.1 |
| Gwynedd | 28256 | 20.4 | 25974 | 18.7 |
| Mid Glamorgan | 14786 | 34.2 | 9801 | 22.7 |
| Powys | 5517 | 24.1 | 5100 | 22.3 |
| South Glamorgan | 7888 | 32.1 | 3028 | 12.3 |
| West Glamorgan | 8810 | 16.9 | 16527 | 31.6 |
| **Wales** | **113236** | **22.3** | **110893** | **21.8** |

**Table 6.8**
**Welsh-speakers: 3–15 years (1981 base)**

| County | 1981 % | 1991 % | 1981* Numbers | 1991* Numbers | 1981–91 % Change |
|---|---|---|---|---|---|
| Clwyd | 18.6 | 27.9 | 13796 | 18167 | 31.7 |
| Dyfed | 40.3 | 47.7 | 23163 | 25811 | 11.4 |
| Gwent | 2.3 | 4.8 | 1921 | 3490 | 81.1 |
| Gwynedd | 69.3 | 77.6 | 28785 | 27889 | -3.1 |
| Mid Glamorgan | 8.6 | 16.1 | 8906 | 14604 | 64.0 |
| Powys | 16.7 | 30.0 | 3284 | 5463 | 66.4 |
| South Glamorgan | 7.4 | 11.9 | 5152 | 7690 | 49.3 |
| West Glamorgan | 9.3 | 15.0 | 6064 | 8719 | 43.8 |

*\* Rounded values based on proportions in County Monitors*

While the results of the 1991 census are encouraging, and have been widely publicized, they need to be treated with some circumspection. Statistics from the Committee for the Development of Welsh Education, for instance, would suggest that the situation is not as solidly based as it might be. Table 6.9 shows the percentages of children between 5 and 11 years of age who in 1988 spoke Welsh at home, who were fluent even though not speaking

Welsh at home, who spoke some Welsh, and finally who had no Welsh at all. The data are not directly comparable of course, but they do indicate that many of those returned as speaking Welsh in the census were likely to have only a rudimentary facility, and this even in the main heartland areas.

**Table 6.9**
**Primary school children (5–11 years) by ability to speak Welsh, 1988/1989**

| County | 1 | 2 | 3 | 4 |
|---|---|---|---|---|
| Clwyd | 4.3 | 5.9 | 24.0 | 65.8 |
| Dyfed | 19.5 | 9.0 | 22.7 | 48.8 |
| Gwent | 0.5 | 1.3 | 0.2 | 98.0 |
| Gwynedd | 39.2 | 19.5 | 32.0 | 9.3 |
| Mid Glamorgan | 1.0 | 9.0 | 5.5 | 84.3 |
| Powys | 5.5 | 4.2 | 21.3 | 59.0 |
| South Glamorgan | 1.3 | 2.6 | 10.6 | 85.5 |
| West Glamorgan | 2.8 | 3.3 | 4.1 | 89.8 |
| **Wales** | **7.0** | **6.4** | **12.6** | **74.0** |

Source: Pwyllgor Datblygu Addysg Gymraeg, 1991

*KEY*
1. *Speak at home*
2. *Fluent but do not speak at home*
3. *Speak but not fluent*
4. *No Welsh*

Figure 6.7 categorizes wards according to the proportion of Welsh-speakers aged between 3 and 15 years. A dominant feature of the distribution is an extensive zone where young Welsh-speakers consistently account for between 15 and 25 per cent of the Welsh-speaking population. By and large, this zone encompasses the main Welsh-speaking areas of rural Wales. Surrounding this core region is a patchwork fringe area where the proportions are generally of a higher order. Although absolute numbers are still small, the patterns draw attention to the significant impact of recent Welsh-language teaching initiatives in areas such as eastern Clwyd, the whole of Radnor, South Pembrokeshire, South Glamorgan, the Cardiff region, eastern parts of Mid Glamorgan, and western Gwent. Here the percentages of young speakers frequently exceed 35; in many wards they are even over 45.

A much more fragmented spatial pattern emerges when reference is made to the proportion of Welsh-speakers that are over 65 years of age (Figure 6.8). The greatest concentrations of older Welsh-speakers are to be found in West Glamorgan and western parts of Mid Glamorgan. A band of wards can be identified extending from the Gower Peninsula through to a zone that embraces the upland plateau and former mining valleys to the south-east of the Vale of Neath. Here more than 40 per cent of the Welsh-speaking population is over 65 years of age. A sharp and telling gradient divides this region from the more youthful Welsh-speaking areas of South Glamorgan. Throughout the main Welsh-speaking areas of rural Wales the proportion of older Welsh-speakers varies locally, ranging generally between 15 and 25 per cent.

**Figure 6.7**

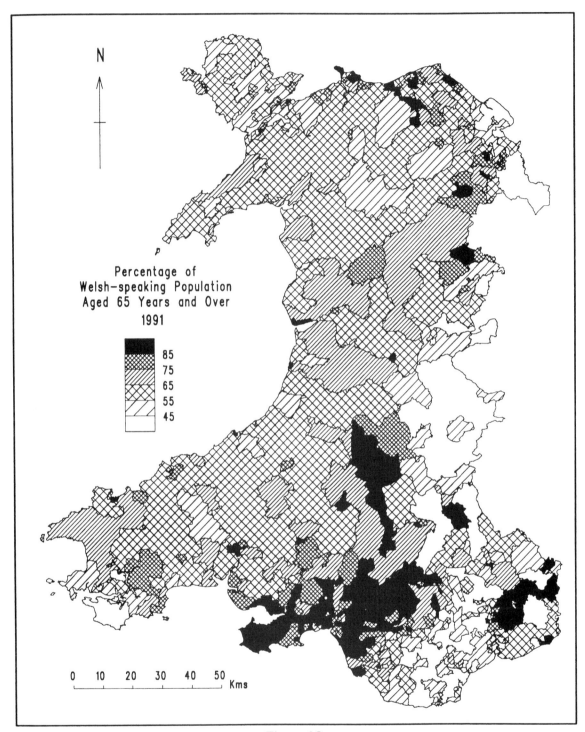

**Figure 6.8**

Finally, in exploring the geography of the language the issue of population movements is clearly of critical significance. Published statistics do not allow a precise evaluation of the impacts of such movements on the language, but some broad insights can be gained through reference to the place of birth of Welsh-speakers. In 1991, of the total resident population in Wales (2,835,073), some 77 per cent were born in Wales (Table 6.10).

**Table 6.10**
**Place of birth by language spoken**

|  | Resident population | |
| --- | --- | --- |
|  | Welsh-speaking | Non-Welsh-speaking |
| Born in Wales | 459179 | 1728520 |
| Born outside Wales | 48919 | 598455 |

Figure 6.9 classifies wards according to the proportion of the resident population born in Wales. One core area dominates the picture: the old industrial and coal-mining region of south Wales. In this region percentages generally exceed 80, with a large cluster of wards actually returning values of more than 90 per cent. Percentages of between 80 and 90 apply in a scattering of wards in various parts of Wales, but for most rural areas values tend to range between 60 and 70. Only along the fringes of the borderland, in the Vale of Powys, and in regions heavily affected by in-migration (e.g., retirement areas along the coast of north Wales) is the non-Welsh-born population dominant.

In terms of the Welsh language it is of interest to note that of the total population able to speak Welsh (508,098), nearly 10 per cent (48,919) were born outside Wales (Table 6.10). This is of some significance for it demonstrates the degree to which incomers have committed themselves to learning the language. Unfortunately it is not possible to break these figures down according to age.

## Conclusion

Although limited in nature, the aggregate data presented in this chapter serve to confirm the persistence of long-standing spatial patterns; at the same time, however, they point to a general consolidation of more recent trends that are having a positive impact on the well-being of the language. Thus, while relative decline is still in evidence, most notably in the traditional heartland, at national level the reduction in numbers of Welsh-speakers is seen to have slackened considerably as a process of rejuvenation begins to assert itself. As far as the future of the language is concerned, however, the situation is not without its uncertainties and complexities. This is forcefully demonstrated if reference is made to more recently published tabulations derived from the 1991 census.

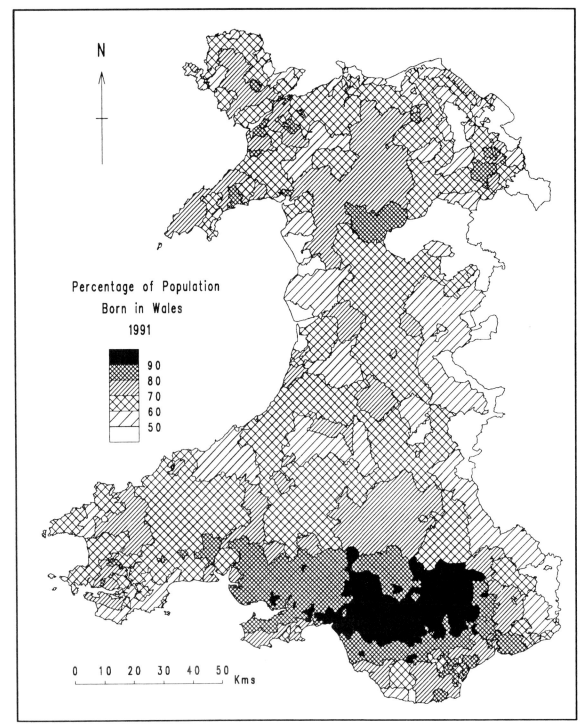

Percentage of Population
Born in Wales
1991

90
80
70
60
50

0  10  20  30  40  50  Kms

**Figure 6.9**

# CHAPTER 7

# Migration, Social Class and Household Structures

While meaningful insights into the changing geography of the Welsh language can be gained through an analysis of basic descriptive data (numbers of speakers, age structures and literacy attributes), it is evident that a more profound evaluation of current and future trends requires more detailed information relating to demographic shifts, social class configurations and household structures. As has been noted previously (Chapter 2), such information, disaggregated according to language, only became available for individuals and households at a later date (after the main census results) through the compilation of the Samples of Anonymized Records and other special cross-tabulations. It is with these records, and the light they shed on language patterns and issues, that this chapter is particularly concerned.

## Migration

In describing the nature of population movements in Wales frequent reference has been made to the impact of in- and out-migration on the numerical strength of Welsh-speaking communities in both rural and urban areas. In this context special consideration has been given to the process of counterurbanization, and the flow of non-Welsh-speakers into even the remoter regions of Wales. Reflecting generally on population trends in Britain, Stillwell has noted that, 'During the 1970s and 1980s in-migration has led to a reversal of the long term population decline in many parts of rural Wales. A clear tendency towards an increase in net in-migration in the 30–44, 45–54, and over 55 age groups is also apparent from the mid-80s' (Stillwell, 1991, 30). He adds that 'by 1988–9, the focus of high net in-migration had shifted to Wales and the west of England' (Stillwell, 1991, 17) and that, 'The in-migration of people into rural Wales, many of them from outside the Principality, and the impact of such in-migrants on the destination communities is seen by many as a great threat to Welsh culture . . . the rural "revival" is widely regarded as having the potential to destroy the linguistic and cultural traditions of these rural areas' (Stillwell, 1991, 30). In evaluating the social implications of these trends it should be emphasized that they are not solely a Welsh phenomenon. Thus, Allen and Mooney write of 'a particular vocabulary associated with counterurbanisation in which terms such as "locals", "incomers" and "settlers" have become common parlance'. They continue:

groups such as 'Scottish Watch' and 'Settler Watch' have projected images of harmonious rural life which is being disrupted and destroyed by incoming populations . . . The use of the term 'White Settler', in particular, conveys feelings of colonisation where local culture is interpreted as being usurped by a more dominant 'English' culture.(Allen and Mooney, 1998, 281–2)

Such difficulties are not unknown in England (Capstick, 1987).

Given earlier data on migration it has been possible to infer ('seen by many' in Stillwell's quotation) the impact upon the Welsh language as outlined above (Carter, 1988), but the critical word is 'infer' since none of the data on population movement included language indicators. Much of the comment, therefore, has been anecdotal or inferential; hence the significance of the new data that has been released following the publication of the basic census information.

There are three main sources of information on which assessments of migration can be based. The first is by reference to data generated in often more broadly based local or community surveys. An example of such surveys is the study of rural deprivation undertaken by Cloke, Goodwin and Milbourne (1998). They write:

Our respondents in Wales, however, strongly associate community change with cultural change due to the influx of 'foreigners' . . . Moreover, there is no doubt that many of our Welsh-speaking respondents, particularly within the area of Y Fro Gymraeg, clearly identify the influx of the foreign with an invasion of 'the English'. Here we can view 'Englishness' as a 'significant other' . . . which is perceived by local Welsh-speaking residents as threatening the existence of their everyday language and culture. (Cloke, Gooodwin and Milbourne, 1998, 141)

In a more focused survey of households in three neighbouring villages located within the traditional Welsh-speaking heartland of Ceredigion, Ackroyd (1996) was concerned specifically with the impact of in-migration on language profiles. His study generated revealing quantitative information regarding the use of the Welsh language at two points in time – 1973 and 1996. As has been noted, migration into the remoter regions of west Wales gathered momentum during the latter part of the 1970s. Data for the three villages confirm that in 1973 the communities concerned were still largely Welsh-speaking. In almost three-quarters of households all members were Welsh-speaking (Table 7.1). Over the next thirteen years the number of new properties in the area increased by 25 per cent. That the majority of these, together with existing properties, were eventually built by, sold or rented out to, non-local people is shown by the data recorded in Table 7.2. They indicate that in 1996, in two of the villages, 56 per cent of household members had been brought up outside Wales, while in the other village the equivalent figure was 33 per cent. The impact of these movements on the language is highlighted in Table 7.1. Here the fall in the percentage of wholly Welsh-speaking households and changes in the percentage of Welsh-speaking households is dramatic. Notable increases were recorded in the percentages of households that were either partly Welsh-speaking or wholly non-Welsh-speaking.

**Table 7.1**
**Villages in Ceredigion: language attributes**

|  | Number of households | % Households | | |
|---|---|---|---|---|
|  |  | Wholly Welsh-speaking | Partly Welsh-speaking | Wholly non-Welsh-speaking |
| 1973 |  |  |  |  |
| Village 1 | 39 | 74.4 | 10.3 | 15.4 |
| Village 2 | 17 | 76.5 | 11.8 | 11.8 |
| Village 3 | 79 | 74.7 | 10.1 | 15.2 |
| 1996 |  |  |  |  |
| Village 1 | 56 | 46.4 | 16.1 | 37.5 |
| Village 2 | 23 | 21.7 | 30.4 | 47.8 |
| Village 3 | 90 | 52.2 | 25.6 | 22.2 |

**Table 7.2**
**Villages in Ceredigion: place of birth and upbringing (1996)**

|  | Place of birth (%) | | | Upbringing (%) | | |
|---|---|---|---|---|---|---|
|  | In Ceredigion | Elsewhere in Wales | Outside Wales | In Ceredigion | Elsewhere in Wales | Outside Wales |
| Village 1 | 30.0 | 6.0 | 64.0 | 36.0 | 8.0 | 56.0 |
| Village 2 | 34.8 | 13.0 | 52.2 | 39.1 | 4.4 | 56.5 |
| Village 3 | 54.4 | 8.9 | 36.7 | 57.0 | 10.1 | 32.9 |

Although not directly helpful as far as the evaluation of language trends *per se* is concerned, it is worth noting that a second potential source of information on migration patterns is the National Health Service Central Register. Here evidence of population movements can be derived from registrations with medical practitioners. These data are collated for Family Practitioner Committee Areas (Family Health Service Authorities) which generally conform to counties. The material is valuable in that it provides a continuous monitor of change. Whilst such data have been used to determine rates of population change through migration, they include no reference to the language characteristics of the individuals concerned.

A third source of data relating to demographic movements is of course the main census itself. Unfortunately the data generated here is somewhat limited, being based simply on change of address in the year before the census. Thus, it is only a snapshot of one year, not a review of the decade. Again, change of address is not a particularly satisfactory way of interpreting migration. Thus a move 'next door' in the same street must be interpreted as migration; perhaps logically and properly it is, but it has limited significance in the general

113

interpretation of migration. That said, for the first time data from the 1991 census have at least been subsequently disaggregated according to the language of household members. Even so, there are limitations which undermine efforts to ascertain the net effect of migration on the numbers of Welsh-speakers. Thus, as Table 7.3 shows by way of illustration, in 1991 there were 3,583 persons who had been residents of Gwynedd one year before the census, but who were now living elsewhere in Great Britain (specifically, outside Wales). Since questions pertaining to the Welsh language applied only to those living in Wales at the time of the enumeration, there is no way of identifying the precise impact of this migratory loss on the Welsh-speaking community.

Some insight into possible linguistic shifts relating to language can however be made using differing assumptions concerning those who have migrated outside Wales. Table 7.3 includes data derived from two such assumptions (imputations, as the census authorities would call them). The first assumes that the proportion of Welsh-speaking out-migrants would be equal to the proportion of Welsh-speakers in Gwynedd, that is 61 per cent. The second assumes that the proportion moving to the rest of Great Britain would be the same as that moving to the other Welsh counties where data as to language is available, that is 39.2 per cent. These are two very different proportions and the conclusions clearly no more than tentative. All that can be said is that whichever figure is taken, there was still a net out-migration of Welsh-speakers and hence a loss to the county. But on one assumption the absolute loss was 1,440 and on the other 659. If, perhaps illegitimately, the single year is extrapolated to the decade then the differences at 14,400 and 6,596 are considerable.

**Table 7.3**
**Migration of Welsh-speakers out of and into Gwynedd 1991**

| Associated county | Migrants out | Migrants in |
|---|---|---|
| Clwyd | 314 | 272 |
| Dyfed | 85 | 81 |
| Gwent | 10 | 4 |
| Mid Glamorgan | 18 | 15 |
| Powys | 50 | 45 |
| South Glamorgan | 90 | 58 |
| West Glamorgan | 14 | 12 |
| Rest of Great Britain | ? | 840 |

Assumption 1: Numbers for rest of Britain equate to the percentage of Welsh-speakers in Gwynedd (61 per cent of 3,583 = 2,186).
Assumption 2: Numbers for rest of Britain equate to the percentage of Welsh-speakers migrating to other Welsh counties (39.2 per cent of 3,583 = 1,405).
Total out-migrants under assumption 1    2,767
Total out-migrants under assumption 2    1,986
Total in-migrants                        1,327

There are further problems with the main census data in that they have only been formally published on a county basis (pre-1997). Thus, for example, the joining of Ceredigion, Llanelli and South Pembrokeshire in the county of Dyfed considerably undermines the value of the returns, almost to the point of rendering them useless for purposes of interpretation. If more spatially sensitive data are required then a special request needs to be made to the Office for National Statistics. Unfortunately, the acquisition of such information can be very costly. Here, additional data were secured, detailing migration patterns between districts and counties. Charges for a district by district matrix are excessive, so more detailed movements of population cannot be considered. In the discussion that follows, and to avoid dominance of very local movements, migration from the county in which the district is located is ignored. This approach might be questioned, but unless it is followed minor local movements, of little import for language, would swamp the larger-scale migration which is crucial to the language situation in Wales. In evaluating the resultant data it should also be noted that the in-migrants concerned were already part of the resident population for census purposes, and therefore have figured in the enumeration of numbers of Welsh-speakers. This needs to be taken into account when the pattern of migration is related to the characteristics of the *in situ* population.

Given the complexity of the matrix concerned, the simplest way to analyse the special migration statistics is to divide Wales into zones according to language status. The division is arbitrary rather than statistical, but the procedure is more useful especially as even the district level does not avoid problems related to the extent of the areas involved. Thus Montgomery reaches from the most Anglicized parts of the Welsh border across to the west coast and Welsh-speaking Wales.

The first zone includes those districts that lie within the remaining core areas of dominant Welsh speech as identified in Chapter 6. Table 7.4 provides relevant data for the two northern cores, Ynys Môn and Arfon-Dwyfor, along with Meirionnydd which forms the third core and Ceredigion together with Preseli.

**Table 7.4**
**Migration data for the districts of Welsh-speaking Wales (*Y Fro Gymraeg*)**

| District | % Welsh-speaking | % Welsh-born | Numbers of in-migrants | % from outside Wales | % in-migrants Welsh-speaking |
|---|---|---|---|---|---|
| Ynys Môn | 62.0 | 67.7 | 1726 | 88.5 | 17.3 |
| Arfon | 74.6 | 76.6 | 1183 | 82.8 | 27.6 |
| Dwyfor | 75.4 | 71.5 | 640 | 87.2 | 28.4 |
| Meirionnydd | 65.4 | 64.3 | 1026 | 78.7 | 24.1 |
| Ceredigion | 59.1 | 64.2 | 2052 | 81.2 | 21.3 |
| Preseli | 24.4 | 71.8 | 2070 | 83.3 | 8.9 |

These districts highlight the problems which have characterized the heart of Welsh-speaking Wales over recent times. One flow of in-migrants dominates all others, virtually to their exclusion. Thus, in each of the districts, except for Meirionnydd, over 80 per cent of in-migrants are seen to have been from outside Wales. No Welsh county contributed more than 10 per cent to the total flow. The highest proportions were essentially cross-border movements; thus, Clwyd contributed 7.6 per cent to Arfon, 7.4 to Ynys Môn and 6.1 per cent to Dwyfor. In these northern cores the greatest absolute numbers of in-migrants were registered by Ynys Môn, a condition reflected in the lower percentage of Welsh-speakers in the district as well as the lower proportion born in Wales. An aspect missed, because of the scale adopted for the analysis, was the process of suburbanization spreading from Bangor across the Menai Straits. There were 3,681 in-migrants from Gwynedd into Ynys Môn, but of those only 2,062 or 56 per cent spoke Welsh, well below the proportion recorded for the island. Indeed, only Dyfed, which accounted for only 27 in-migrants recorded a proportion of Welsh-speakers above that of the district, and that was only 63 per cent.

It would seem that the two districts which make up the second node in the north, Arfon and Dwyfor, have been somewhat more resilient, possibly because of a location more removed from the A55 and its particular impact. Again, however, the basic pattern is similar to that for Ynys Môn with a high degree of dominant migration from outside Wales. Again no Welsh county accounted for more than 10 per cent. In Arfon, only Clwyd with 90 movers contributed more than 5 per cent at 7.6 per cent, but of these only 57.8 per cent were Welsh-speakers, well below the district level. Dwyfor showed a similar pattern again, with 39 migrants (6.1 per cent) of whom only 48.7 per cent spoke Welsh. When local movement is considered, 3,031 from Gwynedd were recorded in Arfon, of whom 1,999 or 66 per cent spoke Welsh, whilst the figures for Dwyfor were 1,073 and 75.8 per cent. Inevitably, since these are the districts within Wales with the highest proportions of Welsh-speakers, it is likely that a lower proportion of Welsh-speaking in-migrants will be recorded. But the overall flows show a quite significant Anglicizing process. If internal movement within Gwynedd is ignored then the overall external movement into the districts returned percentages of Welsh-speakers at 17.3 per cent (Ynys Môn), 27.6 per cent (Arfon) and 28.4 per cent (Dwyfor). These are dramatically below the proportions of speakers within the districts and must inevitably have accounted for a decline in the 'Welshness' of these areas.

Meirionnydd demonstrates a pattern similar to that of Ynys Môn, again with a dominant in-migration from outside Wales. Possibly as a result of its location and extensive borders with neighbouring counties, it shows some evidence of rather greater flows from Welsh sources, with 85 or 8.3 per cent from Clwyd and 64 or 6.5 per cent from Powys. This is standard cross-border movement, but in each case the Welsh-speaking proportions, at 52.9 and 50.7 per cent respectively, are both lower than the district's 65.4 per cent. When all movements are considered the percentage of Welsh-speakers amongst these migrants was only 24.1 per cent.

Since of all the pre-1997 counties Gwynedd was the only one which bore some relation to a distinctive language area, it is worthwhile considering the data for the county as a whole. These are set out in Table 7.5. The conclusions drawn from the district data are reaffirmed. Some 80 per cent of the in-migrant flow came from outside Wales and only 16.6

per cent of the 5,060 spoke Welsh in comparison with the county's figure of 58.8 per cent. As would be expected the largest flow from within Wales came from neighbouring counties, especially Clwyd to the east with 824 or 13.1 per cent, but with only 272 or 33 per cent Welsh-speakers amongst them, and Powys with 99 of whom 45.5 per cent were Welsh-speakers. Dyfed, to the south, provided 132 but the proportion of Welsh-speakers was 61.4 per cent, higher than the proportion in Gwynedd itself. However, only South Glamorgan out of the other counties provided an equally high percentage of Welsh-speakers, though only a small number. The proportion amongst all in-migrants was a mere 21.1 per cent.

**Table 7.5**
**In-migration to Gwynedd, 1990–1991**

| Source of migrants | Numbers of in-migrants | % of migrants | Numbers Welsh-speaking | % Welsh-speaking |
|---|---|---|---|---|
| Clwyd | 824 | 13.1 | 272 | 33.0 |
| Dyfed | 132 | 2.1 | 81 | 61.4 |
| Gwent | 15 | 0.2 | 4 | 26.7 |
| Mid Glamorgan | 33 | 0.5 | 15 | 45.5 |
| Powys | 99 | 1.6 | 45 | 45.5 |
| South Glamorgan | 95 | 1.5 | 58 | 61.1 |
| West Glamorgan | 34 | 0.5 | 12 | 35.3 |
| Outside Wales | 5060 | 80.4 | 840 | 16.6 |
| **Totals** | **6292** | **100** | **1327** | **21.1** |

Although analysis is confounded by the statistical limitations already noted, it is appropriate to consider patterns of out-migration for Gwynedd. As Table 7.6 shows the dominant outflow, some 3,853 or 72.2 per cent was to areas outside Wales. Unfortunately it is not known how many of these were Welsh-speakers. The main destination within Wales was Clwyd, again a neighbouring county. But it is especially worth noting that 149 moved to South Glamorgan, 103 to Cardiff and 46 to the Vale of Glamorgan. This gives some indication of the attraction of the capital and its hinterland – a movement the significance of which has already been highlighted.

**Table 7.6**
**Out-migration from Gwynedd 1990–1991**

| Destination of out-migrants | Numbers of out-migrants | % of out-migrants | Numbers Welsh-speaking | % Welsh-speaking |
|---|---|---|---|---|
| Clwyd | 963 | 18.1 | 314 | 32.0 |
| Dyfed | 161 | 3.0 | 85 | 52.8 |
| Gwent | 36 | 0.7 | 10 | 27.8 |
| Mid Glamorgan | 36 | 0.7 | 18 | 50.0 |
| Powys | 104 | 1.9 | 50 | 48.1 |

(Table 7.6 continued)

| Destination of out-migrants | Numbers of out-migrants | % of out-migrants | Numbers Welsh-speaking | % Welsh-speaking |
|---|---|---|---|---|
| South Glamorgan | 149 | 2.8 | 90 | 60.4 |
| West Glamorgan | 33 | 0.6 | 14 | 42.4 |
| Rest of UK | 3853 | 72.2 | ?? | ?? |
| **Totals** | **5335** | **100** | **??** | **??** |

These county-level data draw attention to the same crucial issue as did those for the districts. There is a two-pronged problem for language maintenance. The first is a clear loss of Welsh-speakers through out-migration, a loss compounded by the predominance in the inflow of non-Welsh-speakers, both from outside and inside Wales.

The southern part of *Y Fro Gymraeg*, south of the Dyfi estuary, is made up of Ceredigion, but it extends also into the northern part of Preseli, Pembrokeshire. Unfortunately the district boundary does not coincide with the Landsker, the historical boundary between Welsh- and English-speaking Pembrokeshire, but in spite of that the district is joined with Ceredigion in this analysis. From the data in Table 7.4 a clear parallel between Ceredigion and Meirionnydd is evident. It is possible that the somewhat lower proportion of Welsh-speakers in Ceredigion at 59.1 per cent can be related to the higher total of in-migrants from outside Wales at 1,667 or 81.2 per cent of the total. But given the contrast in populations, 63,940 in Ceredigion as against 33,583 in Meirionnydd, then the totals, like the proportions, are more in line with each other. It is also significant that both districts lost population by an excess of deaths over births, to the extent of -2.3 per cent in Ceredigion and -3.3 per cent in Meirionnydd over the decade. There is no way of knowing whether or not that loss had any effect on language, although all the evidence suggests that the elderly were more likely to be Welsh-speakers. Even so, the situation in terms of natural processes made the impact of migration all the more pertinent. If the migration from outside Wales into Ceredigion for the one year of the census migration table is extrapolated to the decade of the population figures, then a total of 16,670 would represent an increase on the 1981 population of the district of some 29 per cent. While such a calculation is statistically questionable, it serves to indicate the very considerable impact which this migration process possibly had on the decrease of the proportion speaking Welsh in Ceredigion from 65.5 per cent in 1981 to 59.1 per cent in 1991. It also accounts for the relatively low proportion who were Welsh-born (64.2 per cent ). The percentage of Welsh-speakers amongst all in-migrants was 21.3, with only Ynys Môn of the districts analysed showing a lower percentage of Welsh-speaking in-migrants. Little can be added in regard to Preseli for the reasons stated, but the high number from outside Wales, together with the very low proportion of Welsh-speakers, a mere 8.9 per cent, testify to the same processes at work.

Despite deficiencies in the quality of available data, as far as the districts which make up 'Welsh Wales' are concerned, the general conclusion is very evident and beyond challenge, that the heartland of the Welsh language was being discernibly weakened by the movement into the area of non-Welsh-speaking populations from outside the country. If the numbers of in-migrants from outside Wales in the districts are added together then for the one year 1990–91 some 7,262 moved into these parts of Wales. If the admittedly unacceptable procedure of extrapolating this figure for the decade is followed then the total for the decade is 72,620, a figure higher than that of the populations of any of the districts. Only 14.8 per cent spoke Welsh. If the border area of Preseli is taken out then the 1990–91 figure is 5,538 giving a decadal total of 55,380, out of which some 955 or only 17.2 per cent spoke Welsh.

From a review of the heartland of the language it is appropriate to move to consider the area where Welsh-speaking proportions are lowest, that is the borderland or marchland zone (Table 7.7). Here difficulties again arise because of the internal linguistic diversity that characterizes the areas concerned. Thus, the district of Montgomery includes at one extreme wards such as Glantwymyn where 71.2 per cent spoke Welsh, and at the other Churchstoke where the proportion was 4.6 per cent. Brecknock, though not to the same extent, presents similar problems. Moreover, it includes part of the northern fringes of the western coalfield. The true marcher lands extended along the south coast and, therefore, the Vale of Glamorgan is included in this group although its relation to Cardiff creates very different conditions. Gower, unfortunately is part of the district of Swansea, but south Pembrokeshire is appropriately added.

**Table 7.7**
**Migration data for borderland and marcher districts.**

| District | %<br>Welsh-speaking | % born<br>outside Wales | Migrants from<br>outside Wales | % of migrants<br>from outside Wales | % of in-migrants<br>Welsh-speaking |
|---|---|---|---|---|---|
| Rhuddlan | 16.2 | 51.3 | 1222 | 90.7 | 7.2 |
| Delyn | 17.8 | 60.9 | 1332 | 93.3 | 9.6 |
| Alyn and Deeside | 9.6 | 45.7 | 1708 | 94.2 | 5.8 |
| Wrexham | 13.4 | 74.2 | 1552 | 90.0 | 8.3 |
| Montgomery | 23.3 | 56.4 | 1288 | 82.4 | 15.4 |
| Radnor | 8.3 | 51.1 | 715 | 85.0 | 6.2 |
| Brecknock | 23.0 | 71.2 | 1094 | 70.2 | 11.0 |
| Monmouth | 2.0 | 61.3 | 1952 | 82.1 | 2.7 |
| Vale of Glamorgan | 6.8 | 75.9 | 2607 | 78.5 | 5.6 |
| South Pembrokeshire | 8.2 | 66.3 | 894 | 80.1 | 4.7 |

All these districts show similar features, the exceptions being Montgomery and Brecknock due to their size and articulation across the east–west language gradient. They all show low percentages of Welsh-speakers and generally, though not universally, low proportions born in Wales. There is an overwhelming predominance of in-migrants from outside Wales, the consequence of an expected cross-border shift. It is significant that every district, with the exception of Monmouth, shows an in-migrant flow where the proportion speaking Welsh was lower than that for the district. It would seem, therefore, that any language regeneration which has taken place in these areas is due to internal change rather than to incoming populations. There would appear to be little impact of movement from the more Welsh-speaking areas. Thus, in Alyn and Deeside, of the 1,814 in-migrants 1,708 came from outside Wales, with only 75 from Gwynedd and no other county contributing more than 10. Even then only 28 or 38.4 per cent of the Gwynedd movers spoke Welsh. All the evidence seems to suggest that there was only very limited north–south movement in Wales and the dominant flows were east–west. What is notable is that there is apparently little evidence of distance decay in the migratory pattern. True, the districts of the north-east show greater proportions from outside Wales, but the differences are slight and Ynys Môn returns greater proportions and greater numbers than most of the border districts. This emphasizes the reach of migration into the Welsh-speaking heartland.

The third zone to be considered is somewhat ragged and ill-defined, largely again because of the configuration of the districts (Table 7.8). Thus, Dinefwr which is included takes in the northern part of what once would have been called the anthracite coalfield and which forms part of the fifth Welsh-speaking node earlier identified, the section of the Tywi valley which forms the break between that area and the rural node of Ceredigion and, indeed, part of the southern margins of that node itself. Clearly, against such variety general conclusions are difficult to abstract. But the area generally can be seen as an intermediate one which constitutes the transition between the heartland and the border country. Since the language itself is characterized by a sharp gradient of change across what is often very thinly peopled upland, there is little relation between the language transition and the districts. Properly this area should include parts of Montgomery and Brecknock, but for reasons already adduced these have been treated elsewhere.

**Table 7.8**
**Migration characteristics of districts along the language transition**

| District | % Welsh-speaking | % Welsh-born | Number of in-migrants outside Wales | % from outside Wales | % of migrants Welsh-speaking |
|---|---|---|---|---|---|
| Aberconwy | 36.0 | 57.4 | 1189 | 69.3 | 15.8 |
| Colwyn | 25.5 | 49.9 | 1238 | 67.8 | 12.6 |
| Glyndŵr | 39.9 | 65.3 | 762 | 83.3 | 20.0 |
| Dinefwr | 66.5 | 79.2 | 579 | 63.1 | 26.0 |
| Carmarthen | 58.0 | 75.6 | 907 | 72.0 | 20.5 |

As might be expected, there is considerable variation within this group of areas as shown in Table 7.8, but there are also a number of common characteristics. The first is the intermediate status of the language as denoted by the Welsh-speaking proportions, although Dinefwr for the reasons noted above returns a higher figure. The proportion of Welsh-born varies considerably, the very low figure for Colwyn probably being a result of the influence of the coastal resorts and retirement, although the proportion of migrants from outside Wales is not as high as might be expected due to some 30.8 per cent coming from Gwynedd. However, the high number confirms the significance of inward movement from outside Wales, as does the low percentage of Welsh-speakers amongst them. In all cases the Welsh-speaking percentage amongst migrants is considerably lower than that in the districts themselves. Given the unsatisfactory nature of the area identified it is difficult to generalize, but certainly all the evidence suggests that the long-standing language frontier between 'Welsh Wales' and Anglicized Wales is being pushed westward by the streams of in-migrant flows. Thus if Glyndŵr is taken as an example, the predominant flow within Wales was from Gwynedd with 86 movers of whom 51 or 59.3 per cent spoke Welsh, a figure considerably higher than the district's 39.9 per cent. The next highest flow was from Powys with a total of 27, with 16 speaking Welsh, oddly providing the same percentage of 59.3 as for Gwynedd. Indeed all the Welsh counties provided proportions of Welsh-speakers in excess of the district's figure, apart from Gwent which provided no migrants at all. But all these were swamped by the 762 from outside Wales of whom only 94, or 12.3 per cent, spoke the language. This meant that the overall figure for migrants was reduced to 20 per cent. This seems to be the universal feature all along this transitional zone.

The next zone to be considered is that of the old industrial areas of south Wales. There is no need for an extensive review of the data set out in Table 7.9 since they suggest that migration does not play a large part in language change in these areas. There is the evident increase of Welsh speech from east to west, and a contrast in that in the eastern valleys the proportion of Welsh-speakers amongst the in-migrants is higher than that of the districts themselves, so that there is some indication of the language advance in these highly Anglicized parts. Elsewhere the opposite holds. However, Taff-Ely is an exception, no doubt because of the suburban extension of Cardiff. But the most significant features are the low numbers of movers from outside Wales which is reflected in the high proportions born in Wales, everywhere near 90 per cent, and reaching 93 per cent in the Rhondda. In short, there is no attraction to migrants in these declining industrial areas of high unemployment. At the 1991 census Rhondda, with 15.4 per cent unemployed, recorded the highest district figure for Wales followed by Cynon Valley at 14.5 per cent. There were minor exceptions. Ogwr, which extends south to take in Bridgend, with its newer industries, and part of the western Vale of Glamorgan, recorded a much higher number of in-migrants and the lowest proportion of Welsh-born, but generally its pattern is similar to the rest of the area.

To complete the picture reference must be made to the three large urban agglomerations of south Wales (Table 7.10). At first sight there seems little justification for isolating these three towns. Newport certainly would not look out of place with the groups of 'Eastern valleys' districts detailed above. It does, however, show a greater number of in-migrants, a lower proportion Welsh born and the lowest proportion of Welsh-speaking in-migrants of

**Table 7.9**
**Migration characteristics of southern coalfield districts**

| District | %<br>Welsh-speaking | %<br>Welsh-born | Number of<br>in-migrants from<br>outside Wales | % from<br>outside Wales | % of migrants<br>Welsh-speaking |
|---|---|---|---|---|---|
| EASTERN VALLEYS | | | | | |
| Blaenau Gwent | 2.3 | 91.8 | 752 | 63.0 | 3.5 |
| Islwyn | 3.4 | 91.1 | 387 | 49.1 | 4.4 |
| Torfaen | 2.5 | 85.1 | 700 | 71.8 | 3.7 |
| CENTRAL VALLEYS | | | | | |
| Cynon Valley | 9.5 | 91.0 | 404 | 56.5 | 6.2 |
| Merthyr Tydfil | 7.5 | 92.0 | 381 | 63.2 | 5.0 |
| Rhondda | 8.2 | 93.8 | 389 | 64.2 | 5.8 |
| Rhymney Valley | 7.6 | 90.0 | 688 | 43.6 | 6.1 |
| Taff-Ely | 9.7 | 87.7 | 865 | 47.2 | 9.8 |
| Ogwr | 8.3 | 84.8 | 1351 | 59.8 | 7.4 |
| WESTERN VALLEYS | | | | | |
| Port Talbot | 8.6 | 91.7 | 311 | 54.4 | 7.7 |
| Neath | 13.0 | 90.6 | 447 | 58.5 | 10.0 |
| WESTERN NODE | | | | | |
| Lliw Valley | 36.9 | 87.2 | 589 | 53.4 | 24.1 |
| Llanelli | 46.5 | 87.7 | 715 | 61.1 | 21.0 |

all the districts. Perhaps the closest association is with Monmouth as part of the border country. Swansea, again, is similar to the 'Western valleys' grouping, but with a much larger number of in-migrants and a significantly higher percentage from outside Wales. The gravitational attraction of the second largest town in Wales is apparent, but flows into the area are evidently affected by its less accessible western location. Cardiff, however, is clearly different. The capital city is also seen to have attracted large numbers of in-migrants, but in this case a surprisingly low proportion are from outside Wales. As might be anticipated, the greatest numbers were from the neighbouring counties, especially Mid Glamorgan with 1,388 or 17.3 per cent. But Dyfed accounted for 338 and Gwynedd for 103. Most significantly, all the counties, with the exception of Gwent, returned proportions of Welsh-speakers amongst the migrants higher than that for Cardiff itself. Thus, of the migrants from Dyfed 139 or 41.1 per cent spoke Welsh, and 76 or 73.8 per cent from Gwynedd. These offset the low proportion of 4.4 per cent of the migrants from outside Wales. Here then is the direct evidence of that move of Welsh-speakers from the language heartland which has been such a distinctive feature of the capital city over recent decades.

Although offering only a 'snapshot' insight, the data presented in Tables 7.4 to 7.10 confirm the significant impact of migration from outside Wales upon the language. The impact manifests itself in a pushing back of the frontier between 'Welsh Wales' and Anglicized Wales on the one hand, and in serious disruptions to the integrity of the

**Table 7.10**
**Migrants characteristics of three south Wales urban agglomerations**

| District | % Welsh-speaking | % Welsh-born | Number of migrants from outside Wales | % of migrants from outside Wales | % of migrants Welsh-speaking |
|---|---|---|---|---|---|
| Newport | 2.3 | 81.1 | 1591 | 71.5 | 1.9 |
| Cardiff | 6.4 | 79.2 | 5244 | 65.5 | 8.6 |
| Swansea | 10.0 | 82.3 | 2798 | 76.9 | 8.5 |

heartland on the other. Unfortunately, the full net effect of migration cannot be assessed since Welsh speech is not recorded outside Wales. Elsewhere migration has little effect since attractions are limited, the only exception being the M4 corridor to Bridgend. The one exception is Cardiff where in-flows of Welsh-speakers have contributed to the growing strength of the language within the city and its immediate environs. Perhaps it is worth adding here that South Glamorgan records the lowest percentage of migrants within households over the age of 65, at some 3.2 per cent, as against the highest proportions for Gwynedd at 8.6 per cent and Dyfed at 7.6 per cent. The movement to South Glamorgan, or Cardiff which is its main constituent, is of young, active populations. It is this young migrant population which has provided the dynamic for the language in the capital city.

**Social Status**

As Giggs and Pattie (1992a and 1992b) have noted in their critical analyses of Welsh identity, Wales has long been a plural society composed of distinct ethnic and linguistic groupings. A feature of this plurality, and one that has attracted considerable, and often contentious, debate are the profound shifts in socio-economic status that these various groupings have experienced over time, and the tensions that have been generated as a consequence. An academic question that can be asked is whether or not in contemporary Wales a cultural division of labour can be said to apply, with the three main ethno-linguistic communities – bilingual Welsh, Anglo-Welsh and incomers born outside of Wales – being characterized by differing class profiles.

Such matters have never been easy to address, not least because of the limited availability of objective information. All too often the quality of argument has been diminished by the partial and frequently anecdotal nature of the supporting evidence. In this regard the special SARs data (Chapter 2) that have been made available since the initial publication of the basic census information are particularly helpful for they allow a more detailed examination of the relationship between language and social class divisions in Wales.

The SARs data set for the sample of individuals contains information on 11,152 Welsh-speakers (for convenience, 'speakers' also include those individuals who claimed that they could read and/or write Welsh but did not actually speak it), and 44,574 non-Welsh-speakers. These main groups can be further disaggregated on the basis of other variables, including social class attributes. It is to be appreciated that the SARs are sample statistics, and like all samples have certain built-in errors (sampling errors). These are important for they can affect the interpretation of data and the statistical validity of conclusions (e.g., concerning the significance of differences between sets of percentages). Accordingly, for purposes of reference, ranges of standard errors are included with the various tabulations that are presented here.

The concept of social class is difficult to define in operational terms, and over the years various categorizations have been proposed. For the 1991 census the Office for Population Censuses and Surveys (as it then was) designed its own classification based on the occupations of individuals. Although regarded by some as deficient, it does serve to distinguish broad class variations within the economically active population. Table 7.11 identifies an ordered set of six class categories, and records the proportions of Welsh- and non-Welsh-speakers within each.

**Table 7.11**
**Social class: Welsh-speaking and non-Welsh-speaking population**

| Class | % Employed | |
|---|---|---|
| | Welsh-speakers | Non-Welsh-speakers |
| Professional | 3.5 | 3.4 |
| Managerial/technical | 31.6 | 23.9 |
| Skilled: non-manual | 21.2 | 22.0 |
| Skilled: manual | 20.1 | 23.1 |
| Part-skilled | 16.9 | 19.4 |
| Unskilled | 6.7 | 8.1 |

*Unadjusted standard errors for the percentages in this tabulation range between 0.54 per cent and 1.33 per cent.

The results are revealing for they show that, contrary to certain opinion, a relatively high proportion of the Welsh-speaking workforce in Wales (35 per cent) is engaged in professional or managerial/technical occupations. This compares with an equivalent figure of 27 per cent for non-Welsh-speakers. Thus, at a national level it would appear that Welsh bilinguals have a stronger representation in the higher social classes than English monolinguals. The difference between the two sets of percentages, which can be shown to be statistically significant, suggests that facility in the Welsh language could be instrumental in securing higher class locations. This confirms the findings of the local surveys discussed in Chapter 5 and is contrary to the once widely held belief that an ability to speak Welsh is of limited consequence (even a hindrance) in terms of social and economic advancement.

Further insights into ethno-linguistic differences can be gained through the division of the non-Welsh-speaking category into two subgroups, distinguishing those born in Wales (Anglo-Welsh) and those born outside Wales. This classification is helpful since it addresses in part the frequently encountered assertion that it is incomers who have gained control of the most prominent class locations, to the detriment of indigenous (especially Welsh-speaking) sectors of the population. That said, it should be stressed that to regard non-Welsh-speakers born outside Wales as 'incomers' is, for the purposes of the immediate debate, rather crude. This is largely because the category is too broad, and cannot be deemed to distinguish those in the population who have entered Wales relatively recently as a career move, and who might be described as 'upwardly mobile' (spiralists). It is to such a socio-economic grouping that the arguments relating to a cultural division of labour directly apply. Whilst this is the case the category does serve a purpose, and allows general patterns to be discerned.

Thus, it is evident from Table 7.12 that as a group non-Welsh-speaking incomers tend to have a much stronger representation in the higher social classes than both Welsh-speakers and, most certainly, indigenous non-Welsh-speakers. The statistics could clearly be used to support the notion that a cultural division of labour does indeed apply in Wales. That said, the data also show that the most disadvantaged section of Welsh society is not so much the Welsh-speaking community (as is frequently argued) but the Anglo-Welsh. The Anglo-Welsh would appear to be doubly disadvantaged. On the one hand they cannot compete for often high-level positions in which an ability to speak Welsh is either a necessity or a distinct asset; on the other, even where the language is not an issue, they have to face strong competition from both incomers and indigenous Welsh-speakers.

Table 7.12 shows that nearly 39 per cent of non-Welsh-speaking incomers belong to the top two social classes, compared with 35 per cent for Welsh-speakers and a mere 22 per cent for the Anglo-Welsh. This last grouping is seen to contain relatively high proportions of skilled manual, part-skilled and unskilled workers. Although percentages are only small, it is noteworthy that the proportion of the active population classed as professional in the incomers category was nearly double that for Welsh-speakers and treble that for the Anglo-Welsh.

Academic discussions pertaining to the cultural division of labour have in the main failed to highlight the fact that situations can vary from region to region. Thus, particular ethno-linguistic groups may be disadvantaged in one area but favoured in another. This is certainly the case in Wales. As Aitchison and Carter have argued elsewhere (1987) there are marked differences in the socio-economic positions of Welsh-speakers in rural areas, as opposed to those in the more dynamic urban centres of Wales. To illustrate this, albeit at a crude county level, Table 7.13 records within-group proportions in each of three categories of social class. The 'upper' class category includes professional and managerial/technical employees, the 'middle' category refers to skilled manual and non-manual workers, while

**Table 7.12**

| Social Classes | % Employed Ethno-linguistic groups | | |
|---|---|---|---|
| | W | AW | NW |
| Professional | 3.5 | 2.2 | 6.2 |
| Managerial/technical | 31.6 | 20.1 | 32.6 |
| Skilled: non-manual | 21.2 | 22.1 | 21.7 |
| Skilled: manual | 20.1 | 25.2 | 18.3 |
| Part-skilled | 16.9 | 21.1 | 15.7 |
| Unskilled | 6.7 | 9.3 | 5.5 |

*Key:* W: Welsh-speakers; AW: Anglo-Welsh; NW: Non-Welsh-speakers born outside Wales. Unadjusted standard errors for percentages in this tabulation range between 0.67 per cent and 1.33 per cent.

the 'lower' grouping includes those who are part-skilled or unskilled. Although the data need to be treated circumspectly because of the small size of the samples for certain cells in the tabulation, they draw attention to interesting regional variations in class profiles. They show, for instance, that in four counties – Gwent, South Glamorgan, Mid Glamorgan (especially Taff Ely) and Clwyd – there is a stronger relative representation of the upper class locations within the Welsh-speaking category than each of the other two categories. This would appear to underline the importance of the growth in job opportunities for bilinguals in the more vibrant regions of Wales. Ironically, and as has already been noted in previous chapters, it is in these long-Anglicized areas that the language is now gaining ground – a development that is not unrelated to the expansion of employment in local authorities and other public services. The associated establishment of Welsh-medium primary and secondary schools in these borderland and more urbanized environments is a further manifestation of the prevailing social trends.

An equally pertinent insight that emerges from Table 7.13 is the fact that in the main heartland regions of the Welsh language, it is non-Welsh-speaking incomers who have the highest representation of upper class locations. In Dyfed, Gwynedd and West Glamorgan nearly 40 per cent of this group are in professional or managerial/technical positions. Equivalent figures for Welsh-speaking sectors of the population range from 29 per cent in Gwynedd to 34 per cent in Dyfed. It is in these fragile rural areas and the declining industrial region of West Glamorgan, if anywhere, that Hechter's concept of the cultural division of labour applies.

Finally it can be noted that in all counties it is the Anglo-Welsh that have the lowest proportionate representations in the upper class category. Here proportions range between just 20 per cent and 25 per cent.

Although only based on simple categorizations, the results presented in Table 7.13 would suggest that the general thesis proposing a close relationship between language and

**Table 7.13**

| | | Upper | | | Ethno-linguistic groups<br>% employed<br>Middle | | | Lower | |
|---|---|---|---|---|---|---|---|---|---|
| Counties | W | AW | NW | W | AW | NW | W | AW | NW |
| Clwyd | 35 | 20 | 34 | 43 | 48 | 43 | 21 | 32 | 23 |
| Dyfed | 34 | 25 | 41 | 41 | 45 | 37 | 25 | 30 | 22 |
| Gwent | 54 | 22 | 41 | 34 | 46 | 41 | 12 | 33 | 18 |
| Gwynedd | 29 | 22 | 41 | 42 | 50 | 38 | 29 | 28 | 22 |
| Mid Glamorgan | 40 | 20 | 35 | 41 | 48 | 42 | 19 | 32 | 24 |
| Powys | 38 | 33 | 39 | 36 | 41 | 38 | 26 | 26 | 23 |
| South Glamorgan | 53 | 27 | 44 | 37 | 50 | 38 | 10 | 24 | 18 |
| West Glamorgan | 36 | 20 | 39 | 42 | 48 | 38 | 23 | 32 | 23 |

*Key:* W: Welsh-speakers; AW: Anglo-Welsh; NW: Non-Welsh-speakers born outside of Wales.
Unadjusted standard errors for percentages in this tabulation range between 1.08 per cent and
8.12 per cent.

social class, with Welsh-speakers tending to occupy more lowly locations, is far too
simplistic and requires a number of qualifications. Not least among these is the fact that the
situation varies regionally. In this regard the contrast between the emerging Welsh-
speaking areas (Outer Wales) and the traditional core zones (Inner Wales) is particularly
striking. They are differing realms – the one belongs to the dynamic postmodern urban
world, the other to a remoter but increasingly exposed hinterland where economic opportunities are that much more constrained, and where competition from incomers has had a
considerable impact. As in the past, when the rural heartland served as a labour reservoir
for the coalfields and metal-working industries, so now these same areas help prepare a
well-educated, aspiring and bilingual workforce for the transactional cities and towns of
the south and east. Perhaps the reversal of the Hechter model implied by these trends marks
a critical and formative stage in the rehabilitation of the language in areas from which it
has long been disinherited. For mobile Welsh-speaking spiralists the future seems that
much brighter. But in all this, what of the Anglo-Welsh – the disadvantaged majority? As
Giggs and Pattie have also demonstrated (1992), and as the data presented here reaffirm,
the plural society that defines Wales is characterized by sharp inequalities of opportunity.

## Household Structures

Of all the domains that are central to the maintenance and reproduction of language none is
more critical than that of the family – the hearth around which discourse takes place and
socialization is nurtured. Any evaluation of the condition and vitality of a language must
therefore accord special attention to the home environment.

The SARs data for Wales contain information on 10,939 households. The enumerated resident population for this 1 per cent sample is 27,752. This figure includes those household residents who were present for the census as well as those who happened to be absent, but were normally resident in the household. Within the household SARs, of those persons aged 3 years and over, 20 per cent claimed that they had some knowledge of the Welsh language. Of that group the great majority (69 per cent) could speak, read and write the language (i.e. were fully literate), while 17 per cent indicated that they could only speak it. The rest could either speak and read, speak and write, or simply read and write Welsh. Taking account of sampling errors, these sample percentages broadly mirror those recorded in the full population census of 1991. For simplicity these various literacy classes can be collectively defined as a Welsh-speaking sub-population.

In summarizing the character of Welsh-speaking households it is convenient and meaningful to identify a nested hierarchy of types. The classification presented here recognizes four main types, some of which contain sub-categories (see Table 7.16). At the most general level a basic distinction can be drawn between those households that have *at least* one Welsh-speaker (henceforth referred to as 'Welsh-speaking' households), and those that have no Welsh-speakers (Types 1(i) and 1(ii)). The SARs suggest that some 26 per cent of all households in Wales fall into the first of these two types. While this figure is greater than that for individuals who speak Welsh (20 per cent), Table 7.14 indicates that just over half of these households (51 per cent) have just one Welsh-speaker within them. This is a very high ratio and is clearly of significance for the long-term well-being of the language; in less than half of Welsh-speaking households are household members able to communicate through the medium of Welsh within the home environment. Thus, it would appear that, nationally, one of the most crucial domains for the promotion of the language is strongly circumscribed. It should be added that households with a single Welsh-speaker account for 28 per cent of the total Welsh-speaking population, and that of these nearly 37 per cent are over 65 years of age. Many such households are single-person households (see below). Table 7.14 shows that households with two Welsh-speakers account for 28 per cent of the sample.

**Table 7.14**

| Number of Welsh-speakers in household | Households with Welsh-speakers | |
|---|---|---|
| | Number | % |
| 1 | 1472 | 50.9 |
| 2 | 802 | 27.8 |
| 3 | 335 | 11.6 |
| 4 | 193 | 6.7 |
| 5 and over | 85 | 3.0 |

Having identified this initial broad category of Welsh-speaking households, it is possible to consider the degree to which such households are *wholly* or *partly* Welsh-speaking (i.e. where all or only some of the residents are Welsh-speaking) – Types 2(i) and 2(ii) in Table 7.16. The percentages are again revealing. The data indicate that only 14 per cent of households in Wales are wholly Welsh-speaking; a further 12 per cent are linguistically mixed, but have at least one Welsh-speaker. Table 7.15 summarizes this situation by relating the number of residents within households to the number of Welsh-speakers. A key feature of this matrix are the ratios recorded in its main diagonal. They indicate the proportion of households within the specified size groups for Welsh-speakers where all members of the household are able to speak the language. Thus, it can be seen that nearly 42 per cent of those households with only one Welsh-speaker are actually single-person households (i.e. there is only one resident in the household, and that resident is enumerated as being Welsh-speaking); it follows that the remaining 58 per cent of households with one Welsh-speaker are households with two or more residents. As might be expected, the proportion of Welsh-speaking households that are wholly Welsh-speaking increases with the size of the household. The tabulation shows for instance that 81 per cent of households with four Welsh-speakers are wholly Welsh-speaking; for those with five or more the figure is 100 per cent. Such households clearly provide an environment in which the language can be more effectively nurtured.

**Table 7.15**
**Relationship between numbers of persons within households and numbers of Welsh-speakers**[*]

| Total persons in households | Total number of Welsh-speakers in households (% of households) | | | | | |
|---|---|---|---|---|---|---|
| | 0 | 1 | 2 | 3 | 4 | 5+ |
| 1 | 26.5 | 41.8 | | | | |
| 2 | 37.6 | 29.0 | 61.3 | | | |
| 3 | 17.2 | 14.7 | 15.0 | 59.4 | | |
| 4 | 13.0 | 10.5 | 18.8 | 29.3 | 81.3 | |
| 5 and over | 5.7 | 4.0 | 4.9 | 11.3 | 18.7 | 100.0 |

[*] Column percentages sum to 100 and record proportions of households within particular size categories for Welsh-speakers.

The group of households that are wholly Welsh-speaking can be further sub-divided into those *with* and those *without* children (aged 3–17 years) – Types 3a(i) and 3b(ii) in Table 7.16. The picture that emerges here is again rather disconcerting for the language. Thus, the statistics indicate that only 3 per cent of all households in Wales are wholly Welsh-speaking

**Table 7.16**
**Language attributes and household types**

|  | % Households within type group |
|---|---|
| **Type 1** |  |
| (i) Households without Welsh-speakers | 73.6 |
| (ii) Households with Welsh-speaker(s) | 26.4 |
| **Type 2** |  |
| Households with Welsh-speakers: |  |
| (i) Households wholly Welsh-speaking | 53.6 |
| (ii) Households partly Welsh-speaking | 46.4 |
| **Type 3** |  |
| (a) Households wholly Welsh-speaking: |  |
| (i)With children | 10.9 |
| (ii) Without children | 42.7 |
| (b) Households partly Welsh-speaking: |  |
| (i) With Welsh-speaking children | 18.9 |
| (ii) With non-Welsh-speaking children | 5.8 |
| (iii) Without children | 21.7 |
| **Type 4** |  |
| Households wholly Welsh-speaking: |  |
| (i) With children | 10.9 |
| (ii) Single person households (Welsh-speaking) | 21.3 |
| (iii) Without children – more than 1 Welsh-speaker | 21.5 |
| Households partly Welsh-speaking: |  |
| (a) Households with Welsh-speaking children |  |
| (i) Single Welsh-speaker | 6.2 |
| (ii)More than 1 Welsh-speaker | 12.7 |
| (b) Households without Welsh-speaking children: |  |
| (i) Single Welsh-speaker | 4.9 |
| (ii) More than 1 Welsh-speaker | 0.9 |
| (c) Households without children: |  |
| (i) Single Welsh-speaker | 18.6 |
| (ii) More than 1 Welsh-speaker | 3.1 |

and have children. The vast majority of households that are *wholly* Welsh-speaking (80 per cent) are without children. Also significant is the fact that almost a half of the fully Welsh-speaking households without children are single-person households (Type 4(ii)).

A similar pattern is displayed when consideration is given to the *partly* Welsh-speaking households. Of these nearly two-thirds (64 per cent) have just a single Welsh-speaker (Types 4a(i), 4b(i) and 4c(i)), the majority of whom are in households that have no children. While this is the case, it is noteworthy that 41 per cent of households that are partly Welsh-speaking have one or more children that are able to speak Welsh (Table 7.16).

## Heads of Households and Spouses

In exploring relationships between household structures and language it is pertinent to consider the attributes of heads of households and spouses (including cohabitees). As dominant forces within the household their attitudes and abilities in regard to the use of Welsh will strongly determine the language of the home. Again a hierarchical classification can be adopted which summarizes the situation within Welsh-speaking households.

Once more a primary distinction can be drawn between those households where the head of household is able to speak the language and those where this does not apply. As Table 7.17 shows nearly 70 per cent of all Welsh-speaking households fall into the first of these categories. Such households can be further disaggregated by distinguishing the language characteristics of spouses and cohabitees (if any). Of all Welsh-speaking households nearly 28 per cent have heads of household and spouses (cohabitees) who are both able to speak Welsh (Type 2a(i)). These households account for 7 per cent of all households in Wales. Household types 2a(ii) and 2b(i) identify households where the head and the spouse differ in their ability to speak Welsh. Together these comprise nearly 27 per cent of all Welsh-speaking households. Such a high figure clearly has implications in terms of language transmission within the home. The fact that in a further 12 per cent of households neither the head nor the spouse/cohabitee speaks the language (but at least one other member of the household does) exacerbates the situation considerably (Type 2b(ii)).

Table 7.17 also confirms that a very high proportion of Welsh-speaking households (30 per cent) have heads who are able to speak Welsh, but where there are no recorded spouses/cohabitees (Type 2a(iii)). This is an extremely high ratio and serves to reaffirm the strong preponderance of single-person, and mainly elderly, households among the Welsh-speaking population. Nearly 72 per cent of these households are of this latter type.

An overarching conclusion to be drawn from this set of household analyses is that an extremely high proportion of Welsh-speakers are linguistically isolated within their home environments. Some 28 per cent of Welsh-speakers either live alone or are the only members of their household able to speak the language. Just over half of all households have only one Welsh-speaker. Significantly, 70 per cent of the Welsh-speaking households have no Welsh-speaking children within them. Furthermore in a very high proportion of Welsh-speaking households the head and/or the spouse do(es) not speak Welsh. In general

**Table 7.17**
**Language attributes of heads of households and spouses (cohabitees)**
**in Welsh-speaking households**

|  | %<br>Within type<br>Group | %<br>Welsh-speaking<br>Households |
|---|---|---|
| **Type 1** |  |  |
| (i) Head of household Welsh-speaking | 69.9 | 69.9 |
| (ii) Head of household non-Welsh-speaking | 30.1 | 30.1 |
|  |  |  |
| **Type 2** |  |  |
| (a) Head of household Welsh-speaking |  |  |
| (i) Spouse/cohabitee Welsh-speaking | 39.4 | 27.5 |
| (ii) Spouse/cohabitee non-Welsh-speaking | 17.6 | 12.3 |
| (iii) No spouse/cohabitee | 42.9 | 30.0 |
|  |  |  |
| **Type 3** |  |  |
| (b) Head of household non-Welsh-speaking |  |  |
| (i) Spouse/cohabitee Welsh-speaking | 47.2 | 14.2 |
| (ii) Spouse/cohabitee non-Welsh-speaking | 40.4 | 12.2 |
| (iii) No spouse/cohabitee | 12.4 | 3.7 |

the data would suggest that the potential for language reproduction within the domain of the home is severely constrained. It is for this reason that the major efforts made over recent times to extend teaching and learning opportunities at all levels are so crucial. Developments within the domain of education seek to redress the balance and to compensate for limitations within the domain of the home (see Chapter 8).

While the current domestic situation in regard to the language is problematic it could be viewed as an essentially short-term structural condition, reflecting in the main the current age-profile of the Welsh-speaking population. Despite the surge in numbers of young Welsh-speakers over the past decade in particular, a relatively high proportion of Welsh-speakers are elderly. Within the household population, for example, nearly 19 per cent are over 65 years of age. Furthermore, many of these live in single-person households. However, given that the proportions of Welsh-speakers within younger age groups are well above average, and growing, the future looks more promising. Of course the likely degree of commitment to the language amongst the young, especially once they have left the school environment and established their own homes, is another matter. But statistically at least there can be little doubt that there will be an improvement in the situation over the coming decades, with the number of wholly Welsh-speaking households potentially increasing markedly. For the moment, however, it is evident that the domain of the family and the home cannot be regarded as a major stimulus for the maintenance and reproduction of the language. As has been demonstrated, Welsh-speaking households are fractured and structurally diverse in composition.

# CHAPTER 8

## Reversing Language Shift: Prospects for the Language in the New Millennium

In 1885 D. Isaac Davies looked forward to a Welsh-speaking population of 3 million by 1985; less sanguine about the future, Saunders Lewis in 1962 saw the possibility of the demise of Welsh as a living language by the year 2000. The first prognostication has not been realized, the second will certainly not apply. The future for the language certainly looks brighter, although it is perhaps a little too early to claim either that it is secure or that it will be as deeply rooted (in a cultural sense) as it has been in the past. In discussing the momentous changes since 1961, it has been demonstrated that contradictory forces and trends have been operating, and still continue to operate. While this is the case, it is evident that during the last decade of the millennium the consolidation of a whole series of developments and trends have helped to prepare the ground for a major turnaround in the fortunes of the language. It is with these and their implications that this concluding chapter is particularly concerned.

Predicting and monitoring the future of the Welsh language is made difficult by the rather limited range of data currently available, and their deficiencies when it comes to the tracking of changes over space and time. Without more detailed and consistent statistical information, forecasting is virtually impossible. Although mindful of weaknesses in the quality of the available statistical information, Aitchison and Carter endeavoured to identify movements in numbers and proportions of Welsh-speakers at community level in advance of the 1991 census returns. Based on census returns for the 1961–81 period, their analysis concluded that:

> Numbers of Welsh-speakers will continue to decline until the year 2001, but thereafter there will be a notable reversal of the trend, with numbers increasing sharply. Whilst this scenario augers well for the language, it is based on a major reshaping of the geography of language distribution. It seems that the situation will deteriorate most rapidly in those rural communities where absolute numbers of Welsh-speakers are already rather low. Here it only takes minor movements in population for the linguistic balance to be severely disrupted . . . The predicted overall turnaround in numbers of Welsh-speakers by the year 2001 is explained by a continuance of the rapid advances recently recorded in the borderland areas of Wales, and in particular the increases that could be returned in main urban centres such as Cardiff and its immediate hinterland, Newport, Mold and Llandrindod Wells. Such are the sizes of population in these and other centres that they

could more than compensate for the small absolute losses that are likely to happen in the most vulnerable parts of rural Wales, as well as the more serious decline that could take place in those industrial regions of West Glamorgan and south-east Dyfed which currently have large numbers of Welsh-speakers.

The returns from the 1991 census confirmed the significance of these trends, and the main prediction concerning the historic advances that are likely to be recorded at the next census. As has been demonstrated, the same returns indicate that traditional interpretations of the geographical distribution of the Welsh language are becoming increasingly inappropriate. Though maintainable in a modified form, the bipolar model of an 'Inner' (Welsh-speaking) and an 'Outer' (Anglicized) Wales is now much less of an imperative than it was. In the old core, to use that rather more neutral term, the language is much less dominant, especially in the relative sense which dominance implies. The proportion of Welsh-speakers which could safely be taken to define the core in 1901 was 90 per cent, in 1991 in order to define such a core with equal confidence the limiting proportion must be reduced to 50 per cent.

However, the decline in the heartland has a reciprocal in the resurgence and rejuvenation that has been identified in areas lying outside it. Whilst this is the case the statistics which define and underpin the trend need to be treated circumspectly, especially those relating to the language proficiency of young Welsh-speakers in the new growth regions. Statistical meaningfulness apart, it is appropriate to question whether or not these young 'green shoots' will flourish in what are essentially Anglicized environments. Both these matters may well be crucial for the long-term maintenance and reproduction of the language (Aitchison and Carter, 1997).

In reflecting on the future of the language in Wales the differential status of the language in urban and rural areas is a critical consideration. Welsh is now, and has been since the last century, a predominantly urban language. Because of problems in defining what is urban it is difficult to specify the level of urbanization precisely, but the general proposition is surely undeniable. For the language this urban condition poses a problem, for all towns are, by their very nature, meeting points. As Lewis Mumford has argued:

> In the city remote forces and influences intermingle with the local: their conflicts are no less significant than their harmonies. And here, through the concentration of the means of intercourse in the market and the meeting place, alternative modes of living present themselves: the rutted ways of the village cease to be coercive and the ancestral goals cease to be all-sufficient: strange men and women, strange interests, and stranger gods loosen the traditional ties of blood and neighbourhood. (Mumford, 1938, 4)

Towns are cosmopolitan places where Welsh is inevitably brought face to face with English. It follows that it is much more difficult to live a life wholly in Welsh in an urban area, and the larger the town the more difficult it is, regardless of the number of Welsh-speakers. Thus, if Welsh looks to the marcher and urban areas where it can be thought of as resurgent, it looks to places where it can never be considered truly and properly dominant, that is where it is the mother tongue of a significant majority. Unfortunately, the same can be increasingly said of the traditional rural heartland which has been showing signs of serious attenuation. If only just over a half of the population speak Welsh, as is the case in many such areas, then the basis for a true Welsh-language community in any meaningful sense is hardly present. It is of course true that there are areas where percentages are much higher and where Welsh-speaking communities can be found. But they are now scattered and isolated; there is no longer a solid *Bro Gymraeg* in the sense in which it was originally conceived.

Wales is threatened, therefore, with a situation that could well parallel that in Ireland. While there may be a widespread familiarity with the language, the true Welsh-speaking areas where Welsh is the mother tongue could be reduced, like the Irish *Gaeltacht*, to separated fragments clinging to the north-western shores or the remoter parts of the interior. Such are some of the implications of the current geographical distribution of the language. But there is an obverse side to that gloomy picture. Thus, it might be argued that the array of supportive measures that have been secured over more recent times and the high level of popular commitment to the language that now exists could bring about a bilingual Wales, or at least one where the personality principle could freely operate. That, too, is an implication from the census figures, if a somewhat optimistic one. But it will be a very different Wales, where the cultural associates of language will be greatly changed, for the concomitant life-styles of bilingualism will be transformed from those of traditional Welsh Wales.

It is to be appreciated that this study has been essentially descriptive and interpretative in nature, and that little attempt has been made to offer prescriptions for the future well-being of the language. Although critically important, such matters lie beyond the scope of the present analysis. That said, the patterns and processes that have been displayed and elucidated are clearly of considerable relevance to an understanding of the vitality of the language nationally, and in the various regions of Wales.

It will be recalled that in the opening chapter to this text reference was made to the notion of ethno-linguistic vitality and its associated components. Since this schema has implicitly underpinned the thrust and emphasis of much of the discussion, it is appropriate by way of conclusion to reflect upon the nature and significance of the various components as they currently manifest themselves in Wales, and as they might shape the future. Figure 1.3 identified three main categories of structural variables that determined the vitality of a language: status, demography and institutional support. Each of these is worthy of further summary comment, suitably updated to take account of new data and more recent developments. To complete the picture, however, special reference needs to be made to certain issues concerning local planning and the maintenance of the language, and to the impact that the National Assembly for Wales might have on the primacy of Welsh as a signifier of national identity.

## Status of the Language

The issue of political status has long been central to the language debate in Wales, with calls being frequently made for an Act that would give formal recognition to Welsh as a national language. Persistent pressure from activists culminated in The Welsh Language Act 1993. Although criticized by many as being a weak piece of legislation, the Act does seek to give a full measure of equality to Welsh, at least as far as is possible through the means of government.

Its main purpose is clearly stated in Part 1 of the Act:

> to establish a Board having the function of promoting and facilitating the use of the Welsh Language, to provide for the preparation by public bodies of schemes giving effect to the principle that in the conduct of public business and the administration of justice in Wales the English and Welsh languages should be treated on a basis of equality. (Welsh Language Act, 1993, 2)

The Board, a 'body corporate to be known as Bwrdd yr Iaith Gymraeg or the Welsh Language Board', was to be provided with the necessary finance to make grants and loans to further language interests.

The other parts of the Act can be briefly summarized. Part 2 enacts that every public body in Wales must prepare a scheme to demonstrate how it would give 'effect, so far as is both appropriate in the circumstances and reasonably practicable, to the principle that in the conduct of public business and the administration of justice in Wales the English and Welsh languages should be treated on a basis of equality' (Welsh Language Act, 3 ). To help those bodies concerned with the preparation of such schemes the Welsh Language Board published a document entitled *Welsh Language Schemes: Their Preparation and Approval in Accordance with the Welsh Language Act* (Welsh Language Board, 1996). There it is adumbrated that the basic principle of equality is to be achieved by offering the public in Wales the right to choose which language to use in their dealings with organizations, by recognizing that members of the public express their views and needs better in their preferred language, by recognizing that enabling the public to use their preferred language is a matter of good practice, not a concession, and that denying them the right to use their preferred language could place members of the public at a real disadvantage (Welsh Language Board, 1996, 8). The Annual Report of the Welsh Language Board 1997–8 records the approval of 67 language schemes. All of the 22 local authorities in Wales have schemes in place, and an initiative entitled *Rhwydiaith* has been established to co-ordinate their further development.

Although such schemes are not applicable to the private sector, many organizations in that sector have responded to the spirit of the Act. The Board has also launched a project – *Iaith Gwaith* – which aims to encourage businesses to use Welsh in their dealings with customers.

Part 3 of the Act is headed 'miscellaneous' but deals largely with the use of Welsh in legal proceedings. The Welsh Courts Act of 1942, the Welsh Language Act of 1967 and the

136

Administration of Justice Act of 1977 are all accordingly repealed. The fundamental statement of the 1993 Act is that: 'In any legal proceedings in Wales the Welsh language may be spoken by any party, witness or other person who desires to use it . . . and any necessary provision for interpretation shall be made accordingly.' The Lord Chancellor, now calling himself the Lord Chancellor of England and Wales, has subsequently informally reinforced this condition especially in relation to the provision of Welsh-speaking judges (*Western Mail*, 17 October 1998, 5). In addition, in this section powers are set out to provide Welsh names for statutory bodies and to prescribe the availability of forms in Welsh. There are also provisions for the appropriate use of Welsh by industrial and provident societies, by credit unions, by charities and by companies.

It is to be noted that the Act pointedly avoids the crucial issue of official status for Welsh in Wales. Significantly, this was the key item in a private members' bill introduced by Dafydd Wigley and others, where the first clause was, 'Both Welsh and English shall be official languages in Wales' (Wigley et al., 1986). Though clearly a major step forward, the impact of the Act is likely to be less than was hoped for by language activists. Questions have also been raised with regard to the availability of finance to support the aims and objectives of the Board. Thus, in June 1999 the University of Wales called for more funds to be released to enable it to respond fully to the demands of the Act.

Assessing the economic status of the language is difficult, and differing perspectives on the situation have emerged. Thus, drawing upon special socio-economic tabulations from the 1981 census, but only for the county of Gwynedd, Williams felt able to develop a case for the subservient and dependent condition of Welsh-speakers in the workplace :

> The argument focussing on the cultural division of labour can be substantiated by looking, for example, at an area such as the county of Gwynedd where there have been profound developments of branch plant and new manufacturing industries. The most obvious feature of such developments is that if the employment decisions for both manufacturing and retail are made outside Wales, at head office, then most of the higher level managerial or professional posts will be held by in-migrants. On the other hand, if the objective is the search for cheap labour, the proletarian labour will be local. That is, we envisage two different labour markets for different class locations . . . There is a heavy under-representation of Welsh-speakers in the top four official socio-economic groups used in the census tabulations. (Williams, G., 1986, 187)

As the discussions in Chapter 7 demonstrated, however, a full analysis of the 1991 census suggests that such an interpretation, and the theoretical models that support it, are partial, and need to be suitably qualified to take account of very different situations prevailing in other regions of Wales. Furthermore, it is evident that over more recent times the 'instrumental' value of Welsh in securing employment (of all types and categories) has become widely recognized. Thus, in the school-based questionnaire surveys undertaken by Aitchison and Carter (Chapter 5), the suggestion that being able to speak Welsh offers few advantages when it comes to seeking employment was forcefully rejected by pupils and parents alike. A facility in the language, it was claimed, widened job opportunities considerably. Sceptics might claim that such attitudes reflect hopes and expectations rather than the realities of the situation as far as most economic sectors are concerned. In regard to the highest-level posts in particular, these are often determined by international firms with little or no interest in Wales other than as an advantageous location. This stance is close to the business view, constantly reiterated, that too great an emphasis on the language will deter entrepreneurs from considering investment in Wales, especially where competition from English or Scottish regions is involved. It is part, too, of the argument of those who have reservations concerning the development of Welsh-language education. Thus, in an article in the *Western Mail* (12 June 1999) a Welsh-speaker, Rhodri Clark, voiced fears that 'Wales could become too insular through its passionate commitment to its own language', arguing that the teaching of other European languages was being neglected in the drive to promote Welsh, and that this could have serious consequences both for the image of Wales abroad and for its future economic development. It is evident, therefore, that the sort of nineteenth-century detraction of the language on economic grounds – the central message of the Blue Books – is still extant. But it is by no means as powerful as it was, and there is a widespread awareness of the advantages of a knowledge of Welsh, especially in public employment. With the 1993 Welsh Language Act this is certain to increase. Interestingly, one of the Conservative Party's themes in the National Assembly elections of 1999 was a criticism of Gwynedd County Council for its policy favouring the appointment of Welsh-speakers.

These observations concerning economic status inevitably impinge on the issue of the social status of the language, for there is no easy distinction to be made between the two. The extent of the association of Welsh-speaking with social class is not easy to ascertain, and perhaps the real measure (as examined in Chapter 7) should be with the various socio-economic groups rather than with the rudimentary social class divisions of the census. Since there is no Welsh-speaking aristocracy, it is manifest that Welsh has only an inferior status in the upper ranks of the British class system, which is totally irrelevant to Wales. Certainly it is possible to argue that the old prejudices have gone and there is even an element of social cachet in being able to speak Welsh, at least in Wales. There is a difference of course between class as perceived status and income as a measure of socio-economic well-being. Perhaps it is simply the perceived status of Welsh-speaking within Wales which has risen in recent times.

A further facet of the status component is the perception of the language both within and outside the bounds of the area in which it is spoken. Again, many of the arguments advanced above apply. Certainly, within Wales there is much less of the denigration which was once so widespread. To speak Welsh is seen more widely as the key ethnic symbol of Welshness, and wholly desirable. That is a view often accepted even by non-Welsh-speakers, many of whom greatly regret their inability to speak Welsh. Even those who contest such a notion do not wish to diminish the status of the language as such. Within Wales, therefore, although there are dissenting voices, its status seems more assured than ever. This was certainly affirmed by the results of an attitude survey funded by the Welsh

Language Board and S4C, and conducted by NOP Consumer Market Research, with the assistance of the Central Office of Information in 1996. The survey indicated that 88 per cent of respondents thought that the language is 'something to be proud of', while over 70 per cent believed that Welsh should be used and should have equal status with English (Welsh Language Board, 1996, 12).

The view from outside, essentially from England, rather than from neighbouring Celtic countries, is more difficult to elucidate, for the evidence must be largely anecdotal or even fictional in nature (Faber, 1985). That said, it is certainly difficult to identify much support for the language and all that it stands for. More often there is total incomprehension that a language other than English should be the mother tongue of native British people. Perhaps the crucial factor in all this is that, during the nineteenth century, Welsh population migration, largely dominated by the growth of the coalfields, was internal. There was never the massive emigration which characterized the Irish and the Scots to America for instance. Thus, many Americans are totally unaware of the existence of Wales, and can make no sense of being told that someone is Welsh. Inevitably, this limits the sort of external recognition which other minority languages can claim. The view from outside, therefore, is seldom greatly supportive. While this is the case, it might be expected that a broader commitment to the notion of cultural diversity and a recognition of the need to protect endangered languages worldwide will assure Welsh a much higher profile. The efforts that have been made in Wales to reverse language shift are now seen as a model endeavour, and have been widely acclaimed.

**Demography**

Demographic factors, which constitute the second group of variables impacting on the vitality of the language, have been largely dealt with in the course of the book and need no extensive repetition. At present, there is no evidence that the out-migration of Welsh people will slacken. Indeed, continued de-industrialization and job losses in manufacturing are likely to occur, especially in the linguistically crucial anthracite coalfield in the south. Again, there seems little potential for growth in rural areas as the agricultural and associated service sectors struggle to maintain viability. The wider range of educational and employment opportunities in England will continue to attract younger adults. Property markets are fickle, but it would appear that the purchase of second or holiday homes by outsiders has become less of an issue during the 1990s. This also applies to the process of counterurbanization, although it still continues to affect certain rural communities. But there is a further problem in that the Welsh-speaking population of the heartland is increasingly elderly. Again the census does not permit the derivation of any relationship between natality, mortality and language but there is likely to be little natural increase, and possibly a natural decrease, in the areas with the greatest percentages of Welsh-speakers. In contrast, the areas with the highest proportion of young Welsh-speakers are the marcher and urban areas, those regions where in an Anglicized environment it will be most difficult for school leavers to maintain their fluency and pass it on to their children. The nature of family structures within the Welsh-speaking community, as described in Chapter 7, also points to serious weaknesses as far as the maintenance and reproduction of the language within the crucial home environment is concerned. However, as has been noted, it could be argued that these structural problems are a transitional stage in the evolution of the language, and that they will be superseded as the number of Welsh-speakers increases, and as the very bimodal nature of the current age distribution of Welsh-speakers is transformed (i.e. with more Welsh-speakers being represented in the middle age groups than is the case at present).

## Institutional Support

Of all the influences deemed to affect ethno-linguistic vitality, particularly crucial in the Welsh context is that of institutional support, both formal and informal. In the formal category the general status of the language and the need for complete equality with English within Wales has already been considered. Progress on the latter front has been mixed. Other initiatives, however, have been more successful, and most especially in the domains of education and the media. Needless to say, the establishment of the National Assembly for Wales is a particularly significant institutional development that needs to be factored into the analysis, as is the role of local authorities when it comes to land-use planning and development control.

Developments in education have been extensive and highly significant for the promotion of the Welsh language. It is now possible to pursue schemes of study from pre-school nursery to University of Wales degrees (including postgraduate qualifications) through the medium of Welsh. There are obvious lacunae, for example in the range of degree schemes offering teaching through the medium of Welsh, but progress has been considerable over the last two decades. So widespread has been the development of Welsh-medium education at all levels, including the teaching of Welsh to adults, that no brief summary here can be adequate.

The teaching of Welsh to young children of pre-school age has been spearheaded by the Welsh-medium nursery schools movement (*Mudiad Ysgolion Meithrin*). This movement has been particularly successful in its marketing of the language, and by 1998, 570 nursery groups (*cylchoedd meithrin*) and 386 'you and me' groups (*cylchoedd ti a fi*) had been established, catering for nearly 13,500 children. These schools stimulate an awareness of Welsh at a critical stage, and provide a solid linguistic foundation for those children who then move on into first- or second-language Welsh classes at primary and secondary levels. Significantly some 61 per cent of the children concerned come from non-Welsh-speaking homes.

Data collated by the Welsh Office yield interesting insights into the nature and extent of teaching through the medium of Welsh in grant state-sector maintained primary schools (Welsh Office, 1998a). Four categories of primary schools are differentiated: Class A schools where Welsh is the sole or main medium of instruction, Class B schools where Welsh is a medium of instruction for part of the curriculum, Class C schools where Welsh is taught as a second language only and Class D where no Welsh is taught. Table 8.1 shows that in 1995/6 there were 1,681 primary schools in Wales. Of these some two-thirds are seen to be Class C schools. Welsh is the sole or main language in just over a quarter of schools (27.1 per cent). Table 8.2 confirms that the majority of these Category A schools were to be found in the traditional Welsh-speaking heartland. In Gwynedd 94 per cent of primary schools were of this type, while in Ceredigion, Ynys Môn and Carmarthenshire the equivalent figures were 84 per cent, 79 per cent and 60 per cent, respectively. These five areas together accounted for 64 per cent of all primary schools in Wales where Welsh is the dominant language of instruction. Elsewhere the numbers of Category A schools were of a low order. Thus, the main cities of Cardiff and Swansea each recorded just eight schools of this type.

While the regional data reported here relate to the year 1995/6, it is of interest to note that a comparison of aggregate statistics available for 1994/5 and 1996/7 show a slight but steady decline in the number of Category A and B schools – from 573 to 544. This fall could no doubt partly reflect the closure of small primary schools in the thinly populated and mainly Welsh-speaking rural regions. Over the same period however the number of schools where Welsh was taught essentially as a second language recorded an increase – from 1,091 to 1,136 – while those schools teaching no Welsh whatsoever fell from 27 to just 1. As far as the future of the language is concerned such data could be variously interpreted. However, they do confirm that virtually all children at primary-school level are having some exposure to the language. Of the 251,000 registered primary-school children in 1995/6 nearly a fifth (19 per cent) were taught solely or mainly through the medium of Welsh; for the rest their contact with Welsh was as a second language.

While these statistics could certainly be used to confirm a rejuvenation of the language, it is significant that assessments made by head teachers of language use and fluency present a somewhat different picture. Thus, in 1996/7 only 6 per cent of primary pupils were thought to use Welsh at home. Some 9 per cent of pupils were classed as being fluent in Welsh, but for one reason or another did not speak it at home. Such statistics would appear to reaffirm observations made earlier concerning the fragility of the home domain when it comes to the promotion of the language. The assessments made by head teachers also indicate that nearly 55 per cent of pupils cannot speak Welsh at all, even though, according to the data presented above, they have been following a course in Welsh as a second language. The remaining 30 per cent of pupils were deemed to be able to speak Welsh, but not fluently. Given the importance of the early years for language acquisition these assessments, if accurate, would not appear to bode well for the consolidation of the language long-term.

If the home context is seen to be deficient, then other data raise questions about the environments of the Welsh-medium primary schools themselves for the further promotion of the language. Thus, of the 455 Category A schools less than half (49 per cent) have 80 per cent or more of their pupils who are fluent in Welsh. For a further 39 per cent of these schools the proportion of fluent Welsh-speakers is between 50 per cent and 79 per cent (Welsh Office, 1998, Table 11.3). Aggregate data of this type are difficult to interpret of course, and they may simply reflect the fact that many of the younger pupils (Key Stage 1) are learning Welsh, but are not yet thought to be fluent. That said, the results could be used to reaffirm the conclusions drawn from the surveys of primary schools reported in Chapter 5.

In considering primary education it is worth noting that in 1996/7 there were 2,335 full-time teachers teaching through the medium of Welsh (355 part-time basis). A further 7,160 teachers were teaching Welsh as a second language (320 part-time).

**Table 8.1**
**Maintained primary schools: language categories, 1995/6**

| Welsh language categories | Number | % |
|---|---|---|
| Class A | 455 | 27.1 |
| Class B | 106 | 6.3 |
| Class C | 1109 | 66.0 |
| Class D | 11 | 0.7 |
| **Total schools** | **1681** | **100** |

**Table 8.2**
**Primary school language categories by unitary authority, 1995/6**

| | Category A | | Category B | | Category C | | Category D | |
|---|---|---|---|---|---|---|---|---|
| | Nos. | % | Nos. | % | Nos. | % | Nos. | % |
| Blaenau Gwent | 1 | 2.6 | 2 | 5.1 | 36 | 92.3 | - | - |
| Bridgend | 4 | 6.5 | 1 | 1.6 | 57 | 91.9 | - | - |
| Caerphilly | 8 | 8.6 | 3 | 3.2 | 81 | 87.1 | 1 | 1.1 |
| Cardiff | 8 | 7.3 | 1 | 0.9 | 100 | 91.7 | - | - |
| Carmarthenshire | 84 | 59.6 | 24 | 17.0 | 33 | 23.4 | - | - |
| Ceredigion | 65 | 84.4 | 9 | 11.7 | 3 | 3.9 | - | - |
| Conwy | 31 | 47.0 | 13 | 19.7 | 22 | 33.0 | - | - |
| Denbighshire | 18 | 32.1 | 5 | 8.9 | 33 | 58.9 | - | - |
| Flintshire | 5 | 6.6 | 1 | 1.3 | 70 | 92.1 | - | - |
| Gwynedd | 100 | 94.3 | 3 | 2.8 | 3 | 2.8 | - | - |
| Merthyr Tydfil | 2 | 6.1 | 1 | 3.0 | 30 | 90.9 | - | - |
| Monmouth | 1 | 2.3 | 2 | 4.5 | 39 | 88.6 | 2 | 4.5 |
| Neath and Port Talbot | 12 | 16.7 | 1 | 1.4 | 59 | 81.9 | - | - |
| Newport | 1 | 1.8 | 2 | 3.6 | 51 | 92.7 | 1 | 1.8 |
| Pembrokeshire | 25 | 27.2 | 11 | 12.0 | 56 | 60.9 | - | - |
| Powys | 15 | 13.9 | 11 | 10.2 | 82 | 75.9 | - | - |
| Rhondda Cynon Taff | 14 | 10.0 | 4 | 2.9 | 122 | 87.1 | - | - |
| Swansea | 8 | 8.6 | 2 | 2.2 | 83 | 89.2 | - | - |
| Torfaen | 2 | 4.9 | 2 | 4.9 | 30 | 73.2 | 7 | 1.1 |
| Vale of Glamorgan | 4 | 7.5 | 1 | 1.9 | 48 | 90.6 | - | - |
| Wrexham | 6 | 8.2 | 1 | 1.4 | 66 | 90.4 | - | - |
| Ynys Môn | 41 | 78.8 | 6 | 11.5 | 5 | 9.6 | - | - |
| **Wales** | **455** | **27.1** | **106** | **6.3** | **1109** | **66.0** | **11** | **0.7** |

As has already been noted, the inclusion of Welsh in the National Curriculum is of crucial importance for the promotion of the language in the secondary schools of Wales:

In 1988 the Education Reform Act came into force, giving Welsh the status of a core subject in Welsh-medium schools and the status of a foundation subject in the rest of the schools of Wales. At the same time, the Secretary of State for Wales established a working party to advise . . . on suitable Attainment Targets and Programmes of Study for the Welsh language. As a result, a Statutory Instrument was published as part National Curriculum to be operated from the start of the 1990/1991 academic year. This gives the language an enhanced status, better than ever before in its history. (National Language Forum, 1991, 19–20)

Welsh-speaking secondary schools, as defined in the Education Act 1996, Section 354(b) include those schools where more than one half of subjects (including religious education and those subjects other than English and Welsh which are foundation subjects) are taught wholly or partly through the medium of Welsh (Welsh Office, 1998a, 89). On this basis 49 of the 229 secondary schools in Wales – 21 per cent – were classed as Welsh-speaking in 1996/7. Together they were responsible for nearly 33,400 pupils. Just over 70 per cent of secondary schools taught Welsh as a second language only. In 21.8 per cent of schools Welsh was taught both as a first and a second language; in just 7.9 per cent was it taught only as a first language. Welsh is taught in all secondary schools, but this does not mean that all pupils are actually taught the language. In fact in 1996/7 some 22 per cent of pupils in years 7–11 (nearly 40,000) received no tuition whatsoever in Welsh. The great majority of these were in years 10 and 11. Furthermore for some 65 per cent of pupils Welsh was taught only as a second language. Only 12.6 per cent of pupils were taught Welsh as a first language.

Interestingly, of the pupils in years 12 and 13 (sixth form) only 5 per cent were taught Welsh as a first language. Nearly 90 per cent of sixth formers were not taught Welsh at all. Together, these figures are revealing, and say much in regard to the level of Welsh being achieved nationwide. However, it is evident that the situation varies from region to region. Disaggregated data available for the year 1995/6 (Table 8.3) indicate that two authorities – Gwynedd and Monmouth – mark extreme situations. In the county of Gwynedd nearly 75 per cent of all pupils in year groups 7–11 were being taught Welsh as a first language; in Monmouth 83 per cent were being taught no Welsh at all. For the majority of counties between 60 and 70 per cent of pupils were taught Welsh as a second language.

In 1996/7 276 teachers (full-time and part-time) in maintained secondary schools taught Welsh as a first language; for the teaching of Welsh as a second language the equivalent figure was 672 teachers. The number of teachers teaching other subjects through the medium of Welsh totalled 1,478. In 1997 3,809 pupils took GCSE examinations in Welsh as a first language, and 8,326 as a second language.

A notable part of the educational campaign to promote the language is the network of courses and other opportunities offered to adults to learn Welsh. They are provided both by

**Table 8.3**
**Maintained secondary schools: year groups 7–11**

| | Percentage of pupils | | |
| | Taught Welsh | | Not taught |
| | First language | Second language | Welsh |
| --- | --- | --- | --- |
| Blaenau Gwent | - | 66.1 | 33.9 |
| Bridgend | - | 67.6 | 32.4 |
| Caerphilly | 6.7 | 66.0 | 27.3 |
| Cardiff | 6.2 | 67.0 | 26.8 |
| Carmarthenshire | 27.2 | 64.1 | 8.7 |
| Ceredigion | 47.1 | 52.0 | 0.9 |
| Conwy | 14.8 | 74.5 | 10.8 |
| Denbighshire | 17.1 | 68.0 | 14.9 |
| Flintshire | 4.0 | 69.7 | 26.3 |
| Gwynedd | 74.7 | 25.2 | 0.1 |
| Merthyr Tydfil | - | 74.5 | 25.5 |
| Monmouth | - | 16.6 | 83.4 |
| Neath and Port Talbot | 8.5 | 70.2 | 21.3 |
| Newport | - | 59.8 | 40.2 |
| Pembrokeshire | 7.9 | 60.3 | 31.8 |
| Powys | 7.1 | 74.8 | 18.1 |
| Rhondda Cynon Taff | 17.0 | 62.7 | 20.3 |
| Swansea | 5.0 | 68.1 | 26.8 |
| Torfaen | 7.0 | 48.7 | 44.3 |
| Vale of Glamorgan | - | 74.2 | 25.8 |
| Wrexham | 7.5 | 70.4 | 22.0 |
| Ynys Môn | 43.9 | 56.0 | 0.1 |
| **Wales** | **12.4** | **63.2** | **24.4** |

public and private bodies, and provision is extensive. Few can claim major difficulties in gaining access to language classes for learners. Amongst the many organizations offering courses, CYD (*Cymry Cymraeg a Dysgwyr ar y Cyd*) has been especially successful. Funded by the Welsh Office and from local authority and private sources it was founded in 1984 with the aim of providing adult learners with social settings in which to make active use of the language (Jones, R. W., 1994). In 1990 there were 50 branches of CYD; by 1999 this had expanded significantly to 119.

While developments in the sphere of education have been generally welcomed, there have been local movements in opposition, such as Education First which in the early part of the 1990s opposed Dyfed's policy of classifying schools by language status and thereby constraining parental choice concerning the language in which their children would be taught at primary school level. Problems such as this still continue in certain localities (such as Monmouth) and have even been the subject of debate within the Assembly. There have been other retrogressive steps, such as the Secretary of State's abolition of the Committee for the

Development of Welsh Education (Pwyllgor Datblygiad Addysg Gymraeg); but these have proved to be relatively minor issues in a domain of general progress.

Further institutional support derives from the objective of strengthening Welsh as a community language. This is identified as a key priority in the strategy document of the Welsh Language Board. Singled out for special recognition are community language initiatives (*mentrau iaith*), the first being Menter Cwm Gwendraeth in 1991. These initiatives are aimed at creating social environments which will engender positive attitudes to the language, encourage a genuine bilingualism and associate the whole nexus of social and economic development, as well as environmental concerns, with the language. The Board notes:

> To date, the most exciting development in the field of language planning has been the establishment of local language initiatives (*mentrau iaith*). Their main strength is their potential to raise the profile of the Welsh language locally, and to promote and facilitate its use by causing new activities to be organised and by co-ordinating existing activities. Unitary authorities, in particular, together with the Board and other relevant agencies should be prepared to meet the demand for the establishment of new initiatives; at the same time, they should be prepared to develop those initiatives which are already operational. (Welsh Language Board, 1996, 15)

Williams and Evas (1997) have proposed adding to these community-based initiatives a hierarchy of support in County Resource Centres and a National Language Resource Centre. These are recommendations which will presumably pass to the National Assembly for consideration. It is clear that the scale of community support is crucial for the future of the language, especially in those areas where it is most under threat.

Particularly significant for the promotion of the language during the 1990s has been the proliferation of transmissions and publications in Welsh. The flagship role of S4C (Sianel Pedwar Cymru) is supported by an increasingly wide array of national (Radio Cymru) and local radio programmes, and the publication of Welsh-language books, newspapers and magazines.

Although it is not appropriate to enter into a lengthy discussion of the matter here, it is worth noting that these various media have a vital role to play in safeguarding the linguistic integrity of the language. This is a matter that has caused some consternation given the grammatical, lexical and syntactical trends that are discernible in the everyday use of the language. In a recent commentary Aitchison and Carter have observed:

> There are many studies devoted to what is called the death of language, or more circumspectly, language contact and language degeneration. Many of these aspects can be directly related to contemporary Welsh. Thus Craig writes, 'a category of speakers most typical of the situation of language death is that of the "semi-speakers" defined by Dorian as imperfect speakers with very partial command of the receptive skills required to speak it, but almost perfect command of the skills required to understand it' (Craig, 1997, 259). Such a condition, though measured on a different basis, that of the ability to read and write

as well as to speak, is undoubtedly characteristic of Welsh where in the 1991 census although 508,098 claimed to speak the language only 369,609 returned an ability to speak, read and write it. This is not illiteracy in its conventional meaning but indicative of 'semi-speakers' noted above. The only reservation which needs to be made is that 'semi-speakers' could be equally characteristic of language growth, that is of the ability to speak before the competence to write for example is acquired. But other features of language degeneration can apparently be identified in Welsh. Amongst those usually set out (Craig, 1997, 261–4) are: loss of registers, lexical loss (where the loss of native lexicon is accompanied by replacement from the dominant language), loss in phonology (where modification of pronunciation occurs), loss in morphology (where insecurity develops over structures), and loss in syntax. Of these, whereas loss of registers was at one time a characteristic of Welsh, where the language was used for informal communication as against English for formal contacts, that has largely been reversed by the language movement. Loss of phonology has not occurred. But all the other features have: Lexical loss, with a widespread use of English words, is widely marked. So is loss in morphology where, for example, the gender of words is often unrealised and mutations certainly insecure. Numbers have always been complex in Welsh and now simplified forms are almost universally used. Loss in syntax is apparent too, especially where morphological tense is dropped in favour of periphrastic forms, and where the more esoteric forms of the verb are simply ignored. Internal vowel changes are abandoned (Cenwch–canwch, for example). All this comes to a head in the nature of the language used in popular television programmes such as Heno on S4C where the modifications outlined above are accepted, much to the chagrin of language purists. But there is one important reservation which must be made. All these features are seen as evidence of language degeneration, but they can equally be seen as evidence of regeneration as learners struggle to bring their language up to standard. Certainly, the one point which needs to be stressed is that the language is not static but changing, and that change can be seen as much as evidence of vitality as of decay. It is also likely that the Welsh of the twenty-first century will be a somewhat different language from that even of the recent past. (Aitchison and Carter, 1999c, 108–9)

The Welsh Language Board Strategy notes in regards to the broadcasting media:

> Welsh medium and non-Welsh medium broadcasting both have tremendous potential to influence the public's attitudes and patterns of language use. It must be ensured that such influence has a positive effect. These media can also play an important role in the work of promoting the use of the Welsh language and nurturing confidence among its speakers. (Welsh Language Board, 1996, 13–14)

Significant advances have been made with the publication of local community newspapers (*Papurau Bro*), national magazines and books in Welsh. In 1975 the number of books published was 308; in 1997 it was 636, nearly two-thirds of which were for children and young adults. Again the Welsh Language Board have highlighted the very special role played by the publishing media:

The promotion of reading is an essential part of any strategy to promote the language and there are no doubts concerning the value of reading as a means of building confidence in people to use language on paper as well as orally. We cannot, therefore, over-emphasise the need for a wide-ranging provision of books, magazines and newspapers of the highest quality, and also vigorous schemes to market them. The considerable successes in this area over the past decade should be noted, particularly in the field of books for children and young people where the greatest growth has been seen. The quality and presentation of these books compare favourably with that which is available in other countries. (Welsh Language Board, 1996, 14)

Even before the implementation of the Welsh Language Act (1993) government services were assuring their institutional support for the Welsh language in major policy statements. The stance taken by the Central Council for Education and Training in Social Work (CCETSW), which is responsible for the training of social and care workers, exemplifies the situation. In 1987 CCETSW's Committee in Wales proposed that a Welsh-language policy should be formulated for the Council. The policy, the work of a special subcommittee, was approved in 1989 and issued as a document *Welsh Language Policy* (CCETSW, 1990). The principles of the policy were forcefully stated:

CCETSW should promote and encourage equal status for the Welsh and English languages in its work in Wales . . . A client has a basic right to choose the language of interaction with the social work agency and its workers and there is, therefore, a consequent need for social workers and care workers who can offer a professional service through the medium of Welsh in all parts of Wales. CCETSW should seek to ensure that Welsh medium education and training is available for students who wish to study and practice in Welsh, and that English medium education and training is culturally and linguistically sensitive. (CCETSW, 1990, 2)

While formal areas of institutional support for the language have been effectively articulated during the 1990s, less convincing have been efforts in the informal sector, particularly within industry and business. In more local terms most of the large supermarket chains at least make a token effort at bilingualism with notices in their stores, a trend which is growing. But the opposition to the mandatory use of Welsh by industry and business on grounds of practicality and profitability remains strong and consistent. Recognizing the importance of the private sector in the promotion of the language, the Welsh Language Board in its strategy document notes:

It is important that private companies see the benefits of using the Welsh language, and as a result become more willing to extend their provision to customers for whom Welsh is their preferred language. In addition, a bilingual image can be an advantage beyond Wales, particularly in those markets where a unique image is of vital importance, or where demonstrating an understanding of multilingualism enables the company to identify itself with the indigenous market. (Welsh Language Board, 1996, 10)

In contrast to the situation in the business sector the support for the language in the voluntary sector is much more evident.

## Planning, Development Control and Language

In discussing the forces that are likely to shape the future of the Welsh language it is appropriate to make reference to the direct and indirect impact that a formal planning system can have, and already has had, on the vitality of the language at a local level.

In order to clarify the relation between planning and language a very brief comment on the development of planning in Britain is needed. Formal planning is usually seen as reaching back to the middle of the nineteenth century. It appears in the form of the series of acts concerned with housing and the sanitary and social conditions of what were called until as late as 1903, the labouring or working classes. The earliest was the Lodging Houses Act of 1851, although the Labouring Classes Dwelling Houses Act of 1866 was of much wider application, as was the Artisans' and Labourers' Dwelling Improvement Act of 1875, usually called the Cross Act (Merrett,1979). As is evident these were concerned with the provision of public housing. The first act to use the term 'town planning' was the Housing and Planning Act of 1909. A major step forward to a broader base occurred during and immediately after the Second World War with the formation in 1943 of the Ministry of Town and Country Planning and, after some interim measures, with the passing of the Town and Country Planning Act of 1947. This was the act which required all local authorities (counties) to prepare plans for their areas which set out allocations of land for specific uses and initiated development controls so that all proposals for change were subject to vetting against the plan.

All this, of course, referred specifically to physical planning, and it is perhaps not surprising (given its emanation from Westminster) that at the time no consideration was given to the possible impact of particular types of development upon socio-cultural attributes such as language. Indeed, it was never envisaged as an issue since it was assumed that physical planning in the form of land-use manipulation was not pertinent to cultural matters. Thus no directly relevant measures appeared in the Town and Country Planning Act of 1971, although indirectly measures relating to housing were seen to carry implications for community integrity. This was an issue which was taken up by the Lake District National Park Planning Board in England, which was particularly concerned with the impact that incomers were having on local housing markets, through the purchase of properties as second or holiday homes. Similar concerns were expressed in Wales. Thus, in 1987 Gwynedd County Council, together with other local authorities, formally noted that

> Unless the Secretary of State is prepared to approve policies and practices which enable local planning authorities to ensure that land which is released for the development of housing to meet local demand is actually used for that purpose, rather than to meet some other demands from outside the area, then the basic policies are quite meaningless. (Gwynedd County Council et alia, 1987)

But the Secretary of State had been unwilling to approve such policies in his response to the Menai Straits, Ardudwy and Llanelltyd, and Rural Dwyfor Local Plans. Furthermore, he had refused to approve policies regarding the use of agreements under Section 52 of the Town and Country Planning Act of 1971 to limit the occupation of new dwellings to local residents. He also insisted that any definition of the term 'local needs' should be deleted from the local plans.

Against this background it followed that very little attention was paid to language in the series of planning documents that appeared to deal with economic development in Wales. Reviewing the situation in 1986 and referring to the language changes in the period 1961–81 James wrote:

> All these changes . . . have taken place within the context of one of the most comprehensive land use planning systems in the world, one which however ignores social aspects. The 13 county development plans produced for the pre-1974 counties contain only in 4 cases any mention at all of the Welsh language and none of these attempts to relate the language to land use planning. (James, 1986, 70)

He noted the same absence of any significant reference to language in the series of Welsh Office planning studies published during the mid 1960s and early 1970s and in the Labour government's document *Wales: the Way Ahead* (1967). James referred also to the fact that between 1971 and 1973 the Welsh Council produced three planning studies of rural, Welsh-speaking Wales. He observed that of these, 'Two totally ignore the language and the third contains only one derisory sentence'(James, 1986, 71).

It must be added, however, that by the late 1970s the relevance of planning was becoming more apparent. The report of the Council for the Welsh Language, *A Future for the Welsh Language*, published in 1978, did contain one paragraph (Para.45) on 'planning'. The paragraph concluded: 'We share the view that has been put to us several times that the Welsh language and the culture associated with it should be given special consideration in planning in Wales.' But it was very much of a token mention in response to representations, rather than a statement with insight as to what formal steps were needed and their effective adumbration.

The reasons for this situation are not difficult to ascertain. The way that planning had developed meant that the physical issues of housing and land use dominated, with little notion that developments in those spheres could have much wider cultural repercussions. Futhermore, the period of the formation of county plans came mainly before the main thrust of language concern began to assert itself after the 1962 radio lecture of Saunders Lewis, *The Fate of the Language* (*Tynged yr Iaith*) and the founding of the Welsh Language Society (*Cymdeithas yr Iaith Gymraeg*). It was eventually force of circumstances which brought the relevance of planning for the well-being of the language to the fore. The growth of second homes in Wales and the increasing pace of in-migration made it apparent that physical planning and the integrity of Welsh-speaking communities were intimately related. This situation was clearly set out in a special *Report of Survey* written by Cyril Parry for the Anglesey Structure Plan. James summarizes:

His conclusions, typical of the other findings, were that threats to the language included: second homes, large towns, large scale industry and development of large scale residential estates; encouragement of an influx of non Welsh speaking labour; and increase in the percentage of non Welsh speaking children in schools. Of the various planning options: large scale employment-led growth would lead to an influx of immigrants and flood the language away; too restrictive a plan would not halt depopulation and in retaining rural tranquillity would attract persons for retirement; residential-based growth would have a serious effect upon language in the areas where it was concentrated. The latter might be mitigated by concentrating such developments in already anglicised areas. (James, 1986, 71)

Here was a clear statement of the relation between planning strategies and language interest, although the number of pre-existing valid residential planning permissions on Anglesey undermined any policy that might have been derived from it. Even so, as the relation became more evident and pertinent, a period of contention developed between the Welsh Office, concerned with its responsibilities to see that housing allocation was fair and reasonable as British law demanded and, as has been noted, consistently refusing to interpret local needs as having any cultural implications, and local authorities more and more aware of the critical role of planning in the welfare of the language. Although it involves a movement forward in time it is worth considering these different views. In 1986 an all-party group of MPs, aware of the need to introduce new legislation to support the language, introduced a Welsh Language Bill (Wigley et al., 1986). In the Bill, Part V dealt with 'Planning'. It consisted of two modifications of existing sections of the Town and Country Planning Act, 1971, introducing a need to consider the language in both districts and counties and then added a new section which read:'The Welsh Language in Wales 58(A) – The effects of a proposed development on the linguistic character of a community may be a material consideration for the determination of planning applications by planning authorities in Wales.' This private members' bill was lost, but it was the forerunner of the Welsh Language Act of 1993. But one will search in vain for any mention whatsoever of planning in the 1993 Act. The issue was quite simply ignored. This was in spite of the fact that in October 1986, in reply to a parliamentary question put by Dafydd Elis Thomas, the Under-Secretary of State (Wyn Roberts) had replied that it was appropriate for local planning authorities, when considering applications for planning permission, to have regard to policies which reflect the needs and interests of the Welsh language. Similarly, at the announcement of the establishment of the Welsh Language Board in 1988, Peter Walker, the then Secretary of State for Wales, had noted that amongst the matters to be considered was 'the place of the Welsh language in planning matters', adding that in the past 'there have been misunderstandings and clarification will be needed' (Welsh Office, 1988, 3). Significantly, the issue of planning does not figure prominently in the *Strategy for the Welsh Language* published in 1996 by the Welsh Language Board. Therein, none of the twenty objectives refers directly to planning as such, although there are oblique implications in Objective 18. This follows a consideration in Section 8 where it states that 'it should be ensured that the effects on language of any proposed community developments are fully considered by the relevant planning and economic development authorities at an early stage in the statutory planning process' (Welsh Language Board, 1996, 15).

These problems and the misunderstandings, referred to by Peter Walker in 1988, had largely emerged from two sources. The first was that in a number of public inquiries the Welsh language had been introduced as a pertinent issue, and was recognized as such by inspectors. The other was that local planning authorities began to introduce language matters into their planning procedures.

A characteristic example of the planning inquiries generated by development proposals which were seen as inimical to the language was that for the transformation of a former army site at Tŷ Croes near Aberffraw on Anglesey into a holiday camp with some 100 holiday units and associated recreation facilities. Here, there was certainly local disagreement as the possible advantages of employment in the area were set against the impact on the local community. The development was opposed by Ynys Môn, the Isle of Anglesey Borough Council, with its Bilingual Policy Subcommittee noting on 8 October, 1986, 'that the threat to the language and culture of the district outweighed any advantage that could arise from the scheme and therefore recommended strongly to the Planning Committee that the application be refused' (statement submitted by Ynys Môn. Para. 2.15). The inspector who officiated at the public inquiry noted opposition on the basis of the impact on language and observed:

> the permanent introduction of large numbers of English speakers into a Welsh speaking community would appear to be the most important aspect of this concern. Such circumstances could certainly have a profound effect on the social fabric of the indigenous population and as such may be considered material to any assessment of the planning impact of a development proposal. (Inspector's report, 10 Feb. 1988, Para. 72)

In the end the inspector did not consider that the language grounds were in themselves sufficient to reject the proposal, but the significant point is his view that it could 'be considered material to any assessment'. More and more, in response to mounting concerns, social impact assessments of proposed developments would make reference to the implications for the language. Thus a proposal for the establishment of a time-share complex at Bryn-Afon near Llanrug, south of Caernarfon, in 1988 included a Section 13 entitled 'Impact on Welsh Language and Culture'. Again, in 1987, Mid Wales Development appointed Wyn Thomas and Partners to carry out an independent study of future prospects for the development of Newtown, evaluating the degree to which the growth of the town had met the broad aim of creating an economically viable urban centre in mid-Wales, and examining the costs and benefits of continuing Newtown's growth as against maintaining the *status quo*. The final report contained a section on 'The growth of Newtown and the Welsh Language' which began:

although not one of the objectives we were asked to assess, we have thought it appropriate to consider the effects of development at Newtown on the Welsh language as any proposal for population growth in rural Wales at the present time must be sensitive as to the possible impact on the language. (Newtown Study, 1989, 17)

It thus became apparent from these studies and inquiries that the language issue was highly pertinent to the planning process in Wales. The constant pressure to bring consideration of language into the planning field led the Welsh Office to publish Circular 53/88 in 1988 entitled 'The Welsh Language: Development Plans and Planning Control'. Its prime statement was 'where the Welsh language is part of the social fabric of the community, it is obviously appropriate to take this into consideration when drawing up land-use policies expressed in structure and local plans'. But the circular offered no guidelines as to how the recommendations were to be applied in practice and endeavours to restrict the sale of housing through the use of Section 106 (local needs) agreements were consistently overturned by the Welsh Office on the grounds that they interfered with individual liberties and could undermine economic development if applied. Discussions with local authorities led the Welsh Office to intimate that the authorities might identify settlements which were 'culturally sensitive' and where specific regulation could be accepted. The crucial problem was that no effective and acceptable definition of 'culturally sensitive' was set out. In its draft district plan, before the present unitary authorities were created, Ceredigion's response was to propose a highly provocative policy whereby new housing was to be restricted to people either born in the county or who had lived within a distance of twenty-five miles for at least five years. This was initially proposed to apply in those areas where at least 70 per cent of the population spoke Welsh (i.e. were deemed to be culturally sensitive), but to the concern of many the threshold was subsequently set at 50 per cent. No doubt in an attempt to reduce confrontation, and mindful of the practical implications, certain areas, mainly the urban centres and their suburban extensions, were exempted. Perhaps not surprisingly, pressure from the Welsh Office and local interests, forced the authority to revise this radical policy. Accordingly, in the Ceredigion Local Plan the policy is now encapsulated in the much more general statement that 'Proposals for development which can be demonstrated to be beneficial to the needs and interests of the Welsh language will be supported', and that 'every encouragement should be given to the development of facilities and opportunities which specifically strengthen or promote the interests of the Welsh language'. But it continues: 'This policy should not however be interpreted as justifying development which would not normally be acceptable. Proposals should still conform to other planning policies contained in the plan' (Ceredigion Local Plan, Vol.1 Written Statement, 33–4). A manifest and revealing retreat from a clear and unequivocal statement in the initial draft plan to an anodyne generalization in the final document.

Even so, many authorities have used the guidelines of Circular 53/88 to give the language a significant role in their local plans. Thus, Dwyfor (Dwyfor District Council, 1995) began its statement of main strategy with 'two fundamental principles' the first of which, Principle A1, reads: The Welsh Language – The Council will ensure, through the policies of the Local Plan, that new developments recognize, support and strengthen the social, cultural and linguistic identity of the plan area.' The plan also recognizes:

> The need to consider, safeguard and foster the Welsh language is an important and valid matter for the Dwyfor Local Plan, and the Council will therefore ensure that the proposals and policies for the development and use of land in the area will take this into full consideration.

That this policy was significant can be seen in the inspector's report on the Dwyfor Local Plan. In relation to a proposed low-density residential development of a site in Cricieth he wrote:

> there is firm evidence from the Censuses of 1981 and 1991 that the cultural fabric is being undermined, and that the position of the Welsh language is becoming increasingly fragile. The percentage of Welsh speakers in Criccieth fell from 72.1% in 1981 to 69.4% in 1991. 30% of the resident population was born outside Wales, and are mainly in the older age groups, suggesting that the area continues to be popular for retirement. There is also a high percentage of housing which is not used permanently (20%) . . . The release of land, over and above that already committed and allocated, would be likely to attract more inward migration, further contributing to an unacceptable change in the social fabric of the area, of which the Welsh language is a significant component . . . I conclude that there are clear-cut reasons for rejecting the inclusion of the site

It is evident from this example that the impact of planning decisions on language is now clearly recognized, and that it is being taken into account in the planning system. With the creation of unitary authorities, following the local government reorganization of 1994, a new set of guidelines has been issued in draft form for consultation. These were circulated in October 1998 as a technical advice note under the title, *The Welsh Language: Unitary Development Plans and Planning Control*. To a large extent they are still very general in their application although stating unequivocally that 'the land use planning system should also take account of the needs and interests of the Welsh language' (Para. 3). And again, 'where the use of the Welsh language is part of the social fabric of a community, it is appropriate that the needs and interest of the language be taken into account in the formulation of the policies set out in the Unitary Development Plans'. Furthermore, it affirms that 'it may be possible in some local authority areas to provide for the broad distribution and phasing of development so that it reflects the ability of different communities to accommodate it without eroding the position of the Welsh language'. These sorts of general statements are repeated throughout the document, but the crucial circumscribing limitations appear in Paragraphs 10 and 12. Thus, Paragraph 10 states that: 'Unitary development Plan policies which take into account the needs and interests of the Welsh language should not seek to introduce any element of discrimination between individuals on the basis of linguistic ability. Planning policies should not seek to control housing occupancy on linguistic grounds.' Few would disagree with the sentiment, but its application could undermine much of the generality in the guidelines. Paragraph 12 adds that 'decisions on individual planning applications where the needs and interests of the Welsh language may be a material consideration must, as with all other planning applications, be based on planning grounds only and be reasonable'. These sections do much to offset the generally supportive tenor of the rest of the document. Thus in the last sentence 'planning grounds only' and 'reasonableness' are question-begging statements, their definitions clearly open. Undoubtedly the new guidelines do introduce the opportunity for the new unitary authorities to give a significant place to the language in their new plans, but in much more specific terms the crucial local development proposals are still hedged round with limitations on action.

## Devolution and the National Assembly for Wales

It is appropriate to conclude this analysis of the changing fortunes of the Welsh language in the twentieth century with a brief consideration of the devolution referendum and the subsequent establishment of the National Assembly for Wales. Needless to say, the Assembly constitutes a major institutional development and it is to be expected that its policies and decision-making within a whole variety of socio-economic spheres will impact significantly on the language; and not only those policies that may focus specifically on the language itself. Of course, the place of the language within the Assembly is an issue in its own right.

But before considering such matters it is worth noting that Welsh-language protagonists have also been at the forefront of campaigns to secure a greater degree of autonomy for Wales. This derives in part from the fact that the language was seen as the prime ethnic indicator of Welsh identity; an identity that was all but lost following the early assimilation of Wales to England, and one that was being seriously weakened as the language itself continued to decline. Decentralization of power, it was argued, was vital if Wales was to break free and reassert its identity. A question that arises from this line of argument is whether or not in the new Wales an ethnic nationalism based strongly on the language will be replaced by an emergent and much more broadly based civic or institutional nationalism. The implications of such a development for the language are difficult to determine, but could be problematic. It might be argued for instance that the language could become no more than a 'marginal and optional' indicator of ethnic identity (Fishman, 1997), as Wales fashions a political unity founded on national institutions. As far as the Assembly is concerned, much will no doubt depend upon conflicts that might arise as to the allocation of scarce resources, and whether or not the language is seen as a divisive issue (see below). If this were to be the case it would be ironic in the extreme since in large part the Assembly owes it very existence to the Welsh-speaking vote.

This was most evident in the Devolution Referendum which took place on 18 September 1997. While the overall turnout was low at 50.3 per cent, it was significantly greater than this national average in the four main Welsh-speaking authorities of Gwynedd (60.0 per cent), Ceredigion (57.1 per cent), ), Ynys Môn (57 per cent) and Carmarthen (56.6 per cent). However, in terms of actual voting patterns, the 'ecological' relationship between the percentage who voted 'yes' to the establishment of an Assembly and the percentage of Welsh-speakers in the areas concerned is less clear-cut. That said, there is a very broad correlation between the two variables. Apart from Ynys Môn, each of the authorities within the Welsh-speaking heartland voted strongly in favour of an Assembly (Table 8.4). Only Neath Port Talbot (66.5 per cent) returned a higher proportion in favour than Gwynedd (64.1 per cent), Carmarthen (65.3 per cent) and Ceredigion (59.2 per cent).

**Table 8.4**

| Unitary authorities | % voting Yes | % Welsh-speaking |
| --- | --- | --- |
| Blaenau Gwent | 56.1 | 2.2 |
| Bridgend | 54.4 | 8.2 |
| Caerphilly | 54.7 | 6.0 |
| Cardiff | 44.4 | 6.6 |
| Carmarthenshire | 65.3 | 54.8 |
| Ceredigion | 59.2 | 59.1 |
| Conwy | 40.9 | 30.6 |
| Denbighshire | 40.8 | 26.7 |
| Flintshire | 38.2 | 13.5 |
| Gwynedd | 64.1 | 72.1 |
| Merthyr Tydfil | 58.2 | 7.5 |
| Monmouth | 32.1 | 2.1 |
| Neath and Port Talbot | 66.5 | 17.8 |
| Newport | 37.4 | 2.3 |
| Pembrokeshire | 42.8 | 18.3 |
| Powys | 42.7 | 20.5 |
| Rhondda Cynon Taff | 58.5 | 9.0 |
| Swansea | 52.0 | 13.3 |
| Torfaen | 49.8 | 2.5 |
| Vale of Glamorgan | 36.7 | 6.9 |
| Wrexham | 45.3 | 13.7 |
| Ynys Môn | 50.9 | 62.0 |
| **Wales** | **18.7** | **50.3** |

Most significantly, in the general election to the National Assembly itself, Plaid Cymru – The Party of Wales – secured control of the seven constituencies within the traditional Welsh-speaking heartland, as well as Rhondda and Islwyn, these last two probably due to special local circumstances.

As far as the use of Welsh in the National Assembly is concerned, this was set out in Clause 46 of the Government of Wales Bill (1997). It states:

1. The Assembly shall in the conduct of its business give effect as far as is both appropriate in the circumstances and reasonably practical, to the principle that English and Welsh languages should be treated on a basis of equality.
2. In determining how to comply with subsection (1), the Assembly shall have regard to the spirit of any guidance under section 9 of the Welsh Language Act 1993.
3. The standing orders of the Assembly shall be made both in English and Welsh.

In a paper entitled 'The Welsh language and the National Assembly: operating through two languages', prepared for the Institute of Welsh Affairs' *Handbook for the National Assembly's Agenda*, Williams (1999) has set out a framework for a national language policy. It is based on what are stated as three unchallengeable principles. First, that the links between language and citizenship, including bilingual provision in all public services, should be ensured. Second, that economic and regional policies should be such as to secure the well-being of Welsh-speaking communities. Third, that the variety of initiatives which generally come under the heading of town and country planning should be directed towards the interests of the language. He then writes:

> Holistic language planning rather than sectoral approaches are to be encouraged as is the conception that bilingualism in Wales is an integral element in an emerging civic identity. It is argued that the Assembly is potentially the single most important agency whereby the normalisation of Welsh can be realised in society. (Williams, 1999)

Such a statement raises once again the issue of the link between language, ethnicity and national identity – 'bilingualism in Wales as an integral element in an emerging civic identity'. There is a strong and consistently presented argument to the contrary that the Welsh language is a divisive symbol in Welsh identity, and, at the extreme, that it is a barrier to the real unity of Wales based on a common Welshness, however that may be defined. Here, at the point of definition, one returns to the contrast between an ethnic nationalism and an institutional nationalism, for the moment accepting the congruence of ethnic and national identity. It is argued that what must grow in Wales in order to ensure a real measure of unity is not the divisive language, spoken by less than a fifth of the population, but the firm adherence to a growing panoply of institutions. These have already been noted earlier in this book, and range from the National Museum and Museum of Welsh Life, through the University, to a national orchestra, a national opera and a variety of national sports teams. But the central building block in such a concept, physically and symbolically is now the National Assembly. If all these institutions become an effective and a sufficient representation of Welshness, then the language is in danger of being relegated to a secondary role and eventually to an anachronistic one, the symbol of the past rather than the future. Implicitly this view challenges Williams's assertion above that the language is an 'integral element in an emerging civic identity'.

In an article in the supplement published by the *Western Mail* to commemorate the opening of the Assembly, one significantly entitled, 'Chance at last to unite a deeply-divided nation' (*Western Mail*, 'Wales 2000', Issue 18, 'History in the Making. The Assembly Assembles', May 1999, 36). Toby Mason begins by noting the divisions between north and south and between those areas with high investment and those with lagging economies. But he adds, 'Some commentators detect a deeper civic malaise characterising the Welsh identity'. He then proceeds to quote

> The Director of the Institute of Welsh Affairs, John Osmond, a prominent commentator on Welsh issues [who] sees the assembly's influence over time as creating a new Welsh citizenship. 'If you compare the Welsh identity with the Scottish identity, then the main difference is that the Scottish identity is very much a civic one, bound up with separate institutions such as the legal system and the church, as well as banking and so on. But in Wales, identity has had to be understood in terms of a more diffuse cultural sense, based on a sense of place, as well as a linguistic identity – whether or not you speak the language. The Assembly as an institution should over time, build up a new sense of citizenship in relation to Wales'. (Mason, 1999, 36)

The implication of such a development is not made explicit, but it must surely be that language would as a result become more and more a marginal matter to this new sense of citizenship uniting the people of Wales. Moreover, a parallel exists for the achievement of independence by the Irish republic did not result in a resurgence of language but rather the opposite, to such an extent that it was possible to write of 'The Death of the Irish Language'(Hindley, 1990). Already warning notes are being struck through a comparison with Ireland. In a pamphlet '*Pa Ddiben Protestio Bellach?* (What need to protest further?) Dylan Phillips has outlined the fate of Irish:

> Yng nghymal 4 o gyfansoddiad y Wladwriaeth Rydd cyhoeddwyd mai'r Wyddeleg fyddai iaith genedlaethol Iwerddon . . . Uchafbwynt y polisi iaith blaengar a hyderus hwn oedd sefydlu Gweinyddiaeth yr Iaith Wyddeleg, a phenodi llywydd y mudiad iaith cenedlaethol yn Weinidog yn y Dail. Gyda'r fath ewyllys da o'i phlaid, a'r wladwriaeth newydd yn datgan yn rhwysgfawr mai un o'i hamcanion pennaf oedd diogelu hen iaith y Gwyddyl fel prif iaith eu rhyddid cenedlaethol, 'roedd gobaith mawr yr adferid yr Wyddeleg yn brif iaith Iwerddon unwaith eto. Ond nid felly y bu. [In clause 4 of the constitution of the Free State it was stated that Irish would be the national language. The major purpose of this progressive and confident policy was to establish Irish as the language of administration and to nominate the president of the national language movement as a minister in the Dail. On the basis of such goodwill, the firm declaration of the new state that one of its main objectives was to restore the old language of the Irish as the leading language of national freedom, there was great hope that Irish would become the main language of Ireland once again. But such was not to be]. (Phillips, 1998, 11–12)

157

There is no need here to trace the decline of Irish, but the overarching reason was that with independence and the creation of political and other institutions, national identity became in no way dependent on language (Mac Giollo Chriost and Aitchison, 1998). The possibility follows that Wales could follow the same track. There is clearly a danger that, like Scotland and Ireland, a Welsh identity could develop, that would owe little to language which could well atrophy for reasons very different from those which led to decline in the twentieth century. Language and culture could then be seen as having performed an interim function of preserving identity only to become of secondary significance in a new Welsh identity based on those institutions of growing dominance in Welsh life.

Finally, Roderick (1999) also draws attention to the fact that in the future the Assembly may not be as susceptible to pressures concerning language matters. After tracing all the positive developments that have underpinned the regeneration of the language, he notes: 'There is, though, no guarantee that the Assembly will choose to continue all these policies. Armed with a democratic mandate, it will be far easier for an elected body to withstand the activities of pressure groups, should it choose to do so.' The above scenario is put too baldly to be a likely outcome of the presence of an Assembly. But it is most certainly one that cannot be ignored. It is still possible to regard the Assembly as providing a new impetus to the substantial progress made by the language over the last decades of the twentieth century, but that simple assumption of a *fait accompli* is fraught with danger. The future holds as many challenges as the past, and much will depend on whether or not the Welsh-speaking élite, who so effectively gained control over the levers of power in the recent past, are able to maintain that hold and ensure as high a profile as possible for the language (Aitchison and Carter, 1999a, 1999b).

## Conclusion

Any effort, such as this, to summarize the congeries of forces that is currently impacting on the Welsh language must inevitably be highly selective and partial. A comprehensive and integrated evaluation would require very extensive elaboration. What is certain, however, is that since the 1960s an enormous amount has been achieved in revitalizing and rejuvenating the national language of Wales. However, for those seeking to protect and promote the language, it is particularly frustrating that so many of the influences that will determine its future vitality are virtually beyond control. Continually overshadowing the massive internal efforts to turn the tide of decline are powerful worldwide trends, both economic and social, which are bound to impact upon Wales and which even a devolved government would have difficulty in offsetting. To date, few of those trends in a megalopolitan world are supportive of lesser-used languages. Globalization has little truck with regional diversities. Be this as it may, as the new century begins, it is possible to discern as many positive tendencies. The end of the nineteenth century saw a supposed golden age dissolve into lack of interest and disillusion; a new golden era is not yet certain, but the prospects certainly appear much brighter as we enter the new millennium. The future of the language seems assured, but as always much will depend upon the degree to which it can continue to capture the minds and hearts of the people of Wales, and to represent their feelings of distinction and identity.

# APPENDIX

## *Number and Percentage of Welsh-speakers by Census Ward, 1991*

| Ward | Welsh-speakers No. | % | Ward | Welsh-speakers No. | % | Ward | Welsh-speakers No. | % |
|---|---|---|---|---|---|---|---|---|
| **CLWYD** | | | Uwchaled | 1092 | 77.4 | Llanfair Dyffryn Clwyd | 707 | 54.0 |
| | | | **Delyn** | | | Llangollen | 638 | 20.2 |
| **Alyn and Deeside** | | | Bagillt East | 327 | 12.7 | Llangollen Rural | 446 | 19.8 |
| Aston | 332 | 9.6 | Bagillt West | 147 | 12.7 | Llanrhaeadr-ym-Mochnant | 489 | 51.2 |
| Buckley Bistre East | 348 | 10.1 | Caerwys | 628 | 28.1 | Llanrhaeadr-yng-Nghinmeirch | 829 | 62.4 |
| Buckley Bistre West | 380 | 8.6 | Castle | 221 | 10.2 | Llansilin | 357 | 43.3 |
| Buckley Mountain | 140 | 7.1 | Cilcain | 382 | 20.7 | Llanynys | 623 | 60.5 |
| Buckley Pentrobin | 254 | 7.6 | Coleshill | 406 | 11.4 | Ruthin | 2166 | 44.7 |
| Caergwrle | 148 | 8.8 | Ffynnongroyw | 576 | 27.5 | **Rhuddlan** | | |
| Connah's Quay Central | 304 | 9.6 | Greenfield | 329 | 12.8 | Bodelwyddan | 300 | 18.5 |
| Connah's Quay Golftyn | 436 | 10.4 | Gronant | 252 | 16.9 | Dyserth | 521 | 22.6 |
| Connah's Quay South | 473 | 10.8 | Gwernaffield | 303 | 17.2 | Meliden | 321 | 16.1 |
| Connah's Quay Wepre | 188 | 8.9 | Gwernymynydd | 392 | 23.8 | Prestatyn Central | 620 | 19.0 |
| Ewloe | 281 | 8.9 | Halkyn | 946 | 25.6 | Prestatyn East | 573 | 15.6 |
| Hawarden | 138 | 7.4 | Holywell East | 475 | 15.4 | Prestatyn North | 489 | 10.6 |
| Higher and East Shotton | 336 | 8.2 | Holywell West | 526 | 19.1 | Prestatyn South West | 391 | 12.9 |
| Higher Kinnerton | 169 | 11.0 | Leeswood | 324 | 16.2 | Rhuddlan | 790 | 22.6 |
| Hope | 291 | 13.2 | Mold Bron Coed | 279 | 20.6 | Rhyl East | 607 | 13.7 |
| Llanfynydd | 361 | 21.6 | Mold Central | 364 | 22.2 | Rhyl South | 583 | 16.7 |
| Mancot | 219 | 7.5 | Mold East | 214 | 15.8 | Rhyl South East | 881 | 14.2 |
| North and East Broughton | 138 | 7.0 | Mold North | 284 | 18.1 | Rhyl South West | 620 | 12.4 |
| Penyffordd | 388 | 11.6 | Mold South | 469 | 28.2 | Rhyl West | 562 | 12.0 |
| Queensferry | 118 | 6.5 | Mold West | 185 | 14.1 | St Asaph East | 443 | 26.0 |
| Saltney | 318 | 7.4 | Mostyn | 443 | 24.3 | St Asaph West | 296 | 18.5 |
| Sealand | 158 | 5.6 | Mynydd Isa East | 354 | 12.2 | Tremeirchion | 529 | 37.4 |
| South Broughton | 219 | 6.8 | New Brighton | 394 | 13.7 | **Wrexham Maelor** | | |
| Treuddyn | 494 | 33.0 | Northop | 595 | 14.8 | Acton | 305 | 9.9 |
| West Shotton | 168 | 8.8 | Oakenholt | 327 | 11.0 | Borras Park | 401 | 14.8 |
| **Colwyn** | | | Trelawny | 436 | 12.8 | Bronington | 225 | 7.8 |
| Betws yn Rhos | 483 | 52.4 | Trelawnyd and Gwaenysgor | 511 | 31.2 | Brymbo | 322 | 12.5 |
| Colwyn | 991 | 23.8 | Whitford | 515 | 22.7 | Bryn Cefn | 165 | 9.6 |
| Dinarth | 429 | 16.5 | **Glyndŵr** | | | Caia Park | 374 | 7.1 |
| Eirias | 920 | 27.6 | Ceiriog Ganol | 617 | 36.2 | Cefn | 564 | 12.0 |
| Gele | 990 | 23.8 | Chirk North | 239 | 10.9 | Coedpoeth | 994 | 21.4 |
| Glyn | 773 | 19.0 | Chirk South | 138 | 8.4 | Esclusham | 377 | 13.3 |
| Kinmel Bay | 375 | 8.6 | Corwen | 1332 | 58.9 | Garden Village | 321 | 16.5 |
| Llanddulas | 386 | 24.6 | Denbigh Central | 772 | 40.5 | Gresford East and West | 216 | 8.3 |
| Llanfair Talhaearn | 841 | 56.1 | Denbigh Lower | 1930 | 50.3 | Grosvenor | 252 | 12.8 |
| Llangernyw | 1017 | 74.8 | Denbigh Upper | 952 | 39.2 | Gwenfro | 135 | 8.0 |
| Llansannan | 943 | 74.1 | Efenechtyd | 644 | 53.1 | Gwersyllt East and South | 287 | 7.9 |
| Llysfaen | 546 | 22.8 | Gwyddelwern | 530 | 69.6 | Gwersyllt North | 191 | 7.8 |
| Mochdre | 517 | 27.1 | Henllan | 344 | 47.6 | Gwersyllt West | 243 | 8.9 |
| Pentre Mawr | 1043 | 19.8 | Llanarmon-yn-Ial | 412 | 25.2 | Holt | 125 | 6.3 |
| Rhiw | 840 | 16.7 | Llanbedr Dyffryn Clwyd | 431 | 32.9 | Johnstown | 712 | 23.2 |
| Rhos | 642 | 14.7 | Llandegla | 315 | 39.7 | Little Acton | 317 | 13.5 |
| Towyn | 166 | 8.9 | Llandrillo | 723 | 70.6 | Llay | 346 | 7.4 |
| Trefnant | 569 | 33.8 | Llandyrnog | 433 | 35.8 | Maesydre | 288 | 14.5 |

| Ward | Welsh-speakers No. | % | Ward | Welsh-speakers No. | % | Ward | Welsh-speakers No. | % |
|------|------|------|------|------|------|------|------|------|
| Marchwiel | 162 | 7.8 | Llanarth | 820 | 63.4 | Llangennech | 2048 | 53.3 |
| Marford and Hoseley | 217 | 9.9 | Llanbadarn Fawr | 645 | 45.0 | Lliedi | 1880 | 36.9 |
| Minera | 447 | 19.7 | Llandyfriog | 1052 | 64.4 | Llwynhendy | 1522 | 35.4 |
| New Broughton | 274 | 10.1 | Llandysiliogogo | 935 | 56.3 | Pembrey | 1464 | 41.1 |
| Offa East | 816 | 15.0 | Llandysul Town | 1003 | 75.5 | Pontyberem | 2162 | 80.5 |
| Offa West | 376 | 11.5 | Llanfarian | 667 | 59.6 | Swiss Valley | 975 | 38.6 |
| Overton | 224 | 8.6 | Llanfihangel Ystrad | 1207 | 66.0 | Trimsaran | 1667 | 64.2 |
| Pant | 798 | 37.9 | Llangeitho | 855 | 60.3 | Tumble | 2770 | 78.0 |
| Penycae | 777 | 23.5 | Llangybi | 739 | 54.7 | Tycroes | 1385 | 64.4 |
| Plas Madoc | 238 | 10.9 | Llanrhystyd | 839 | 67.7 | Tyisha | 1275 | 31.3 |
| Ponciau | 1841 | 50.8 | Llansantffraid | 1282 | 62.4 | **Preseli Pembrokeshire** | | |
| Queensway | 317 | 6.7 | Llanwenog | 1161 | 71.4 | Brawdy | 477 | 35.0 |
| Rhosnesni | 319 | 11.5 | Lledrod | 1308 | 65.6 | Burton | 113 | 8.3 |
| Rossett | 197 | 6.9 | Melindwr | 1020 | 58.1 | Camrose | 266 | 11.9 |
| Ruabon | 377 | 12.5 | New Quay | 453 | 50.6 | Castle | 230 | 12.5 |
| Stansty | 227 | 10.4 | Penbryn | 1065 | 54.7 | Cilgerran | 1102 | 65.0 |
| Whitegate | 153 | 8.0 | Penparc | 1338 | 60.8 | Clydey | 858 | 64.5 |
| **DYFED** | | | Tirymynach | 986 | 65.3 | Crymych | 1487 | 68.8 |
| | | | Trefeurig | 795 | 60.2 | Dinas Cross | 967 | 61.4 |
| **Carmarthen** | | | Tregaron | 887 | 78.4 | Fishguard | 1197 | 39.3 |
| Abergwili | 1146 | 60.4 | Troedyraur | 791 | 63.3 | Garth | 497 | 10.9 |
| Carmarthen Town North | 2286 | 44.8 | Ystwyth | 1032 | 64.2 | Goodwick | 587 | 31.6 |
| Carmarthen Town South | 1689 | 50.1 | **Dinefwr** | | | Hakin | 252 | 5.2 |
| Carmarthen Town West | 1632 | 48.3 | Ammanford | 1017 | 70.8 | Johnston | 156 | 7.6 |
| Cenarth | 1205 | 63.4 | Betws | 1116 | 66.9 | Letterston | 793 | 42.5 |
| Clynderwen | 816 | 62.4 | Brynamman | 734 | 81.1 | Llangwm | 145 | 7.8 |
| Cynwyl Elfed | 943 | 59.6 | Castle | 446 | 55.9 | Maenclochog | 911 | 59.4 |
| Gorslas | 2602 | 78.4 | Cynwyl Gaeo | 814 | 60.1 | Merlin's Bridge | 210 | 11.7 |
| Laugharne Township | 215 | 17.5 | Ffairfach | 731 | 64.3 | Milford Central and East | 244 | 5.6 |
| Llanboidy | 858 | 53.5 | Garnant | 1563 | 77.5 | Milford North and West | 237 | 6.1 |
| Llanddarog | 1262 | 69.6 | Glanamman | 1604 | 77.0 | Newport | 651 | 57.0 |
| Llanddowror | 371 | 23.1 | Llandeilo | 481 | 58.7 | Neyland East | 126 | 7.1 |
| Llandyfaelog | 826 | 68.3 | Llandovery | 927 | 46.9 | Neyland West | 113 | 5.5 |
| Llanfihangel-ar-Arth | 1403 | 68.6 | Llandybie | 2377 | 68.8 | Prendergast | 272 | 15.7 |
| Llangeler | 2004 | 67.2 | Llanegwad | 1031 | 61.2 | Priory | 193 | 8.1 |
| Llangunnor | 1199 | 52.6 | Llanfair-ar-y-Bryn | 490 | 49.1 | Rudbaxton | 331 | 16.3 |
| Llangyndeyrn | 2062 | 71.9 | Llanfihangel Aberbythych | 929 | 61.5 | St David's | 828 | 43.2 |
| Llanllwni | 645 | 62.7 | Llangadog | 1109 | 65.8 | St Dogmaels | 1009 | 55.6 |
| Llansteffan | 1010 | 54.7 | Llynfell | 752 | 81.8 | St Ishmael's | 100 | 6.9 |
| Llanybydder | 1035 | 69.7 | Manordeilo | 808 | 55.3 | Scleddau | 637 | 46.5 |
| Newchurch | 711 | 62.6 | Myddfai | 378 | 60.1 | Solva | 857 | 50.9 |
| Pencarreg | 821 | 67.2 | Myddnfych | 711 | 62.4 | The Havens | 121 | 8.7 |
| St Clears | 1798 | 62.1 | Pantyffynnon | 793 | 67.3 | Wiston | 486 | 32.2 |
| St Ishmael | 680 | 51.7 | Penygroes | 1677 | 78.5 | **South Pembrokeshire** | | |
| Trelech | 995 | 67.8 | Pontamman | 821 | 65.7 | Amroth | 68 | 6.1 |
| Whitland | 693 | 47.3 | Quarter Bach | 827 | 79.1 | Begelly | 120 | 7.1 |
| **Ceredigion** | | | Saron | 2141 | 68.9 | Carew | 74 | 5.9 |
| Aberaeron | 1040 | 71.2 | Talley | 519 | 56.3 | East Williamston | 101 | 5.3 |
| Aberporth | 1026 | 49.6 | **Llanelli** | | | Hundleton | 88 | 7.8 |
| Aberystwyth East | 583 | 55.7 | Bigyn | 1946 | 32.7 | Lampeter Velfrey | 302 | 23.0 |
| Aberystwyth North | 884 | 44.9 | Burry Port | 1682 | 39.9 | Lamphey | 132 | 8.3 |
| Aberystwyth South | 1153 | 40.9 | Bynea | 1175 | 43.3 | Manorbier | 83 | 4.6 |
| Aberystwyth West | 976 | 43.4 | Cross Hands | 1086 | 80.4 | Martletwy | 167 | 13.6 |
| Beulah | 882 | 60.0 | Dafen | 1031 | 37.5 | Narberth Rural | 130 | 12.4 |
| Borth | 831 | 43.9 | Elli | 1300 | 42.1 | Narberth Urban | 326 | 18.1 |
| Capel Dewi | 759 | 60.9 | Felinfoel | 682 | 33.9 | Pembroke Dock Central | 111 | 7.3 |
| Cardigan | 2707 | 63.9 | Glanymor | 1099 | 25.3 | Pembroke Dock Llanion | 185 | 7.5 |
| Ceulanamaesmawr | 1054 | 61.7 | Glyn | 1438 | 73.2 | Pembroke Dock Market | 121 | 7.1 |
| Ciliau Aeron | 973 | 62.4 | Hendy | 1621 | 61.6 | Pembroke Dock Pennar | 137 | 5.3 |
| Faenor | 864 | 50.9 | Hengoed | 1462 | 41.0 | Pembroke Monkton | 91 | 5.3 |
| Lampeter | 1410 | 72.6 | Kidwelly | 1831 | 59.7 | Pembroke St Mary | 223 | 7.2 |

| Ward | Welsh-speakers No. | % | Ward | Welsh-speakers No. | % | Ward | Welsh-speakers No. | % |
|---|---|---|---|---|---|---|---|---|
| Pembroke St Michael | 222 | 10.5 | Priory | 66 | 2.6 | Wainfelin | 94 | 4.5 |
| Penally | 96 | 7.0 | Raglan | 30 | 1.7 | **GWYNEDD** | | |
| Saundersfoot | 131 | 5.0 | Rogiet | 12 | 1.2 | | | |
| Stackpole | 71 | 10.6 | Severn | 86 | 2.0 | **Aberconwy** | | |
| Tenby | 296 | 6.4 | Shirenewton | 33 | 1.4 | Betws-y-Coed | 457 | 55.7 |
| | | | St Arvans | 23 | 1.6 | Bro Machno | 739 | 68.4 |
| **GWENT** | | | St Christopher's | 22 | 1.2 | Bryn | 637 | 51.0 |
| | | | St Kingsmark | 54 | 2.2 | Bryn Rhys | 509 | 42.3 |
| **Blaenau Gwent** | | | St Mary's | 14 | .9 | Caerhun | 964 | 50.1 |
| Abertillery | 53 | 1.2 | Thornwell | 55 | 2.9 | Capelulo | 607 | 41.8 |
| Badminton | 68 | 2.2 | Trellech United | 37 | 1.6 | Conwy | 1345 | 38.4 |
| Beaufort | 101 | 2.6 | Usk | 56 | 2.6 | Craig-y-Don | 680 | 21.2 |
| Blaina | 65 | 1.5 | Vauxhall | 63 | 1.6 | Crwst | 1081 | 63.3 |
| Brynmawr | 248 | 4.7 | West End | 25 | 1.7 | Deganwy | 810 | 23.5 |
| Cwm | 80 | 2.2 | Wyesham | 14 | .7 | Eglwysbach | 823 | 58.4 |
| Cwmtillery | 69 | 1.4 | **Newport** | | | Fforddlas | 350 | 38.9 |
| Ebbw Vale North | 107 | 2.3 | Allt-yr-yn | 255 | 3.1 | Gogarth | 674 | 18.9 |
| Ebbw Vale South | 93 | 2.2 | Alway | 183 | 2.2 | Gower | 808 | 67.2 |
| Georgetown | 96 | 3.0 | Beechwood | 167 | 2.2 | Lafan | 339 | 46.8 |
| Llanelly Hill | 173 | 4.6 | Bettws | 123 | 1.5 | Marl | 1007 | 29.7 |
| Llanhilleth | 78 | 1.5 | Caerleon | 188 | 2.4 | Mostyn | 637 | 18.1 |
| Nantyglo | 95 | 2.0 | Gaer | 129 | 1.6 | Pandy | 944 | 56.9 |
| Rassau | 107 | 3.1 | Graig | 168 | 3.9 | Pant-yr-afon | 668 | 37.9 |
| Sirhowy | 101 | 1.8 | Langstone | 48 | 1.9 | Penmaenan | 369 | 47.7 |
| Six Bells | 33 | 1.3 | Liswerry | 280 | 3.0 | Penrhyn | 754 | 21.4 |
| Tredegar Central and West | 145 | 2.4 | Llanwern | 91 | 2.7 | Pensarn | 899 | 33.3 |
| **Islwyn** | | | Malpas | 196 | 2.4 | Trefriw | 680 | 54.4 |
| Abercarn | 62 | 1.3 | Marshfield | 67 | 2.3 | Tudno | 945 | 22.1 |
| Argoed | 93 | 3.7 | Pillgwenlly | 124 | 2.4 | Uwch Conwy | 738 | 78.3 |
| Blackwood | 344 | 4.9 | Ringland | 90 | 1.0 | **Arfon** | | |
| Cefn Fforest | 196 | 5.3 | Rogerstone | 214 | 3.0 | Bethel | 1578 | 79.0 |
| Crosskeys | 93 | 3.0 | St Julians | 149 | 1.8 | Bontnewydd | 960 | 85.9 |
| Crumlin | 160 | 2.8 | Shaftesbury | 82 | 1.6 | Cadnant | 1619 | 87.4 |
| Newbridge | 116 | 1.8 | Stow Hill | 127 | 2.9 | Deiniol | 416 | 44.4 |
| Pengam | 248 | 7.0 | Tredegar Park | 64 | 2.2 | Deiniolen | 1110 | 85.0 |
| Penmaen | 98 | 2.3 | Victoria | 132 | 2.2 | Dewi | 939 | 63.8 |
| Pontllanfraith | 242 | 3.2 | **Torfaen** | | | Garth | 344 | 54.1 |
| Risca East | 236 | 3.6 | Abersychan | 190 | 2.8 | Gerlan | 927 | 72.9 |
| Risca West | 156 | 3.2 | Blaenavon | 65 | 1.1 | Glyder | 882 | 56.6 |
| Ynysddu | 153 | 4.1 | Brynwern | 40 | 2.2 | Hendre | 661 | 56.8 |
| **Monmouth** | | | Coed Eva | 101 | 4.1 | Hirael | 774 | 65.8 |
| Caerwent | 43 | 1.9 | Croesyceiliog North | 52 | 1.5 | Llanberis | 1553 | 80.9 |
| Caldicot Castle | 61 | 2.6 | Croesyceiliog South | 57 | 3.0 | Llandwrog | 1837 | 77.9 |
| Cantref | 94 | 3.1 | Cwmyniscoy | 30 | 2.0 | Llandygai | 1586 | 66.6 |
| Castle and Grofield | 42 | 2.1 | Fairwater | 189 | 3.9 | Llanllechid/Aber | 686 | 66.7 |
| Croesonen | 30 | 2.0 | Greenmeadow | 149 | 3.2 | Llanllyfni | 751 | 74.7 |
| Crucorney | 38 | 2.1 | Llantarnam | 116 | 2.8 | Llanrug | 2055 | 82.8 |
| Dewstow | 24 | 1.7 | Llanyrafon North | 56 | 2.8 | Llanwnda | 1447 | 81.4 |
| Goetre Fawr | 63 | 2.8 | Llanyrafon South | 90 | 3.8 | Marchog | 1381 | 55.0 |
| Lansdown | 36 | 2.2 | New Inn Lower | 55 | 2.1 | Menai (Bangor) | 534 | 43.0 |
| Larkfield | 26 | 1.8 | New Inn Upper | 71 | 2.4 | Menai (Caernarfon) | 1875 | 84.5 |
| Llanbadoc | 24 | 1.9 | Panteg | 101 | 1.5 | Ogwen | 1675 | 83.5 |
| Llanfoist Fawr | 41 | 2.7 | Pontnewydd | 66 | 1.2 | Peblig | 2108 | 90.9 |
| Llangybi Fawr | 38 | 2.4 | Pontnewynydd | 27 | 1.9 | Penisarwaun | 921 | 72.4 |
| Llanover | 51 | 2.3 | Pontypool | 50 | 2.6 | Pentir | 1400 | 64.9 |
| Llantilio Crossenny | 22 | 1.4 | Snatchwood | 21 | 1.1 | Penygroes | 1566 | 89.8 |
| Llanwenarth Ultra | 58 | 4.0 | St Cadocs and Penygarn | 17 | 1.0 | Rachub | 679 | 84.5 |
| Magor with Undy | 76 | 2.0 | St Dials | 115 | 2.9 | Seiont | 2559 | 89.2 |
| Mardy | 64 | 2.7 | Trevethin | 48 | 1.3 | Talysarn | 945 | 76.2 |
| Mitchel Troy | 20 | 1.7 | Two Locks | 164 | 3.6 | Waunfawr | 1103 | 73.0 |
| Overmonnow | 23 | 1.3 | Upper Cwmbran | 155 | 2.7 | Y Felinheli | 1257 | 72.7 |
| Portskewett | 29 | 1.6 | | | | | | |

| Ward | Welsh-speakers No. | % | Ward | Welsh-speakers No. | % | Ward | Welsh-speakers No. | % |
|---|---|---|---|---|---|---|---|---|
| **Dwyfor** | | | Kingsland | 759 | 53.7 | Coity Higher | 409 | 8.3 |
| Aberdaron | 697 | 79.0 | Llanbadrig | 776 | 56.2 | Cornelly | 525 | 8.5 |
| Abererch | 1089 | 84.2 | Llanbedrgoch | 655 | 44.4 | Coychurch Lower | 277 | 10.6 |
| Abersoch | 413 | 52.5 | Llanddyfnan | 963 | 74.6 | Laleston | 389 | 5.7 |
| Beddgelert | 320 | 61.4 | Llaneilian | 1426 | 64.3 | Llangeinor | 127 | 8.9 |
| Botwnnog | 722 | 80.1 | Llanfaethlu | 1121 | 70.6 | Llangynwyd | 333 | 14.4 |
| Buan | 327 | 71.1 | Llanfair Pwllgwyngyll | 2216 | 73.8 | Maesteg East | 551 | 10.8 |
| Clynnog | 631 | 74.8 | Llanfair-yn-Neubwll | 1195 | 46.3 | Maesteg West | 701 | 11.9 |
| Cricieth | 1135 | 67.8 | Llanfihangel Ysgeifiog | 1493 | 78.5 | Morfa | 352 | 7.7 |
| Dolbenmaen | 933 | 72.0 | Llangoed | 720 | 58.8 | Nantyffyllon | 331 | 10.0 |
| Efail-newydd | 635 | 79.6 | Llanidan | 1100 | 70.1 | Nant-y-Moel | 124 | 5.4 |
| Gest | 458 | 52.3 | Llanmerch-y-Medd | 1329 | 78.6 | Newcastle | 434 | 8.3 |
| Llanaelhaearn | 848 | 83.7 | London Road | 940 | 58.4 | Newcastle Higher | 307 | 7.7 |
| Llanarmon | 949 | 71.8 | Maeshyfryd | 996 | 46.7 | Ogmore Vale | 142 | 4.6 |
| Llanbedrog | 573 | 55.1 | Mechell | 960 | 64.9 | Oldcastle | 428 | 10.6 |
| Llanengan | 772 | 68.7 | Moelfre | 655 | 56.1 | Pencoed | 917 | 10.2 |
| Llanystumdwy | 564 | 76.7 | Morawelon | 868 | 52.6 | Pontycymmer | 166 | 6.7 |
| Nefyn | 1908 | 77.1 | Parc a'r Mynydd | 708 | 59.4 | Porthcawl East | 494 | 7.5 |
| Pistyll | 382 | 78.9 | Pentraeth | 947 | 55.5 | Porthcawl West | 905 | 10.0 |
| Porthmadog East | 814 | 89.6 | Porthyfelin | 1199 | 53.6 | Pyle | 434 | 6.9 |
| Porthmadog West | 564 | 78.2 | Rhosyr | 1342 | 66.3 | St Bride's Major | 275 | 8.9 |
| Pwllheli North | 1585 | 83.2 | Trearddur | 978 | 44.2 | St Bride's Minor | 340 | 6.2 |
| Pwllheli South | 1576 | 81.2 | Tudur | 1370 | 86.2 | Ynysawdre | 164 | 6.8 |
| Tremadog | 1186 | 85.7 | Tysilio | 1270 | 63.1 | **Rhondda** | | |
| Tudweiliog | 737 | 84.5 | Valley | 1308 | 57.1 | Cwm Clydach | 198 | 6.3 |
| **Meirionnydd** | | | | | | Cymmer | 299 | 4.9 |
| Aberdovey | 288 | 34.2 | **MID GLAMORGAN** | | | Ferndale | 483 | 10.7 |
| Arthog | 326 | 33.7 | | | | Llwyn-y-pia | 139 | 5.8 |
| Bala | 1531 | 82.2 | **Cynon Valley** | | | Maerdy | 352 | 8.8 |
| Barmouth | 999 | 43.3 | Aberaman North | 404 | 8.1 | Pentre | 442 | 8.5 |
| Bowydd and Rhiw | 1659 | 84.1 | Aberaman South | 370 | 7.8 | Pen-y-graig | 335 | 5.9 |
| Brithdir and Llanfachreth | 493 | 68.8 | Abercynon | 259 | 4.1 | Porth | 503 | 8.4 |
| Bryn-crug | 338 | 60.0 | Aberdare East | 800 | 12.8 | Tonypandy | 193 | 5.6 |
| Conglywal and Maenofferen | 2010 | 84.7 | Aberdare West | 1098 | 16.3 | Trealaw | 217 | 5.3 |
| Corris | 767 | 60.3 | Cwmbach | 456 | 9.7 | Treherbert | 762 | 11.7 |
| Cynfal and Teigl | 590 | 77.1 | Hirwaun | 626 | 15.8 | Treorchy | 1048 | 13.8 |
| Dolgellau | 1843 | 72.8 | Llwydcoed | 216 | 15.8 | Tylorstown | 401 | 6.0 |
| Dyffryn Ardudwy | 727 | 49.8 | Mountain Ash East | 161 | 5.7 | Ynyshir | 271 | 7.6 |
| Harlech | 1185 | 64.6 | Mountain Ash West | 292 | 6.3 | Ystrad | 463 | 7.5 |
| Llanbedr | 596 | 54.9 | Penrhiwceiber | 272 | 4.2 | **Rhymney Valley** | | |
| Llandderfel | 1146 | 76.8 | Pen-y-waun | 223 | 6.4 | Aberbargoed | 200 | 5.4 |
| Llanelltyd | 464 | 69.6 | Rhigos | 335 | 19.3 | Abertysswg | 69 | 4.9 |
| Llangelynin | 526 | 56.5 | Ynysybwl | 423 | 10.1 | Aber Valley | 725 | 11.3 |
| Llanuwchllyn | 749 | 83.4 | **Merthyr Tydfil** | | | Bargoed | 461 | 7.0 |
| Mawddwy | 401 | 70.1 | Bedlinog | 226 | 6.5 | Bedwas and Trethomas | 390 | 6.5 |
| Penrhyndeudraeth | 1799 | 78.2 | Cyfarthfa | 686 | 10.7 | Darran Valley | 184 | 7.1 |
| Trawsfynydd | 1177 | 79.0 | Dowlais | 649 | 9.3 | Gilfach | 133 | 6.2 |
| Tywyn | 1163 | 39.6 | Gurnos | 284 | 4.7 | Hengoed | 233 | 5.0 |
| **Ynys Môn – Isle of Anglesey** | | | Merthyr Vale | 235 | 5.8 | Llanbradach | 309 | 6.9 |
| Aberffraw | 1452 | 60.4 | Park | 316 | 7.8 | Machen | 278 | 7.2 |
| Amlwch | 2483 | 66.7 | Penydarren | 320 | 6.1 | Maesycwmmer | 177 | 7.8 |
| Beaumaris | 732 | 37.2 | Plymouth | 317 | 6.2 | Morgan Jones | 504 | 8.7 |
| Bodffordd | 1203 | 80.2 | Town | 462 | 7.2 | Moriah | 242 | 7.7 |
| Bodorgan | 1087 | 74.2 | Treharris | 446 | 7.8 | Nelson | 356 | 8.8 |
| Bryngwran | 1405 | 78.6 | Vaynor | 284 | 8.8 | New Tredegar | 112 | 2.9 |
| Brynteg | 861 | 47.9 | **Ogwr** | | | Penyrheol | 852 | 8.7 |
| Cadnant | 545 | 53.5 | Bettws | 123 | 4.6 | Pontllotyn | 73 | 3.8 |
| Cefni | 1164 | 82.4 | Blackmill | 177 | 6.5 | St Cattwg | 558 | 8.3 |
| Cwm Cadnant | 1268 | 55.4 | Blaengarw | 121 | 6.7 | St James | 478 | 7.5 |
| Cyngar | 1255 | 85.8 | Brackla | 595 | 7.9 | St Martins | 612 | 10.4 |
| Holyhead Town | 497 | 47.0 | Caerau | 299 | 6.6 | Tir-Phil | 53 | 4.1 |
| | | | Cefn Cribwr | 117 | 7.1 | | | |

| Ward | Welsh-speakers No. | % | Ward | Welsh-speakers No. | % | Ward | Welsh-speakers No. | % |
|---|---|---|---|---|---|---|---|---|
| Twyn Carno | 238 | 9.1 | Yscir | 172 | 19.4 | Llangunllo | 54 | 8.8 |
| Ystrad Mynach | 299 | 8.4 | Ystradfellte | 153 | 26.8 | Llansantffraed-Cwmdeuddwr | 53 | 12.1 |
| **Taff-Ely** | | | Ystradgynlais | 1557 | 59.9 | Llanyre | 82 | 7.9 |
| Beddau | 251 | 8.1 | **Montgomeryshire** | | | Nantmel | 43 | 7.4 |
| Brynna | 357 | 10.9 | Banwy | 531 | 66.9 | New Radnor | 44 | 10.5 |
| Church Village | 281 | 10.0 | Berriew | 112 | 8.9 | Old Radnor | 53 | 7.3 |
| Cilfynydd | 243 | 9.2 | Cadfarch | 494 | 69.7 | Painscastle | 26 | 5.9 |
| Creigiau | 420 | 15.9 | Caersws | 314 | 22.1 | Presteigne | 115 | 5.5 |
| Gilfach Goch | 184 | 5.4 | Carno | 323 | 56.8 | Rhayader Town | 169 | 10.8 |
| Glyncoch | 202 | 6.7 | Churchstoke | 60 | 4.6 | St Harmon | 47 | 6.8 |
| Graig | 145 | 6.4 | Dolforwyn | 170 | 12.8 | | | |
| Hawthorn | 133 | 6.3 | Forden | 103 | 9.4 | **SOUTH GLAMORGAN** | | |
| Ilan | 174 | 9.8 | Glantwymyn | 780 | 71.2 | | | |
| Llanharan | 245 | 8.9 | Guilsfield Within | 138 | 14.0 | **Cardiff** | | |
| Llanharry | 175 | 7.8 | Guilsfield Without | 135 | 15.2 | Adamsdown | 309 | 4.5 |
| Llantrisant Town | 552 | 14.3 | Kerry | 127 | 8.0 | Butetown | 111 | 3.2 |
| Llantwit Fardre | 577 | 11.4 | Llanbrynmair | 569 | 68.3 | Caerau | 411 | 4.2 |
| Pentyrch | 489 | 14.2 | Llandinam | 107 | 12.9 | Canton | 1030 | 8.0 |
| Pont-y-Clun | 464 | 11.1 | Llandrinio | 147 | 9.7 | Cathays | 615 | 6.5 |
| Pontypridd Town | 483 | 16.3 | Llandysilio | 82 | 8.5 | Cyncoed | 933 | 9.2 |
| Rhondda | 291 | 6.8 | Llanfair Caereinion | 587 | 41.0 | Ely | 601 | 4.1 |
| Rhydfelen Central | 290 | 10.7 | Llanfihangel | 513 | 57.9 | Fairwater | 580 | 4.7 |
| Rhydfelen Lower | 116 | 7.5 | Llanfyllin | 486 | 39.6 | Gabalfa | 341 | 6.4 |
| Taffs Well | 407 | 12.1 | Llangurig | 151 | 23.4 | Grangetown | 408 | 3.5 |
| Talbot Green | 214 | 9.1 | Llanidloes East | 330 | 16.7 | Heath | 979 | 8.9 |
| Ton-teg | 588 | 12.2 | Llanidloes West | 139 | 24.9 | Lisvane and St Mellons | 373 | 6.3 |
| Tonyrefail East | 469 | 7.9 | Llansantffraid | 290 | 19.2 | Llandaff | 989 | 11.9 |
| Tonyrefail West | 313 | 7.3 | Llanwddyn | 779 | 60.2 | Llandaff North | 410 | 5.3 |
| Trallwng | 339 | 9.3 | Machynlleth No.1 | 542 | 60.3 | Llanishen | 908 | 6.8 |
| Treforest | 230 | 6.8 | Machynlleth No.2 | 643 | 60.4 | Llanrumney | 322 | 2.7 |
| Tyn-y-nant | 271 | 7.5 | Meifod | 221 | 21.0 | Pentwyn | 735 | 4.6 |
| | | | Mochdre | 126 | 14.7 | Plasnewydd | 973 | 7.2 |
| **POWYS** | | | Montgomery | 74 | 7.1 | Radyr and St Fagans | 572 | 11.7 |
| | | | Newtown Central | 420 | 14.5 | Rhiwbina | 1199 | 10.9 |
| **Brecknock** | | | Newtown East | 245 | 12.9 | Riverside | 973 | 8.4 |
| Aber-Craf | 808 | 56.4 | Newtown Llanllwchaiarn North | 268 | 15.6 | Roath | 918 | 9.1 |
| Bronllys | 55 | 7.5 | Newtown Llanllwchaiarn West | 276 | 16.8 | Rumney | 301 | 3.5 |
| Builth | 195 | 9.8 | Newtown South | 198 | 10.5 | Splott | 306 | 3.0 |
| Bwlch | 63 | 7.2 | Rhiewcynon | 251 | 20.5 | Trowbridge | 430 | 3.6 |
| Crickhowell | 201 | 9.6 | Trefeglwys | 465 | 36.4 | Whitchurch and Tongwynlais | 1435 | 10.1 |
| Cwm-twrch | 1249 | 65.7 | Trewern | 79 | 9.0 | **Vale of Glamorgan** | | |
| Erwood | 58 | 8.5 | Welshpool Castle | 142 | 9.6 | Alexandra | 722 | 6.7 |
| Felin-fâch | 115 | 10.3 | Welshpool Gungrog | 199 | 9.3 | Baruc | 514 | 9.7 |
| Gwernyfed | 108 | 8.1 | Welshpool Llanerchyddoll | 198 | 9.8 | Buttrills | 311 | 5.7 |
| Hay | 71 | 5.3 | **Radnor** | | | Cadoc | 363 | 5.0 |
| Llanafanfawr | 90 | 8.8 | Beguildy | 47 | 6.9 | Castel land | 134 | 3.6 |
| Llanfrynach | 109 | 10.2 | Clyro | 48 | 7.9 | Cornerswell | 299 | 5.7 |
| Llangamarch | 186 | 20.3 | Disserth and Trecoed | 82 | 8.2 | Court | 267 | 5.4 |
| Llangattock | 63 | 6.0 | Gladestry | 50 | 12.0 | Cowbridge | 593 | 9.8 |
| Llangors | 94 | 9.1 | Glasbury | 76 | 9.4 | Dinas Powys | 672 | 7.4 |
| Llangynidr | 89 | 9.3 | Glascwm | 55 | 7.8 | Dyfan | 316 | 6.3 |
| Llanwrtyd Wells | 194 | 30.7 | Knighton | 195 | 7.1 | Gibbonsdown | 226 | 4.2 |
| Llywel | 279 | 40.7 | Llanbadarn Fawr | 62 | 6.9 | Illtyd | 538 | 7.5 |
| Maescar | 283 | 32.0 | Llanbister | 27 | 4.3 | Llandough | 119 | 6.2 |
| St David Within | 157 | 11.4 | Llandrindod East | 50 | 7.6 | Llandow | 206 | 11.3 |
| St John | 454 | 14.3 | Llandrindod North | 201 | 11.3 | Llantwit Major | 595 | 6.3 |
| St Mary | 289 | 10.8 | Llandrindod South No.1 | 49 | 7.9 | Peterston-super-Ely | 204 | 7.9 |
| Talgarth | 148 | 8.4 | Llandrindod South No.2 | 134 | 12.4 | Rhoose | 314 | 7.4 |
| Talybont-on-Usk | 70 | 10.7 | Llandrindod West | 88 | 13.7 | St Athan | 219 | 5.9 |
| Tawe-Uchaf | 625 | 41.0 | Llanelwedd | 21 | 4.3 | Stanwell | 260 | 6.9 |
| The Vale of Grwyney | 46 | 5.7 | Llanfihangel Rhydithon | 44 | 8.7 | Sully | 294 | 7.2 |
| Ynyscedwyn | 1235 | 60.3 | | | | Wenvoe | 233 | 10.4 |

| Ward | Welsh-speakers No. | % | Ward | Welsh-speakers No. | % | | Welsh-speakers No. | % |
|---|---|---|---|---|---|---|---|---|
| **WEST GLAMORGAN** | | | Blaengwrach | 307 | 15.1 | Sandfields East | 329 | 5.5 |
| | | | Briton Ferry East | 199 | 6.6 | Sandfields West | 364 | 5.4 |
| **Lliw Valley** | | | Briton Ferry West | 126 | 4.1 | Tai Bach | 312 | 6.6 |
| Allt-Wen | 891 | 40.1 | Bryn-côch North | 402 | 16.6 | **Swansea** | | |
| Clydach | 897 | 32.5 | Bryn-côch South | 439 | 12.6 | Bishopston | 391 | 8.3 |
| Cwmllynfell | 877 | 76.9 | Cadoxton | 192 | 13.9 | Bonymaen | 607 | 8.6 |
| Dulais East | 615 | 42.2 | Cimla | 380 | 8.9 | Castle | 720 | 6.6 |
| Godre'r graig | 681 | 46.3 | Coedffranc Central | 471 | 12.0 | Cockett | 1500 | 12.2 |
| Gorseinon Central | 397 | 26.6 | Coedffranc North | 273 | 12.1 | Cwmbwrla | 597 | 7.6 |
| Gorseinon East | 320 | 22.9 | Coedffranc West | 250 | 12.5 | Dunvant | 390 | 8.2 |
| Gowerton East | 320 | 16.3 | Crynant | 694 | 33.9 | Killay | 358 | 8.8 |
| Gowerton West | 266 | 14.6 | Dyffryn | 338 | 11.5 | Landore | 450 | 7.1 |
| Graigfelen | 361 | 20.5 | Glynneath | 893 | 24.3 | Llansamlet | 1540 | 15.0 |
| Gwauncaegurwen | 2204 | 79.1 | Neath East | 346 | 5.8 | Mayals | 324 | 12.5 |
| Kingsbridge | 1012 | 25.3 | Neath North | 411 | 10.3 | Morriston | 2755 | 17.2 |
| Llangyfelach | 754 | 25.2 | Neath South | 345 | 7.5 | Mynyddbach | 1093 | 11.3 |
| Lower Brynamman | 1044 | 76.6 | Onllwyn | 328 | 25.8 | Newton | 332 | 9.6 |
| Lower Loughor | 497 | 23.1 | Pelenna | 342 | 26.9 | North Gower | 1160 | 18.4 |
| Mawr | 983 | 53.5 | Resolven | 400 | 12.4 | Oystermouth | 386 | 9.5 |
| Penllergaer | 468 | 21.1 | Seven Sisters | 621 | 27.6 | Penderry | 679 | 5.8 |
| Penyrheol | 1130 | 22.1 | Tonna | 237 | 11.5 | Pennard | 219 | 7.9 |
| Pontardawe | 2093 | 42.2 | **Port Talbot** | | | Sketty | 1428 | 11.2 |
| Pontardulais | 733 | 46.4 | Aberavon | 295 | 5.1 | South Gower | 184 | 8.3 |
| Rhos | 744 | 31.4 | Baglan | 560 | 8.2 | St Thomas | 228 | 3.4 |
| Tal-y-bont | 999 | 51.3 | Bryn and Cwmavon | 1376 | 22.8 | Townhill | 366 | 3.8 |
| Trebanos | 668 | 47.2 | Cymmer | 163 | 5.1 | Uplands | 1298 | 10.8 |
| Upper Loughor | 731 | 26.3 | Glyncorrwg | 75 | 6.1 | West Cross | 512 | 7.8 |
| Vardre | 590 | 24.3 | Gwynfi | 108 | 6.5 | | | |
| Ystalyfera | 2110 | 66.7 | Margam | 139 | 8.5 | | | |
| **Neath** | | | Port Talbot | 501 | 9.3 | | | |
| Aberdulais | 234 | 11.9 | | | | | | |

# References

Ackroyd, R. S. (1996) *The Changing Status of the Welsh Language: Community Studies in Ceredigion.* Undergraduate dissertation, Institute of Geography and Earth Sciences, University of Wales, Aberystwyth.

Aitchison, J. W., J. Baptiste and W. J. Edwards, (1990) *Dyfed Communities: An Analysis of Electoral Registers 1970–1990*, Rural Surveys Research Unit, Department of Geography, University College of Wales, Aberystwyth (mimeo).

Aitchison, J. W. and H. Carter, (1985) *The Welsh Language: An Interpretative Atlas: 1961–1981.* Cardiff: University of Wales Press.

Aitchison, J. W. and H. Carter, (1987) *The Welsh Language in Cardiff: a quiet revolution.* Transactions of the Institute of British Geographers, new series, 12, 482–92.

Aitchison, J. W. and H. Carter, (1988) *The Welsh Language in the Cardiff Region*, Rural Surveys Research Unit, Monograph 1, Department of Geography, University College of Wales, Aberystwyth.

Aitchison, J. W. and H. Carter, (1991) 'Rural Wales and the Welsh language' in *Rural History*, 2, 59–76.

Aitchison, J. W. and H. Carter, (1993) 'The Welsh language in 1991 – a broken heartland and a new beginning?' *Planet*, 97, 3–10.

Aitchison, J. W. and H. Carter, (1997) 'Language reproduction: reflections on the Welsh example', *Area*, 29.4, 357–66.

Aitchison, J. W. and H. Carter, (1999a) 'The regeneration of the Welsh language: an analysis'. *Contemporary Wales*, 11, 167–85.

Aitchison, J. W. and H. Carter, (1999b) 'Cultural empowerment and language shift in Wales'. *Tijdschrift voor Economsiche en Sociale Geografie*, 90(2), 168–83.

Aitchison, J. W. and H. Carter, (1999c) 'The Welsh language today'. In *Wales Today*, eds. D. Dunkerley and A. Thompson, 91–110. Cardiff: University of Wales Press.

Aitchison, J. W., H. Carter and D. Rogers, (1989) *In-migration and the Welsh Language: A Case Study of Tregaron and its Region*, Rural Surveys Research Unit, Monograph 3, Department of Geography, University College of Wales, Aberystwyth.

Allen, J. and E. Mooney, (1998) 'Migration into rural communities: questioning the language of counterurbanisation'. In *Migration into Rural Areas: Series and Issues*, eds. P. Boyle and K. Halfacree, 280–302. London: Wiley.

Baker, C. (1985) *Aspects of Bilingualism in Wales.* Clevedon: Multilingual Matters.

Beard, C. and C. Cerf, (1992) *The Official Politically Correct Dictionary and Handbook.* London: Graffion.

Bowen, E. G. (1959) *Le Pays De Galles.* Trans. Inst. Br. Geogr. 26, 1–24.

Bowen, E. G. (1964) *Daearyddiaeth Cymru fel Cefndir i'w Hanes*. London: BBC.

Bowen, E. G. and H. Carter, (1975) 'Some preliminary observations on the distribution of the Welsh language at the 1971 census'. *Geographical Journal*, 140, 432–43.

Bowen, I. (1908) *The Statutes of Wales*. London: T. Fisher Unwin.

Capstick, M. (1987) *Housing Dilemmas in the Lake District*. Lancaster: Centre for North West Regional Studies.

Carter, H. (1976) 'Y Fro Gymraeg and the 1975 referendum on Sunday closing of public houses in Wales'. *Cambria*, 3, 89–101.

Carter, H. (1988) *Culture, Language and Territory*. London: BBC.

Carter, H. (1988) *Mewnfudo a'r Iaith Gymraeg*. Abertawe: Llys yr Eisteddfod Genedlaethol.

Carter, H. (1989) *Whose City? A View from the Periphery*. Trans. Inst. Br. Geogr. 14, 4–23.

Carter, H. (1992) *Yr Iaith Gymraeg mewn Oes Ôl-Fodern*. Cardiff: University of Wales – Darlith Eisteddfod y Brifysgol.

Carter, H. and J. W. Aitchison, (1986) 'Language areas and language change in Wales: 1961–1981'. In *The Welsh and Their Country*, ed. I. Hume and W. T. R. Pryce, Llandysul: Gwasg Gomer for the Open University.

Carter, H. and J. G. Thomas, (1969) 'The Referendum on the Sunday opening of licensed premises in Wales as a criterion of a culture region'. *Regional Studies*, 3, 61–71.

Carter, H. and S. Williams, (1978) 'Aggregate studies of language and culture change in Wales'. In *Social and Cultural Change in Contemporary Wales*, ed. G. Williams, 143–65. London: Routledge and Kegan Paul.

Central Advisory Council for Education (Wales) (1953) *The Place of Welsh and English in the Schools of Wales*. London: HMSO.

Central Council for Education and Training in Social Work (1990) *Welsh Language Policy*. Bristol: CCETSW

Ceredigion Local Plan (1998) *Vol.1 Written Statement*. Aberaeron: Ceredigion County Council.

Champion, A. G. (1987) *Population Deconcentration in Britain*. Seminar Papers No 49 – Geography Dept., University of Newcastle Upon Tyne, 49.

Champion, T. (1992*) Migration Processes and Patterns. Vol. 1 Research Progress and Patterns*. London: Belhaven Press.

Cloke, P., M. Goodwin and P. Milbourne (1995) ' "There's so many strangers in the village now": marginalization and change in 1990s Welsh rural life-styles'. *Contemporary Wales*, 8, 47–74.

Cloke. P., M. Goodwin and P. Milbourne (1998) 'Inside looking out; outside looking in. Different experiences of cultural competence in rural life-styles'. In *Migration into Rural Areas. Theories and Issues*, eds. P. Boyle and K. Halfacree, Chap. 7, 134–50. Chichester: John Wiley.

Council for The Welsh Language (1978) *A Future for The Welsh Language*. Cardiff: HMSO.

Craig, S. G. (1997) 'Language contact and language degeneration'. In *The handbook of Sociolinguistics*, ed. F. Coulmas, 257–70. Oxford: Blackwell.

Dafis, L. (1992) *Lesser Used Languages – Assimilating Newcomers*. Carmarthen: Joint Working Party on Bilingualism in Dyfed.

Davies, J. (1990) *Hanes Cymru*. London: Penguin.

Davies, R. R. (1991) *The Age of Conquest. Wales 1063–1415.* Oxford: Oxford University Press.

Davies, W. (1982) *Wales in the Middle Ages.* Leicester: Leicester University Press.

Dofny, J. and A. Akiwowo (1980) *National and Ethnic Movements.* Beverly Hills: Sage Publications.

Dunkerley, D. and A. Thompson eds., (1999) *Wales Today.* Cardiff: University of Wales Press.

Dwyfor District Council (1995) Dwyfor Local Plan. Draft deposit. Pwllheli.

Edwards, H. T. (1987) 'Y Gymraeg yn y bedwaredd ganrif ar bymtheg'. In *Cof Cenedl* 2, ed. G. H. Jenkins, 119–52. Llandysul: Gwasg Gomer.

Evans, N. (1989) *National Identity in the British Isles.* Harlech: Coleg Harlech Occasional Papers in Welsh Studies No 3.

Faber, R. (1985) *High Road to England.* London: Faber and Faber.

Fishman, J. A. (1997) 'Language, ethnicity and racism'. In *Sociolinguistics. A Reader and a Coursebook*, eds. N. Coupland and A. Jaworski, 329–40. Basingstoke: Macmillan.

Fishman, J. A. (1997) 'Language and ethnicity: the view from within'. In *The Handbook of Sociolinguistics*, ed. F. Collins. Oxford: Blackwell.

Francaviglia, R. V. (1970) 'The Mormon landscape: definition of an image in the American West'. *Proceedings of Association of American Geographers*, 51–61.

Garrett, P., H. Giles and N. Coupland, (1989) 'The contexts of language learning, extending the intergroup model of second language acquisition'. In *Language, Communication and Culture,* ed. S. Ting-Tooney and F. Korzenny, 201–21.

Gellner, E. (1983) *Nations and Nationalism.* Oxford: Blackwell.

Giggs, J. and C. Pattie, (1991) *Croeso i Gymru. Welcome to Wales. But Welcome to whose Wales?* Working Paper 10. Dept. of Geography, University of Nottingham.

Giggs, J. and C. Pattie, (1992a) 'Croeso i Gymru – Welcome to Wales: but welcome to whose Wales?' *Area*, 24, 268–82.

Giggs, J. and C. Pattie, (1992b) 'Wales as a plural society'. *Contemporary Wales*, 5, 25–64.

Giles, H. (1977) *Language, Ethnicity and Intergroup Relations.* London: Academic Press.

Giles, H., R. Y. Bourhis, and D. M. Taylor, (1977) 'Towards a theory of language in ethnic group relations.' In *Language, Ethnicity and Intergroup Relations*, ed. H. Giles. London: Academic Press.

Gottman, J. (1987) *Megalopolis Revisited: 25 Years Later.* Maryland: Institute of Urban Studies, University of Maryland.

Gudykunst, W. B. (1989) 'Cultural variability in ethnolinguistic identity'. In *Language Communication and Culture*, eds. S. Ting-Tooney and F. Korzenny, 222–43.

Gwynedd County Council (1987) *Language, Planning and Housing in Gwynedd.* Draft Memorandum to the Secretary of State. Caernarfon: Gwynedd County Council.

Harrison, G. J. (1978) Summary Report of a study of 'Bilingual Welsh/English Mothers in Wales, with special regard to those rearing monolingual (English) children'. In *A Future For The Welsh Language, Council for the Welsh Language.* Appendix 3, 67–72. Cardiff: HMSO.

Harris, M. (1968) *The Rise of Anthropological Theory.* London: Routledge and Kegan Paul.

Hechter, M. (1975) *Internal Colonisation: The Celtic Fringe in British National Development, 1536–1966.* London: Routledge and Kegan Paul.

Hindley, R. (1990) *The Death of the Irish Language.* London: Routledge.

HMSO (1927) *Welsh in Education and Life.* London.

HMSO (1964) *Depopulation in Mid-Wales.* London.

HMSO (1965) *Report on the Legal Status of the Welsh Language.* London.

Hume, I. and W. T. R. Pryce, (1986) *The Welsh and Their Country.* Llandysul: Gwasg Gomer for the Open University.

Jackson, P. (1989) *Maps of Meaning,* London: Unwin Hyman.

James, C. (1986) 'Planning for the language'. *Planet,* 55, 67–73.

Jenkins, G. H. (1978) *Literature, Religion and Society in Wales, 1660–1730.* Cardiff: University of Wales Press.

Jenkins, G. H. ed. (1997) *The Welsh Language before the Industrial Revolution.* Cardiff: University of Wales Press.

Jenkins, G. H. ed. (1998) *Language and Community in the Nineteenth Century.* Cardiff: University of Wales Press.

Jones, D. (1998) *Statistical Evidence Relating to the Welsh Language.* Cardiff: University of Wales Press.

Jones, D. G. (1973) 'The Welsh language movement'. In *The Welsh Language Today,* ed. M. Stephens. Llandysul: Gwasg Gomer.

Jones, Elin (1992) 'Economic change and the survival of a minority language: a case study of the Welsh language'. In *Lesser Used Languages – Assimilating Newcomers,* ed. L. Dafis, 120–33. Carmarthen: Joint Working Party on Bilingualism in Dyfed.

Jones, E. and I. L. Griffiths, (1963) 'A linguistic map of Wales: 1961'. *Geographical Journal,* 129, 192–6.

Jones, I. G. (1992) *Mid Victorian Wales. The Observers and the Observed.* Cardiff: University of Wales Press.

Jones, P. N. (1976) 'Baptist Chapels as an index of cultural transition in the south Wales coalfields before 1914'. *Journal of Historical Geography,* 2, 347–60.

Lewis, R. (1973) 'The Welsh language and the law'. In *The Welsh Language Today,* ed. M. Stephens, 195–210. Llandysul: Gwasg Gomer.

Lewis, S. (1962) *Tynged yr Iaith.* London: BBC Publications.

Lewis, S. (1973) 'The fate of the language'. In *Presenting Saunders Lewis,* ed. A. R. Jones and G. Thomas, 127–41. Cardiff: University of Wales Press.

Mac Giolla Chriost, D. and J. W. Aitchison, (1998) 'Ethnic identities and language in Northern Ireland', *Area,* 30.4, 301–9.

McCrone, D. (1998) *The Sociology of Nationalism.* London: Routledge.

Mackey, W. F. (1988) 'Geolinguistics: its scope and principles'. In *Language in Geographic Context,* ed. C. H. Williams, 20–46. Clevedon: Multilingual Matters Ltd.

Mandelbaum, D. G. (1949) *Selected Writings of Edward Sapir.* Berkley, California: University of California Press.

Mason, T. (1999) 'Chance at last to unite a deeply-divided nation'. 'Wales 2000', Issue 18. 'History in the Making. The Assembly Assembles' *Western Mail.* Cardiff: Western Mail.

Meinig, D. W. (1965) 'The Mormon culture region: strategies and patterns in the geography of the American West: 1847–1964'. *Annals Assoc. American Geographers,* 55, 191–220.

Merrett, S. (1979) *State Housing in Britain*. London: Routledge and Kegan Paul.

Morgan, K. O. (1981) *Rebirth of a Nation. Wales 1880–1980*. Oxford: Clarendon Press/University of Wales Press.

Morgan, P. (1981) *The Eighteenth Century Renaissance*. Llandybïe: Christopher Davies.

Morris, D. (1992) 'The effect of economic changes on Gwynedd society'. In *Lesser Used Languages – Assimilating Newcomers*, ed. L. Dafis, 134–57. Carmarthen: Joint Working Party on Bilingualism in Dyfed.

Mumford, L. (1938) *The Culture of Cities*. London: Secker and Warburg.

National Language Forum (1991) *Language Strategy 1991–2001*. Caernarfon: National Language Forum.

Osmond, J. (1989) 'The modernisation of Wales'. In *National Identity in the British Isles*, ed. N. Evans, 73–90. Harlech: Coleg Harlech Occasional Papers in Welsh Studies, No.3.

Parry, G and M. A. Williams. (1999) *The Welsh Language and the 1891 Census*. Cardiff: University of Wales Press.

Pei, M. (1971) *Invitation to Linguistics*. Southbend, Indiana: Gateway Editions.

Phillips, D. (1998) *Pa Ddiben Protestio Bellach?* Talybont: Y Lolfa.

Pryce, W. T. R. (1971) 'Parish registers and visitation returns as primary sources for the population geography of the eighteenth century'. *Transactions of the Honourable Society of Cymmrodorion*, 271–93.

Pryce, W. T. R. (1978a) 'Wales as a culture region: patterns of change 1750–1971'. *Transactions of the Honourable Society of Cymmrodorion*, 229–61.

Pryce, W. T. R. (1978b) 'Welsh and English in Wales: a spatial analysis based on the linguistic affiliations of parochial communities'. *Bulletin of the Board of Celtic Studies*, 28, 1–36.

Pryce, W. T. R. and C. H. Williams (1988) 'Sources and methods in the study of language areas: a case study of Wales'. In *Language in Geographic Context*, ed. C. H. Williams, 167–237.

Rawkins, P. H. (1979) *The Implementation of Language Policy in the Schools of Wales*. Glasgow: University of Strathclyde, Centre for the Study of Public Policy.

Rees, A. D. (1973) 'The Welsh language in broadcasting'. In *The Welsh Language Today*, ed. M. Stephens, 174–94. Llandysul: Gwasg Gomer.

Rees, I. B. (1973) 'The Welsh language in government'. In *The Welsh Language Today*, ed. M. Stephens, 211–30. Llandysul: Gwasg Gomer.

Rees, W. H. (1947) 'The vicissitudes of the Welsh language in the marches of Wales'. Unpublished Ph.D., University of Wales.

Roberts, G. T. (1998) *The Language of the Blue Books. The Perfect Instrument of Empire*. Cardiff: University of Wales Press.

Roderick, V. (1999) 'Building a nation: the language divide'. BBC Cymru: State of the Nation Web site.

Smith, A. D. (1986) *The Ethnic Origins of Nations*. Oxford: Blackwell.

Smith, L. B. (1986) 'Pwnc yr iaith yng Nghymru 1282–1536'. In *Cof Cenedl*, ed. G. H. Jenkins, 1–34. Llandysul: Gwasg Gomer.

Smith, P. (1975) *Houses of the Welsh Countryside. A Study in Historical Geography*. London: HMSO

Southall, J. E. (1895) *The Welsh Language Census of 1891*. Newport.

Steinfatt, T. M. (1989) 'Linguistic relativity. Towards a broader view'. In *Language, Communication and Culture*, eds. S. Ting-Tooney and F. Korzenny, 33–75.

Stephens, M. (1973) *The Welsh Language Today*. Llandysul: Gwasg Gomer.

Stillwell, J. (1991*) Population Redistribution in the United Kingdom: Internal Migration Trends in the 1970s and 1980s*. Leeds: University of Leeds, School of Geography. Working Paper 91/4.

Stillwell, J., P. Rees and P. Boden. (1992) *Migration Processes and Patterns. Vol 2 Population Redistribution in the 1980s*. London: Belhaven Press.

Tabournet-Keller, A. (1997) 'Language and identity'. In *The Handbook of Sociolinguistics*, ed. F. Collins, 15–326. Oxford: Blackwell.

The Council for Wales and Monmouthshire (1963) *Report on the Welsh Language Today*. London: HMSO.

The Welsh Language Board (1989) *The Welsh Language: A Strategy for the Futur*e. Cardiff: The Welsh Language Board.

The Welsh Language Board (1996) *A Strategy for the Welsh Language*. Cardiff: The Welsh Language Board.

Thomas, B. (1987) 'A cauldron, a rebirth. Population and the Welsh language in the nineteenth century', *Welsh History Review*, 13, 418–37.

Thomas, Dafydd Elis. (1988) 'Ridding Wales of a seige mentality', *Western Mail*, 9 July 1988.

Thomas, J. G. (1956) 'The geographical distribution of the Welsh language'. *Geog. Journal*, 122, 71–9.

Thomas, J. G. (1975) 'The Welsh language'. In *Wales, A Physical, Historical and Regional Geography*, ed. E. G. Bowen, 247–63. London: Methuen.

Thomas, Ned. (1988) 'Can Plaid Cymru survive until 1994?'. *Planet*, 70.

S. Ting-Tooney, and F. Korzenny, (1989) *Language, Communication and Culture*. Newbury Park, California: Sage Publications. International and Introcultural Communications Annual Vol XIII.

Tudur, G. (1989) *Wyt Ti'n Cofio? Chwarter Canrif o Frwydr yr Iaith*. Talybont: Y Lolfa.

Welsh Office (1981) *Welsh in Schools*: Statement by the Secretary of State.

Welsh Office (1988) Statement by the Secretary of State for Wales Mr Peter Walker at a press conference. Cardiff: Welsh Office.

Welsh Office (1998a) *Statistics of Education and Training in Wales: Schools*. Cardiff: Welsh Office.

Welsh Office (1998b) *Digest of Welsh Local Area Statistics*. Cardiff: Welsh Office.

Wigley, D. et alia. (1986) *A Bill to amend the Welsh Language Act 1967; to make further provision relating to the use of the Welsh language in Wales; and for connected purposes*. London: HMSO.

Williams, C. H. (1982) *National Separatism*. Cardiff: University of Wales Press.

Williams, C. H. (1984) *On Measurement and Application in Geolinguistics*. Discussion Papers in Geolinguistics, No 8, Dept. of Geography & Recreation, Stoke on Trent.

Williams, C. H. (1988) 'An introduction to geolinguistics'. In *Language in Geographic Context,* ed. C. H. Williams, 1–19.

Williams, C. H. (1988) *Language in Geographic Context*. Clevedon and Philadelphia: Multilingual Matters.

Williams, C. H. (1991) *Linguistic Minorities, Society and Territory*. Clevedon: Multilingual Matters.

Williams, C. H. (1999) 'The Welsh language and the National Assembly: operating through two languages'. In *Handbook for the National Assembly's Agenda*. Cardiff: Institute of Welsh Affairs.

Williams, C. H. and J. Evas (1997) *The Community Research Project*. Cardiff: Bwrdd yr Iaith Gymraeg/Welsh Language Board.

Williams, D. (1950) *A History of Modern Wales*. London: John Murray.

Williams, D. T. (1937) 'A linguistic map of Wales'. *Geog. Journal*, 89, 146–51.

Williams, E. W. (1989) 'The dynamic of Welsh identity'. In *National Identity in the British Isles*, ed. N. Evans, 46–59. Harlech: Coleg Harlech Occasional Papers in Welsh Studies, 3.

Williams, G. (1979) *Religion, Language and Nationality in Wales*. Cardiff: University of Wales Press.

Williams, G. (1986) 'Recent trends in the sociology of Wales'. In *The Welsh and Their Country*, eds. I. Hume and W. T. R. Pryce. Llandysul: Gwasg Gomer.

Williams, G. (1992) *Sociolinguistics: A Sociological Antique*. London: Routledge.

Williams, G. A. (1979) *When Was Wales?* London: BBC.

Williams, G. A. (1966) 'The Merthyr of Dic Penderyn'. In *Merthyr Politics: The Making of a Working Class Tradition*, ed. G. Williams. Cardiff: University of Wales Press.

Williams, J. (1985) *Digest of Welsh Historical Statistics* (2 vols.). Aberystwyth: Dept. of Economic and Social History, University College, Aberystwyth.

Williams, Jac. L. (1973) 'The Welsh language in education'. In *The Welsh Language Today*, ed. M. Stephens, 92–109. Llandysul: Gwasg Gomer.

Williams, S. R. (1992) *Oes y Byd i'r Iaith Gymraeg. Y Gymraeg yn ardal ddiwydiannol Sir Fynwy yn y bedwaredd ganrif ar bymtheg*. Cardiff: University of Wales Press.

Wuthnow, R. et al. (1984) *Cultural Analysis*. Boston: Routledge and Kegan Paul.

Zelinsky, W. (1973) *The Cultural Geography of the United States*. Englewood Cliffs, N. J.: Prentice-Hall Inc.